In Helen's Kitchen

A PHILOSOPHY OF FOOD

In Helen's Kitchen

A PHILOSOPHY OF FOOD

By Helen Hudson Whiting

EDITED BY DAVE BIRKHEAD

GEORGANN EUBANKS

ROB GRINGLE

KATHY STANFORD

Published by Regulator Bookshop
720 Ninth Street, Durham, North Carolina 27705
919-286-2700
www.regbook.com

Book design by Dave Birkhead
Cover concept by Ray Simone
Cover art by Dabney Smith and Brian Schmidt

Library of Congress Card Number: 00-105675
ISBN 0-615-11842-9

Lovingly dedicated to Helen's family –

Betty and Fred Flemming,

Liz Whiting, Meg Flemming

and Christian Flemming

SHARING FOOD WITH FRIENDS is my favorite way to celebrate anything. No event is too slight nor too momentous that it cannot be enhanced by good food and good company. Neither needs to be fancy but both should be chosen with care.

— *Helen Hudson Whiting*

Contents

Index to Recipes

Index to Recipes

Preface

HELEN HUDSON WHITING, bookseller, knitter, and amateur chef, was also a writer of delightfully witty and informative essays on food and cooking. Over a 19-year period, Helen wrote columns for two local Triangle publications. From 1976 through 1984 she authored the column known as "Oral Gratification" for *The Guide,* and from 1983 through 1995 her byline anchored the Food column in *The Independent.*

The book is organized in two parts. The first section contains Helen's columns from *The Guide,* introduced by Rob Gringle, WDBS *Guide* editor. He outlines a history of the publication and tells of Helen's beginnings as a food writer.

The second section includes Helen's writing for *The Independent,* an award-winning, community oriented weekly newpaper, founded in 1983. Publisher Steve Schewel introduces the columns Helen wrote over her years at the "Indy."

Helen was born in 1946 at Fort Sam Houston, Texas, to Betty and Richard Whiting. Her father, an Air Force officer and fighter pilot, was killed when she was two. Her mother later married Fred Flemming, an Army officer whose postings carried the family to faraway bases in Germany and Japan.

She attended Duke University, and then dropped out for a time that included a short-lived marriage in England, and immersion in all things Navajo as a student in many forms. She returned to graduate from Duke in 1975 with degrees in anthropology and economics, and a passion for ACC basketball. Durham became her home, while she still maintained ties with her close-knit family.

Helen joined the crowd of cultural activists who roosted in the old Monkeytop-Sunnyside

Helen with Johnny Valentine, co-owner of Regulator Bookshop in Durham, NC

neighborhood in the '70s. There she found her place in the community. Helen had a half-dozen careers before she settled into bookselling as partner in the Regulator Bookshop, an independent bookstore in Durham.

Friends and Triangle book lovers knew Helen as an enthusiastic reader, an expert on cookbooks and mysteries, always seeming to know the best book to recommend. She shared her knowledge, offering it as a gift.

Through her various interests, Helen accumulated circles of friends, formed a knitting group, played a formidable game of bridge, and sat on the board of the Regulator Community Fund, distributing grants and scholarships to local groups and students.

All the while, Helen cooked. She cooked for friends and family, gathering recipes from all over the world, refining her tastes and sensibilities. She shared her love and knowledge in her writings. We share them with you now.

— *Kathy Stanford & Dave Birkhead*

In Helen's Kitchen: A Philosophy of Food

Foreword

By Georgann Eubanks

LIKE ITS AUTHOR and her recipe for couscous, this book is many-layered and complex. Although you can use it as a reference — a place to look on occasion for an exotic recipe to surprise your dinner guests — we hope you will stay for more. Sit down with a cup of tea or a glass of wine and spend some time *In Helen's Kitchen*. Before you know it, an hour will have passed, the words flying by. Suddenly you realize you're hungry and have the urge to cook something daring. And now you know more about Latin American cuisine, French country cooking or how to fry a chicken than you ever knew there was to know.

You will also know that you've been in the presence of an original personality — someone you would trust in your own kitchen.

For those of us who knew her over the twenty years represented by these food columns, Helen Hudson Whiting was a leading member of the community in her adopted hometown of Durham, North Carolina. She was the friend you called on when you needed a word of encouragement, a clever pun, a fresh angle on a problem, a recipe or a recommendation for something new to read. No matter what the circumstance, she was unflappable, witty, generous and, above all, wise.

Helen was serious about her pleasures — food, friends, good books, knitting — and she suffered no arrogant or angst-ridden fools. Read this book from end to end, and you'll develop a taste for Helen's philosophy. She had her opinions. Carefully formed. Well read and researched.

Year after year, Helen opened her kitchen to friends and family. To her readers, she offered the eclectic contents of her recipe box and her distinctive spirit. Over three hundred dishes are represented in this book, but there's much more just underneath. I'm pretty sure that what Helen would most like for us to remember from all her words about food preparation is this singular and not-so-simple recipe: "Pay attention. Try something different. Stretch yourself. Don't be so damned serious. Live it up!"

"Live it up!" was the daily mantra Helen offered her fellow staff members at the Regulator Bookshop when they headed out the door to lunch. It is also the lens I train on my own life now, a year after Helen's death from a brain tumor. She was 52.

In the late 1970s, Helen and I worked in the graphics arts business, sharing office space with several others in Durham, wedged between a mom-and-pop grocery and a TV repair shop. The grocery carried pigs' feet and other Southern-style cuts of meat. On the other side of us, the TV repair shop was making a transition to car stereo sales and service. Sometimes the exhaust and blaring woofers from their garage put us on edge. But we were only paying about $34 per person per month for the space. We met with our customers at a red Formica-top table set as far away from the sound of the speaker installations as possible. We laughed a lot.

We didn't recognize at the time that there was more transition going on than in the TV shop next door. Though we would have loathed the term *entrepreneur*, we were involved in building a new wing of the business community — many of us transplants to the town where we'd gone to college. Durham was becoming identified with much more than tobacco manufacturing and family-style barbeque.

Helen, April 1976, Duke Campus　　　photo by Bill Boyarsky

It's only now, in the era of Martha Stewart and a dynamic new multiethnicity in North Carolina, that I fully appreciate the sophistication of Helen's palate at that time. Helen knew celeriac and Belgian endive long before you could find such things at the Kroger. (Tongue-in-cheek, she pronounced it "crow-zhay," rhymes with parfait.) In her column as H. Hudson Whiting, Helen set about to teach us the difference between pinto beans and frijoles refritos long before Durham had its first Mexican eatery. Today, avgolemono is usually the *soup de jour* at one of Durham's nicest lunch spots. Still, first-time diners often ask their waitperson, "Now, what exactly is in that soup?" Helen gave us her recipe in 1977.

With a degree in anthropology and economics and a short stint at married life in London, Helen had long cultivated a keen interest in the world at large. She was devoted to her family and stayed close to them even though geography separated them.

It may seem odd that she first took up typesetting as a way to earn a living, but that, too, was all about words, culture and aesthetics. She read broadly. She consumed books as quickly as her dinner guests worked their way through a plate of her lamb biryani or her salad niçoise. Working with her on a daily basis brought all kinds of new information on current events and history.

No wonder then, that she moved so easily into bookselling in 1982, becoming a principal player in the revitalization of Durham's Ninth Street district as one of the owners of the Regulator Bookshop — an enterprise that has won both local and national awards as an independent bookseller and regularly hosts public readings by authors of inter-national stature.

When I first met her, Helen lived in a mill house behind what had been one of Durham's grand, turn-of-the century residences, known as Sunnyside. Her "West Pettigrew test kitchen" as she refers to it in the early columns, was a closet-sized room on the side of the house, which itself hung precariously on the edge of the canyon that had recently been dug out for the Durham Freeway. On the other side, the railroad tracks that bisect town often halted dinnertime conversation as the trains rattled by.

Helen eventually bought a house in Durham's Watts-Hillandale neighborhood, across the street from the vintage '40s bungalow where I lived. Never the front door, but the door to Helen's kitchen was the one visitors used. The kitchen was also the first room Helen remodeled with new countertops, a gas stove and custom racks for her pots, knives and spices.

Helen's shaggy black lab mix named Pettigrew and my dog, Caledonia, each in their respective fenced yards, barked at passers-by and kept an eye out for each other, as did Helen and I. She planted blueberries, a vigorous asparagus patch, and beau-tiful fruit trees. And year after year, I witnessed the procession of cars and trucks and friends on foot who came calling to Helen's kitchen where she prepared elaborate feasts and simple suppers. A group of women gathered there to knit every other week. Helen owned a loom and also helped inspire the launch of a fiber arts store on Ninth Street in Durham. And she continued writing—her columns on food and a raft of insightful book reviews. She was an expert on mysteries and cookbooks.

In the March 1981 column that inspired the subtitle for this book, Helen tells us that one of the positive aspects of living in a small town like Durham is "having friends I've seen nearly every day for years." That's how it was, indeed. It's a style of life and friendship that's all too easy to take for granted.

Gathering together all of Helen's writings about food from 1976 to 1995 brings the point home. It adds up fast — like calories — and it can be over before you know it. Like a good meal. For those of us who knew and loved her, there were the daily lessons and gifts she brought us. In this book, we now have Helen as our teacher for keeps — everything from encouragement in cutting up a chicken for the first time: "it might be a little ragged, but it gets easier and makes more sense with very little practice" to several elaborate recipes that help you "Say it With Cauliflowers."

There has been another kind of gathering here as well. Old friends who have gone their separate ways — many of us still in Durham and others across the country and abroad — have connected again to produce this book. With it, we can carry Helen's presence into our own kitchens in the same way that Helen shared stories about commu-nity events, little private jokes and the best recipes from her friends and family in her columns.

Finally then, this is a document about a very particular community and how it developed over a specific period of time. Helen's capacity for connecting us through food was a marvel in our midst. Some of us are just now catching up to her. Fortunately, we still have her detailed instructions.

Introduction: Guidelines Revisited

By Rob Gringle

How to begin at the beginning? As I sit, a blank computer screen staring back at me, cursor beating in measured anticipation, I can almost hear Helen Whiting laughing at the very existence of this book, a warm, knowing laughter partially at her own expense in recognition of the quirks and modest turns of events that so often come to shape the human comedy of living a life, leaving a legacy. And through the laughter I hear a question from Helen, partially in mock horror, and partially because she would want to know: "What *is* this?"

What indeed. Helen's thoughts on food and its preparation first appeared in print almost by accident in a most unlikely publication, *The Guide,* which began its own modest, quirky existence as a monthly pamphlet-sized calendar of upcoming programs to be broadcast on WDBS-FM, an eclectic "progressive" radio station in Durham North Carolina, steeped in rock & roll and drawing on a wide, deep variety of new and old music from virtually every genre — much of which was rarely (if ever) heard over the airways — especially the more commercial airways. The programming was broadcast in extended, uninterrupted sets by announcers who were most valued for their abilities to weave individual album cuts into tapestries of musical connections that delighted and nourished an impossibly critical yet loyal community of listeners, Helen among them — but I'm already simultaneously digressing and getting ahead of myself.

Those first printings of *The WDBS Monthly Program Guide* in the mid-70s were offered free at the businesses that advertised on the radio station. They were popular beyond all expectation, disappearing within days of publication.

The radio station's signal reach did not extend far beyond Durham and Chapel Hill, yet the *Program Guide* evolved as its commercial support grew — first with short explanatory notes on featured music, then with some reviews of new recordings and sporadic in-depth critiques of popular musicians and other more random topics loosely aligned with the radio station's programming point of view.

With each geometric growth in circulation, its title shrank into shorter, more inclusive descriptions of its contents, culminating in *The Guide.* More than expanded editorial content was implicit in the truncated title. *The Guide's* circulation had expanded beyond the normal reach of its parent radio station's signal.

Helen Whiting was one of a number of people I asked, as editor, to try their hand at reviewing, and she was the first to write a print-worthy "Retrospectives." It consisted of her critique of a superb Steeleye Span album that had never risen beyond the nether regions of the music sales charts. The review was exactly what was needed: exceptional writing, mixing objective information with personal opinion. I was thrilled, and assumed I had our first regular columnist. Unfortunately, Helen was having second thoughts. She told me that writing just this one review brought her to the realization that her depth of knowledge about lesser-known music was thin, that she would soon run out of material.

"No problem," I replied, attempting to keep the disappointment out of my voice, "I'll give you recordings to review, and you can keep all the ones you like — besides what you'll get paid for the writing."

But this tactic got me nowhere. Helen pointed out that she still would be hampered by lacking a large enough frame of reference to make new, fresh observations over time — not, she gently reminded me, what I would want from a regular columnist. I did not have a ready answer for this honest self-appraisal, and there was an uncomfortably long silence as we sat, facing one another.

"However," Helen eventually said, "I do have this idea for writing a column on a topic I understand quite well, that I am almost never at a loss for words in describing. I must warn you that it has nothing to do with music or broadcasting."

And "Oral Gratification"* was born. It was an instant hit with readers, and served as the gold standard for all *Guide* columns that were to follow, columns that ultimately featured many of the area's leading writers, artists, and thinkers.

Through all this, Helen's work shone, and as she found her voice, I rarely touched what she committed to paper from the standpoint of editing. I was a fan, and read each new column with as much eager anticipation as any of her regular readers.

As WDBS went through ownership changes, *The Guide* survived for awhile, but withered away during the time that *The Independent* was taking root. There was no doubt a collective sigh of relief when *The Independent* requested that Helen continue her writing on food in their pages.

The column's identifying title, "Oral Gratification," was created tongue-in-cheek to differentiate it from the regular music review column, "Aural Gratification."

but I am yet again ahead of myself, rushing to complete a history, still devoid of a cogent sense of Helen Hudson Whiting in those times.

One story may help. Each year in Durham, there was a "Chili Wars" competition to determine the best chili in town. It was set up as a blind taste test with democratic and secret balloting. More than three years into her "Oral Gratification" column, Helen entered, certainly not an action without some risk, as she now had an established foodie reputation. She won, of course, and the next month in "Oral Gratification," she published her recipe, and the recipes for the other two top entries. She made no mention that her recipe had won the contest. In fact, the publication of this book marks the first time her first-place finish is publicly acknowledged. I'm not at all sure H. Hudson would approve. She might dig in her heels, demanding that we honor her original intentions.

It seemed to me that Helen met the world not so much with modesty as with a self-efface-ment based on the security of her own abilities and intellect. She had her first sustained contact with Durham through coming to Duke as a National Merit Scholar, but you would never hear this from her. Helen became a mainstay in a community of the rarest of disaffected Duke alumni, those who call Durham home, and nurse abiding suspicions of the means in obtaining material professional success pursued by most of their former classmates. It's a community that has prospered in Durham — in spite of its own frequent fragmentations and cross-purposes. Helen transcended all squabbles and borders, and she was perhaps the last person to be on speaking terms with all the community's disparate parts.

This, then, is the most telling answer to Helen's imagined question about what this book *is*: In large part because of her transcendence, there has been a clear consensus that this book should be published for those who knew Helen in person, and for those who knew her through her writings in *The Guide* and *The Independent*. But there's more: the multiple merits of H. Hudson Whiting the writer present a compelling case for a wider audience. Her words can't help but make the reader hungry, and not only for the food she recommends or the preparations she details. There's a zest for living, for seeking out the delights to be found in nourishment in its broadest sense that binds these columns together. It's all part of the consistency of who Helen Hudson Whiting will forever be that rendered editing duties not only a labor of love, but (if you'll pardon the expression) a piece of cake.

*This reproduction of the first "Oral Gratification," which appeared in **The Guide,** August 1976, also includes two advertisements of the time. The Bentwood is still in business in Chapel Hill, featuring the same sorts of products if not always the same brand names. The second ad is a somewhat different matter. For our younger readers, if you don't know what an Earth Shoe is, ask your mother. If she draws a blank, ask a grandparent.*

oralgratification
by Helen Whiting

When you reach the point where your tomatoes are ripening faster than you can use them on sandwiches and in salads but there aren't quite enough yet to make preserving worthwhile, try:

TOMATO SOUP

2 lbs. sliced tomatoes
1 small sliced onion
2 tsp. salt
1 tbl. cornstarch
2 cups milk
2 cups chicken stock
chopped parsley or chervil

Put the tomatoes, onion and salt in to a saucepan, cover and cook gently for 10-15 minutes until everything is soft. Puree these ingredients and put them back into the saucepan. Mix the cornstarch with a little of the milk and stir it into the puree. Add the milk and chicken stock and simmer, stirring often, for 15 minutes. Sprinkle with parsley and serve 4.

Or this tomato sauce, which is easily made while the pasta cooks and is especially good with homemade pasta (coming soon in this column):

FRESH TOMATO SAUCE

2-3 tbl. olive oil
1 clove garlic
1 small onion, finely chopped
2 lbs. tomatoes
basil or parsley or mint; chopped

Put the olive oil in a wide pan (an iron skillet works well) on moderately high heat. Squash the garlic clove with the side of a knife and let it brown in the oil while you pour boiling water over the tomatoes to loosen their skins. Peel them and discard the seeds; then chop the tomatoes roughly.

When the garlic is brown, discard it and soften the onion (but don't brown it) in the oil. Add the tomatoes and turn up the heat; stir frequently so they won't stick to the bottom. In about 5 to 8 minutes the sauce is done, when the tomatoes have barely disintegrated. Stir in the herb of your choice.

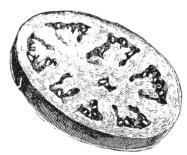

Or as a first course:

LOVE APPLES IN COCOTTE

4 medium tomatoes
butter
1 tsp. sugar
salt and pepper
1½ oz. grated parmesan
2/3 cup whipping cream
chopped parsley

Butter four individual dishes or one large dish. Cut the tomatoes into bite-sized wedges (eighths or so) and put them into the dishes. Sprinkle with salt, pepper, sugar and pour on the cream. Sprinkle on the parmesan (much better when you grate a large piece rather than buying pre-grated cheese). Bake in a 425º oven for 10-15 minutes. The tomatoes should be tender but the cream should not boil away. Sprinkle with finely chopped parsley and serve.

Coming Next Month: The Neglected First Course.

In Helen's Kitchen: A Philosophy of Food

Oral Gratification

The Guide
August 1976

WHEN YOU REACH THE POINT where your tomatoes are ripening faster than you can use them on sandwiches and in salads, but there aren't quite enough yet to make preserving worthwhile, try:

Tomato Soup

> 2 pounds sliced tomatoes
> 1 small sliced onion
> 2 teaspoon salt
> 1 tablespoon cornstarch
> 2 cups milk
> 2 cups chicken stock
> chopped parsley or chervil

Put the tomatoes, onion and salt into a saucepan, cover and cook gently for 10 to 15 minutes until everything is soft. Puree these ingredients and put them back into the saucepan. Mix the cornstarch with a little of the milk and stir it into the puree. Add the milk and chicken stock and simmer, stirring often, for 15 minutes. Sprinkle with parsley. Serves four.

Or this tomato sauce, which is easily made while the pasta cooks and is especially good with homemade pasta (coming soon in this column):

Fresh Tomato Sauce I

> 2 or 3 tablespoons olive oil
> 1 clove garlic
> 1 small onion, finely chopped
> 2 pounds tomatoes
> basil or parsley or mint, chopped

Put the olive oil in a wide pan (an iron skillet works well) on moderately high heat. Squash the garlic clove with the side of a knife and let the garlic brown in the oil while you pour boiling water over the tomatoes to loosen their skins. Peel them and discard the seeds; then chop the tomatoes roughly.

When the garlic is brown, discard it and soften the onion (but don't brown it) in the oil. Add the tomatoes and turn up the heat; stir frequently so they won't stick to the bottom. In about 5 to 8 minutes the sauce is done, when the tomatoes have barely disintegrated. Stir in the herb of your choice.

Or as a first course:

Love Apples in Cocotte

> 4 medium tomatoes
> butter
> 1 teaspoon sugar
> salt and pepper
> 1½ ounces grated parmesan
> ⅔ cup whipping cream
> chopped parsley

Butter four individual dishes or one large dish. Cut the tomatoes into bite-sized wedges (eighths or so) and put them into the dishes. Sprinkle with salt, pepper and sugar, and pour on the cream. Sprinkle on the parmesan (much better when you grate a large piece rather than buying pre-grated cheese). Bake in a 425°F oven for 10 to 15 minutes. The tomatoes should be tender but the cream should not boil away. Sprinkle with finely chopped parsley and serve.

*Coming Next Month: The Neglected First Course.**

*Because we were anxious about trying to establish the first continuous column for **The Guide,** *the three words "Coming Next Month," appearing at the bottom of Helen's original manuscript had a magical effect on our editorial mood. — ed.*

Oral Gratification

First Courses

The Guide
September 1976

IN THE HOMES OF THIS COUNTRY, the first course is often an ignored course. When it is served, it's likely to be tidbits to nibble on while drinking cocktails before a dinner party. There are many dishes which are too messy to eat with fingers while juggling a cocktail, too insubstantial to be a complete meal and too interesting to serve as an aside to other dishes. Here are three first-course ideas that make delicious beginnings to a meal. The portions are large enough to whet, but not sate, the appetites of four.

Tapenade

3 tablespoons capers
a small can of anchovies
½ cup olive oil
juice of a lemon
black pepper

Pound the capers and anchovies together in a mortar and pestle. When they are smooth, add the olive oil as if you were making mayonnaise — drop by drop at first, then in a slow, thin stream, making sure it is amalgamated into a paste. Next mix in the juice of a lemon, and season with freshly ground pepper. The anchovies provide all the salt that is necessary. This recipe comes from the south of France and has an exotic, powerful taste. Serve it with toast, bread (especially good with pita bread) or mix with the yolks of hard-boiled eggs and stuff the whites with the mixture.

Oranges & Olives

4 oranges
4 tablespoons olive oil
1 tablespoon wine vinegar
pinch salt
black pepper
1 can black olives

Grate the peel of two of the oranges, being careful to grate away only the orange part. Mix this with the oil, vinegar and salt. Using a sharp knife, peel the oranges, taking off as much of the white as possible. Slice the oranges thinly and arrange in one layer on a large dish. Pour the dressing over and grind on plenty of pepper. Freshly ground black pepper makes this dish; pre-ground or white pepper will not do. Leave in the refrigerator until very cold. Sprinkle with the black olives (Greek ones have the best flavor) before serving.

Avocados & Apples with Mayonnaise

I recommend making your own mayonnaise for this dish. Though you have to pay attention when you add the oil, it's not hard to make and is superior to any kind you can buy for dishes like this. I use olive oil or a mixture of olive oil and safflower oil (which seems to have a nicer flavor than corn or peanut oils).

MAYONNAISE:
2 egg yolks
1 cup olive oil
1 tablespoon lemon juice
1 teaspoon boiling water

Use either a mortar and pestle or a bowl and wire whisk. Beat the egg yolks thoroughly (about 30 seconds); then beat in the lemon juice and season with salt and pepper. Add the olive oil drop by drop at first, beating all the while. As the sauce thickens, you can increase the oil to a slow, thin stream but work slowly and make sure all the oil is being incorporated. When you are finished, beat in the teaspoon of boiling water to set the mayonnaise. If anything goes wrong with the mayonnaise (if you add the oil too fast and it separates), take a clean bowl and a fresh egg yolk and start again, adding your curdled mayonnaise drop by drop.

2 tart, crisp apples
2 ripe avocados
mayonnaise
lemon juice or cream to thin mayonnaise
3 to 4 finely chopped teaspoons of fresh herbs:
    parsley and tarragon or mint

Thin the mayonnaise to the consistency of very thick cream with lemon juice or cream. Mix in the herbs. Cut the apples in half and core them. Cut the avocados in half, remove the pits and peel them. Cut them both into half-inch slices. Arrange the slices alternately on four plates; cover with the mayonnaise and serve.

Kim Anderson remembers —

I first met Helen in 1974 or '75. She lived across Markham Avenue from me, but I met her at a Monkey-top volleyball afternoon. Our relationship progressed rapidly from acquaintances to the greatest of friends. Over the years, our love of all things food being a constant, she was the kind of friend that I could count on for everything — from helping to plan and host sybaritic alternate community fun, to letting me bunk in with her between grad school years behind Sunnyside during the decadent summer of '78, to serving as the perfect hostess for my mother during her occasional visits. My reciprocation, though likely inadequate, was always warmly appreciated. And a river ran through it — the river being the love of food, drink, and friendship.

Introducing Mexico

The Guide
October 1976

THERE HAS BEEN A DEFINITE TREND toward more cosmopolitan wining and dining in the Research Triangle since I first set foot here. There are more interesting places to eat out and a greater variety of foods to take home and cook. My local supermarket has recently begun carrying a good brand of fresh tortillas, both corn and flour. Now that I don't have to make tortillas every time I need them, I have been doing more Mexican cooking. Here's a taco recipe that includes recipes for guacamole and chorizo.

Tacos

10 flour tortillas
1 can refried beans
1 pound chorizo (recipe below)
guacamole (recipe below)
¼ pound grated Monterey jack or
    muenster cheese
½ chopped onion
1 chopped tomato
1 loose cup chopped lettuce

Wrap the tortillas in a damp kitchen towel or aluminum foil and heat for 10 to 15 minutes in a 325°F oven. Warm the beans over a low heat, stirring frequently. Fry the chorizo until lightly browned. Let everyone assemble their own tacos: tortilla-beans-chorizo-cheese-guacamole-vegetables. If you don't eat meat, these are fine without the chorizo. Serves four.

This filling is also good with fried tortilla shells. Use the masa (corn) tortillas and fry in enough fat to cover. Keep the fat very hot (but not smoking), so the tortillas fry instead of absorbing oil. As the tortillas soften in the fat, fold them in half with kitchen tongs, keeping the opening wide enough to stuff with the fillings.

Guacamole

 1 large ripe avocado
 1 small tomato, peeled, seeded & chopped
 ½ small onion, chopped
 2 hot chili peppers, seeded & chopped
     (more if your taste is hot)
 fresh coriander (if you can get it) or
     pinch dried coriander
 salt, freshly ground pepper
 pinch sugar

Either blend briefly (you don't want a total paste) or mash the ingredients together with a fork. If you make the guacamole ahead of time, seal it very closely as the avocado discolors in the air.

This is delicious served with homemade tortilla chips: Cut up tortillas and fry in hot oil until crisp.

Chorizo

 1 pound lean ground pork
 1 teaspoon salt
 2 seeded, chopped chili peppers
 1 teaspoon cumin
 ½ teaspoon coriander
 1 teaspoon oregano
 2 tablespoons red wine vinegar

Mix all ingredients. Let them stand several hours or overnight in the refrigerator.

If you wish to go beyond the scope of this recipe (perhaps make your own tortillas and refried beans) or try other Mexican dishes, I recommend:

The Complete Book of Mexican Cooking by Elizabeth Lambert Ortiz: Authentic, thorough introduction to Mexican cooking. Takes you way beyond tacos and enchiladas into many less widely known dishes.

Sunset Mexican Cookbook: Good introduction to Mexican foods. Clear directions. Includes instructions on how to build tools you may want, such as a tortilla press. [*Out of print – ed.*]

English Savoury Pies

The Guide
November 1976

ENGLISH SAVOURY PIES come in many sizes and shapes with a great variety of fillings: game, beef, chicken, cheese and vegetables. The pastry is usually a top crust only. Some of the fillings, such as steak and kidney, also appear as puddings when they are put into a soft crust and steamed. Here is a hot water crust, especially good with meat fillings, and three ways to fill it. You can also use short or flaky pastry.

Hot Water Crust

    2 cups unbleached white flour
    3 tablespoons water
    3 ounces lard
    $\frac{1}{4}$ teaspoons salt
    milk or an egg yolk (for glazing)

Sift the flour and salt into a bowl. Bring the water and lard to a boil and pour into the flour, mixing until the dough forms a smooth ball. Add a little water if the dough seems too crumbly, but the object when making pastries is to get the dough to come together with the least amount of liquid possible to insure a crisp crust. Let the dough rest while you make your filling.

Sausage & Apple Pie

This is a very hearty pie and with a salad, will serve six for dinner. Use your favorite cooking apples; I like Staymans because they are tart and crisp.

    I small onion, thinly sliced
    I pound sausage meat, sliced into 12 pieces
    6 apples, peeled, cored and sliced thickly
    generous pinch of thyme
    pinch of rosemary
    pinch salt, freshly ground pepper

Cook the sliced onion slowly in a little bacon fat, butter or other cooking oil until transparent.

Take slightly more than half of the hot water crust and roll it out thinly on a lightly floured board. Gently put it into your pie pan, being careful not to tear the crust and making sure it comes right to the edge of the pan.

Now put in a layer of $\frac{1}{3}$ of the apples; then a layer of $\frac{1}{2}$ of the sausage. Pat the sausage out thinly to cover the apples. Spread on $\frac{1}{2}$ of the onions and sprinkle with the seasonings. Repeat this process and end with the last third of the apples. Roll out the remaining dough to make the top crust. Moisten the edges of the bottom crust and put on the top, pinching the edges together to make a tight seal. Make a couple of slits in the top for the steam to escape and brush very lightly with milk or egg yolk. Bake for one hour at 350°F. If the top is not browning well, turn your oven up to 425°F for the last 5 minutes. Let the pie cool a bit before serving; it tastes best warm, not hot.

Cornish Leek Pie

Leeks are ancient food; this mild member of the onion family appears on Egyptian columns. This pie seems like a quiche turned upside down and serves four.

    $\frac{1}{2}$ recipe of the hot water crust
    I pound leeks
    2 ounces butter
    $\frac{1}{4}$ pound bacon
    8 ounces sour cream
    I egg and I egg yolk
    pepper

Cut off any wilted green portions of the leeks and trim the bottoms. Slice down through the green part into the white and hold under running water to wash them out. Drain and slice them. Cook them gently in butter for 10 to 15 minutes, until they are soft. Cut the bacon into ½ inch bits and mix into the leeks. Put this mixture into your pie pan.

Mix the sour cream, egg, egg yolk and pepper together and pour over the leek mixture. Roll out your crust, making sure it overlaps the edge of the pan as it shrinks during cooking. Put it on top of the pie and cut slits for the steam to escape. Brush with egg yolk or milk to glaze and bake for 30 minutes at 350°F. This pie is also best warm; leftovers are good cold.

Cornish Pasties

I cannot sing the praises of Cornish pasties too highly. They are delicious little pouches, filled with meat and potatoes, easy to make and good hot, warm or cold.

> hot water crust
> ½ pound chuck steak, cut into ½ inch cubes
> ½ pound potatoes, cut into ½ inch cubes
> 1 onion, roughly chopped
> salt, pepper, very small pinch thyme

Mix the meat, potatoes, onion and seasonings together.

Divide the dough into fourths (for largish pasties) or sixths and roll into rounds. Put the filling on one half of the round. Moisten the edges of the crust and fold over. Pinch the edges together well. Glaze them with milk or egg yolk. Bake at 350°F for 40 minutes.

Dale Appleman remembers —

The standard plastic index card box where I find my favorite handwritten Helen recipes is laminated with bits of old New Yorker covers — made for me in the late '60s by my new husband. I had met Helen when traveling to England as a roadie/bride for this hard-driving folksinger. Helen befriended us after a concert and invited us to stay with her when we returned to London at the end of our travels.

And so we did.

I remember Helen and I walking together in her London neighborhood to shop for each meal. This was in radical contrast to my own supermarket routine. We only went to Sainsbury's (the one supermarket) for ordinary house supplies. Otherwise, it was a stop at the greengrocers for salads and vegetables, the fish market to see what was fresh (red mullet would be nice, Helen decided), the butcher, the cheese store and so on. They weren't called "specialty stores," either. I would watch Helen survey the displays. She was open to anything interesting and fresh, always had questions for the storekeeper and opened me to a new way of looking at and preparing food. Helen had cookbooks by Elizabeth David, books about food that were to be read (unlike the heavy illustrated, directional recipe books I had). Europe was all over her cooking — we ate pistous, tians, soup with aioli on crusts. She said courgette for zucchini, aubergine for eggplant and understood English measures and ovens. And Helen captured my heart forever as the only person who ever made enough Hollandaise for my asparagus.

Christmas Sweets

The Guide
December 1976

Sweets before Christmas, and sweets with
Christmas, and after Christmas sweets.

I DID NOT HAVE A SHELTERED YOUTH when it came to dessert. In the finest American tradition, my mother explored all the possibilities for the final course. But there was one experience that I did not have until I was 21 and living in England — Christmas Pudding, a sterling example of Victorian excess at the table. The Puritans found these puddings sinfully rich but were not successful in stamping them out. Elizabeth David believes them to be heavily influenced by dried fruit and nuts from the eastern Mediterranean.

Christmas Pudding

Make your Christmas Pudding as soon as you can locate the ingredients you need. It's traditional (and safe, due to the high sugar content) to let your pudding mature for some time before Christmas. Though several months is more common, I once had a year-old pudding that was quite good. This recipe (from Clement Freud in the *Daily Telegraph,* several years ago) sets out the ingredients in categories. You put it together emphasizing the elements you like best. No matter what proportions you choose, it will be absolutely delicious and worth every bit of time and energy you put into it. It makes three pounds of pudding and is so rich that it will serve everyone at your Christmas table. It fills an English pint-sized pudding basin* (20 American ounces) or can be made in several smaller basins or bowls.

STODGE: 1 pound

6 ounces of shredded suet and 10 ounces of soft white breadcrumbs. (Suet is beef fat. This sounds weird, if you've never had puddings made with it. You can try using other fats, but I recommend getting some fresh looking and smelling beef fat and shredding it yourself. Mrs. Beeton, in her famous *Book of Household Management,* helpfully suggested dusting the suet lightly with flour as you shred it. If you can find boxed, pre-shredded suet, this is fine.)

FRUIT: 1½ pounds

Currants, raisins (both dark and golden — known as "sultanas" in England), dried apricots, prunes, apples, candied peel *(see page 102)* or whole crystallized fruit and about 2 ounces chopped almonds. Chop the large fruit.

SEASONINGS:

4 ounces brown sugar, ½ teaspoon salt, 1½ teaspoons spice (cinnamon, nutmeg, cloves, allspice).

LIQUIDS:

3 whole eggs, well beaten. Twice the volume of eggs in other liquids, one half of which should be molasses or dark cane syrup. The rest can be rum, brandy, lemon juice, Guinness, etc.

METHOD:

Lightly mix together the suet and breadcrumbs. Add the fruit and seasonings; then the liquids. Fingers work best for mixing. Butter your basin(s); pack in the pudding; cover with a circle of buttered paper, then a piece of foil. Lay a clean cloth across the top and tie it securely around the basin. Let it sit in a cool place for a day.

*A pudding basin is a metal bowl with a tightly fitting lid, made especially for steamed puddings. Any metal bowl will do if covered with foil as Helen describes. – ed.

STEAM:

Steam the pudding for six hours. Put the basin on a trivet or jar lid in a large pan. Pour in enough boiling water to come to two-thirds of the height of the basin. Keep the water simmering and top it off with boiling water when necessary. Remove and store the pudding in a cool place until Christmas.

SERVE:

Re-steam the pudding for two hours before serving. Flame it with brandy, if you like spectacular entrances. (Warm the brandy gently, pour it over the pudding and ignite it — very carefully.) Serve the pudding with cream or brandied butter.

BRANDIED BUTTER:

Cream together ½ pound butter and 3 ounces sugar (about ½ cup). Add 2 tablespoons brandy. Make this butter the day you want to use it, as the brandy evaporates.

Norman Kennedy's Shortbread

Norman Kennedy is a Scot and a fine weaver, singer of traditional songs and cook. This is the best shortbread I've ever eaten.

1 pound butter
1 pound white flour (4 cups)
½ pound sugar (2 cups)
½ pound rice flour or farina (2 cups)

Mix the dry ingredients. Knead in the butter as if you were making pastry. The dough should form a ball, with the addition of no liquids. Roll it out to about ⅜ inch and cut it in rounds. Prick each round with a fork a couple of times. Bake at 350°F for 20-30 minutes. The rounds should be lightly colored. Though they are very tempting hot, they are even better cold, when they get crisp.

Winter Salads

The Guide
January 1977

MODERN TECHNOLOGY assures our supply of the same vegetables year round. I don't classify myself as a reactionary, but flavor and texture seem to be the first casualties when technology meets food, if the intent is preservation or availability out of season. An example: the tomatoes in the stores these days. I'd rather do without fresh ones and use canned tomatoes (picked and canned when ripe) for cooking in the winter months.

I also enjoy a seasonal quality in my cooking, making dishes that seem appropriate to the time of year. This month's salads go well with wintry meals and avoid ingredients that are not at their best right now. Try serving them after the main course. (Don't dirty a separate plate — drag the lettuce through gravy or stew liquids just once, and you'll be hooked). The carrot and parsnip salads are also good as a first course.

Vinaigrette

This is a good basic dressing. The flavor of each ingredient is important. Olive oil is my first choice of oil by a large margin; safflower is my second. I don't really care for other readily available oils — they taste too much like their preservatives. Wine vinegar has a more interesting taste than other vinegars. The lemon juice is for a delicate tang. This vinaigrette goes well with simple salads like Romaine or Boston lettuce alone or with one or two other ingredients — Greek olives and/or alfalfa sprouts.

5 to 6 parts olive oil
1 part wine vinegar or lemon juice
pinch of ground mustard seed (optional)
salt and freshly ground pepper

Mix these ingredients well by stirring them in the bottom of the salad bowl, shaking in a jar, using a wire whisk or whatever. Don't mix the dressing with your lettuce until the last minute and the salad will be crisply coated with the dressing instead of limply soaked.

Carrot Salad

8 small carrots
1 scallion or shallot
6 tablespoons of vinaigrette made
**   with lemon juice**

Peel, rinse and grate the carrots. Trim, rinse and grate the scallion or shallot. Lightly coat the salad with vinaigrette. Make this salad well before you are ready to eat it and the flavors will mingle nicely. Serves four.

Parsnip Salad

This salad, for some strange reason, is often called "Poor Man's Lobster" in England. It doesn't taste like lobster at all; it tastes like parsnips — which are very good in their own right. If you have never eaten them before, this recipe is a good introduction.

6 medium parsnips
½ cup mayonnaise or aioli
finely chopped parsley

Peel the parsnips and slice them into ½ inch rounds. Boil them in just enough salted water to cover. They will take about 10 minutes to cook, but start checking them earlier because they must just barely be done. Drain and mix them with

the mayonnaise or aioli. Sprinkle with parsley. Serves four.

Homemade mayonnaise is better for this dish than store-bought because it has a subtler flavor. Aioli is garlic mayonnaise. Completely smash a clove of garlic before starting the mayonnaise (use a mortar and pestle or the side of a big flat knife), and proceed with your favorite mayonnaise recipe. If you have no favorite mayonnaise recipe at present, *Mastering the Art of French Cooking, Volume 1,* by Child, Bertholle and Beck, gives clear instructions for making all types of sauces. It is also very strong on what to do if something goes wrong. (*Or see instructions on page 10.*)

Endive Salad

4 heads endive
4 tablespoons walnut halves
¼ cup vinaigrette (with lemon)

Trim the base of the endives, separate the leaves, wash them and dry them well. Mix the endive, walnuts and dressing just before serving. Serves four.

Couscous

The Guide
February 1977

Couscous is native to North Africa. The name of this dish is couscous, but couscous is actually the grain (wheat) itself which has been ground and treated with flour to prepare it for steaming. Although there are sweet and fish versions of this dish, the most common is a mutton stew with the couscous steamed above it. Recently I've seen distinctive couscous steamers and stew pots for sale in stores in this area. You don't need this special pot; you can use a vegetable steamer or a colander that fits over a pan with boiling water.

In North Africa each family gets wheat ground to their specifications and then works in the flour at home. As we don't have millers, it's handy that prepared couscous is available.

The Algerian version below was given to me by Helene Pruniaux, who grew up there and is one of the best and most hospitable cooks I've known. It's very good for entertaining large groups of people. Helene says this fancy version reflects a French influence on Algerian cooking. I present the various parts of the dish in chronological order.

Chickpeas

Use one ounce dried chickpeas (⅓ rounded cup) per person. Soak the peas for six hours or overnight. Simmer them until done. This will take anywhere from two to six hours, depending on the chickpeas you buy. If the package has instructions, follow them. If you have doubts, do them the day before and warm them up in just enough of the stew stock to cover them for about a half-hour before serving.

Couscous

For each person:
2 ounces couscous
salt

Put the couscous in a bowl and cover with water. Let it sit for 10 minutes. Turn it out onto a clean tea towel or multi-layered cheese cloth and leave it to swell for an hour. Steam it (leaving it in the cloth) uncovered, over boiling salted water for 20 to 25 minutes. Start timing when the steam comes through the couscous. Take the bundle out of the steamer and splash cold, salted water on the couscous, using your fingers or a fork to break apart any clumps. Leave it for another hour. Just before serving, resteam the couscous for 10 minutes.

Chicken & Lamb Stew

For each person:
1 piece chicken
1 lamb chop
½ onion, sliced
½ leek (optional), sliced
½ carrot, sliced
½ turnip or potato, sliced
½ summer squash, sliced
1 tablespoon tomato paste
parsley, bay leaf, thyme
paprika, 1 clove garlic
basil, cumin
fresh mint (when available)
salt and pepper

Brown the meats in a large stew pan, using a small amount of oil. Remove the meat and soften the onions and leeks. Add the paprika and garlic and stir in. Return the meat and cover with water or chicken stock. Stir in the tomato paste. Add a sprig of parsley, a couple of bay leaves, a good pinch of thyme, salt and pepper to taste. The amount of basil and cumin depends on the total volume of your stew. Start out with good pinches of each and taste for them after it's cooked for 15 or 20 minutes. Bring the stew to the boil and reduce to simmer.

You will want to add the other vegetables about 45 minutes before the stew is ready (except for the squash which should wait until 20 minutes before serving) so that they will not be overdone. The total cooking time will be about one-and-a-half hours, unless you are using stewing hen, when it may take two to three hours for the meats to be tender. When fresh mint is available, add a sprig 10 minutes before the end.

 Go easily, Helen, draped in an impeccable black voile dress from the 1940s. When I first saw you, you looked exactly like . . . Ava Gardner.

Go with your intractable poise, Helen, fashioning hollandaise sauce over a high flame without a double boiler and quoting Elizabeth David.

Go imperiously, Helen, an island of precocious sanity in a sea of bewildered hedonism, grinning through it all like Delbert McClinton fronting a 90-decibel boogie band.

Go, fixing your own Volkswagen and hardly even getting dirty.

Go, baking astonishing muffins without a recipe using random ingredients from the pantry of a kitchen that didn't even have one.

Go with a detective novel in your hand.

Go, Helen, in a chenille bathrobe humming a song by Martin, Bogan & Armstrong with your mouth curled in a bashful grin.

Go with your determined stride. You also resembled Susan Hayward.

Go with tablecloths and napkins.

Go in Keds.

Go, gracious, kind, and laughing, an emissary from an unsuspected place of wisdom and style.

Go, writing out, by hand and from memory, instructions that read:

> *"Put the couscous in a bowl and cover with water. Let sit 10 minutes. Turn out into a clean tea towel and leave to swell for one hour. Steam over boiling H_2O for 20 minutes. Start counting when the steam comes through the couscous. Splash cold, salted water on couscous, using your fingers to break up clumps. Before serving, resteam for 10 minutes." And expecting me to do it.*

Go, Helen, standing with one leg cocked, arms folded, scudding across a persimmon-colored sky holding a small fluted glass.

Go, Helen, with Django Reinhardt playing in the background.

With you gone there's a great big hole in the world.

— Steve Emerson, memorial tribute to Helen

Couscous

Merquez (Meatballs)

8 ounces ground beef or lamb
1 small onion, finely chopped
1 thin slice of bread, soaked in milk and
**   squeezed dry**
1 tablespoon parsley, finely chopped
1 tablespoon peanut oil
1 egg
small pinch each: saffron, powdered ginger,
**   nutmeg**

This will be enough meatballs for about four people. Alter to suit the number you are feeding.

Mix all the ingredients together and form into smallish meatballs. Roll them in flour and then a beaten egg. Fry them in a small amount of oil until brown. Drain away the oil and add enough stew stock to barely cover. Simmer for 20 minutes.

Harissa (Hot Sauce)

Crush cayenne pepper into pieces and cover with peanut oil. This mixture keeps a long time and just gets hotter with age.

TO SERVE: Take a large platter with edges or a flattish bowl. Put in the couscous and moisten with a bit of the stock. Arrange the chickpeas evenly over the surface. Arrange the meats and vegetables over the surface, moistening with a bit more of the stock. Serve more of the stock separately to pour on each serving. The harissa is to sprinkle, to taste. Don't worry about any leftovers. They are very good reheated.

Homemade Soups

The Guide
March 1977

HOMEMADE SOUPS are worth every bit of effort they may take. Simple recipes will amaze you with how easily delicious soups can be made, and the complicated ones will most likely be soups you couldn't find in cans. Besides, the soups in cans usually taste too much like flavor enhancers, and the ones you make at home are fresh and need no enhancement.

Chicken Stock

Many soup recipes call for some sort of meat stock. When I'm cooking chicken, I buy a whole one and make a stock from unused parts — the backs and innards when I'm cutting up the chicken or the carcass of a whole one when the meal is over. You can boil up the pieces with an onion, carrot, herbs and spices or you can brown the pieces before boiling for a richer flavor. I usually throw in a pinch of thyme, a bay leaf, parsley, peppercorns and a little salt. Be sparing with the salt, because if you reduce the stock it may end up too salty. Simmer for 1 to 2 hours. Strain out all the bits and store the stock in the refrigerator until you need it. It's safe for up to a week.

Carrot Soup

½ pound sliced carrots
1 medium onion, chopped
1 tablespoon rice
4 cups chicken stock or water
pinch thyme (1 sprig, if you have fresh)
salt and pepper
1 stick (4 ounces) butter
2 slices bread

Soften the onions and carrots in two ounces of the butter. Stir a couple of times and don't let them brown. Add the rice, liquid and thyme and bring to a simmer. Salt and pepper to taste. Cook until the carrots are soft (20–30 minutes) then sieve or blend the soup. A vegetable ricer or food mill is perfect for this sort of soup. If you use a blender, be brief so there is some texture to the soup. Return the soup to the pan, taste for seasonings and reheat.

Before the soup is done, cut the crusts off the bread and cube it. Fry until crisp in the other 2 oz. of butter. Sprinkle the fresh croutons into the soup as it's served.

Creamed Onion Soup

4 large onions
4 tablespoons butter
5 cups chicken stock
salt and pepper
½ pint whipping cream
3 egg yolks
grated Swiss cheese

Melt the butter. Let the onions soften (but not color) in the butter for about 10 minutes. Add the stock and bring it to a simmer. Salt and pepper to taste. Let it simmer for 30 minutes. Beat the egg yolks and cream together. Add a ladleful of hot soup and beat again. Now add the yolk and cream mixture to the soup. Heat gently, stirring all the while, until the soup thickens slightly. Do not let it come to a boil or the yolks will scramble. Serve and let everyone sprinkle their soup with the grated cheese.

Pistou I

This soup is named for the mixture of garlic, basil and tomato that is stirred in before serving.

4 cups water
1 small leek, chopped (optional)
1 onion, chopped
3 tomatoes
salt and pepper
1 potato, diced
1 zucchini, sliced
½ pound green beans
1 ounce vermicelli
1 clove garlic
1 tablespoon basil
grated parmesan cheese

Pour boiling water over the tomatoes. Peel and seed them. Set one aside and chop the other two. Put the tomatoes, leek, onion and water in a pan and bring to a simmer. Salt and pepper to taste. After 10 minutes add the diced potato. Five minutes later, add the zucchini and green beans. When the soup simmers again, add the vermicelli. The soup is ready when the vegetables and pasta are done, in about 10 minutes.

In the meantime, make the pistou: smash up a clove of garlic with a tablespoon of basil. A mortar and pestle are good for this, although you can use a blender. Add and smash up the remaining tomato. When the soup is done add 3 tablespoons of soup stock and mix well, then mix the pistou into the soup. Serve the soup and pass the cheese.

A Weakness for Chocolate

The Guide
April 1977

Q UEEN ISABELLA financed Columbus's voyage to find a short cut to the profitable spice trade with India. He missed, but the obstruction he found changed a great many things; for one thing the tables of Europe were never the same. All manner of exotic food and drink were being consumed in the New World: potatoes, pineapples, tomatoes, corn, a great variety of squashes, peppers and beans, maté, and chocolate. Bernal Díaz del Castillo, traveling with Cortez, wrote of the "cacao" served "all frothed up . . . in cup-shaped vessels of pure gold." Chocolate was a royal drink, served only to certain classes; I've read that it was prepared by women to be drunk by men and that the Spanish continued that custom for a time.

Today in Mexico, the drink is still served, and chocolate turns up in some dishes we'd think unlikely. Molé sauce, often served with turkey, is a mixture of seeds and chiles and contains several squares of bitter chocolate. My Texan mother uses bitter chocolate as the secret ingredient in her chili.

Sinful Chocolate Cake

I have a weakness for chocolate, which may be inherited, so the first recipe is my mother's chocolate cake. It's a beautiful, three-layer cake that is perfect for special occasions. Sometimes I've made it even more impressive by cutting each layer in half and having a six layer cake.

THE CAKE:
1 cup cocoa
2 cups boiling water
1 cup butter (2 sticks)
2½ cups sugar
4 eggs
½ teaspoon vanilla
2¾ cups flour
2 teaspoons soda
½ teaspoon baking powder
½ teaspoon salt

Pour boiling water over the cocoa. Whisk until smooth and allow to cool. Combine dry ingredients. Cream the butter and sugar. Beat in the eggs and vanilla. Mix in the flour mixture a quarter at a time; the cocoa mixture, a third at a time. Put into three greased and floured 9-inch cake pans and bake in a 350°F oven for 35 minutes.

THE FILLING:
1 cup whipping cream
¼ cup powdered sugar
1 teaspoon vanilla

Whip the cream with the sugar and vanilla. Spread it between the layers of the cooled cake.

THE ICING:
16 ounce package of chocolate chips
½ cup whipping cream
1 cup butter
2½ cups powdered sugar

Betty Flemming remembers —

While living in London, Helen telephoned me one morning during the days when it was fairly expensive for international calls. We caught up on each other's news, then she asked for the "Sinful Chocolate Cake" recipe. This has been our family birthday cake for years.

I told her I would jot it down and get it in the mail the next day. "No, Mom. I need the recipe today because I must bake the cake for a friend's birthday party tomorrow evening!" Getting the recipe cost Helen £30-35, but the response at the birthday party was "worth every pence"!

Melt the chocolate with the cream and butter. Let this mixture cool. Set it into a container of ice and beat with the powdered sugar until thick enough to spread. Spread it on the top and sides of the cake.

Chocolate Mousse

This is a simple chocolate mousse recipe, rich and delicious.

Per serving:
1 ounce semi-sweet chocolate
1 egg
½ tablespoon butter at room temperature
Optional: 1 tablespoon strong coffee,
orange juice or liquor

Melt the chocolate in a dish in a 250°F oven, or in a double boiler. (The reason recipes tell you to melt chocolate in one of these ways is that it burns easily.) Separate the eggs and beat the yolks well. Stir the yolks into the chocolate, then mix in the butter. Add the flavoring of your choice; Cointreau is especially nice. Beat the egg whites until they're stiff and gently fold them into the chocolate mixture. Put into individual glasses or serving dishes and refrigerate for several hours before serving.

Chocolate Chinchilla

This recipe is adapted from Elizabeth David's *Spices, Salt and Aromatics in the English Kitchen* (the answer to those who think the seasonings in English cooking are water and a lot of heat applied over a long period of time). She points out that it is a "splendid" way to use left over egg whites. You can freeze the whites until you accumulate enough for this recipe.

5 to 7 egg whites
½ cup + 1 tablespoon unsweetened cocoa
scant ½ cup sugar
1 heaping teaspoon ground cinnamon

Mix the cocoa, sugar, and cinnamon. Whip the egg whites until stiff. Fold the cocoa mixture gently into the whites. Turn the mixture into a buttered ring mold or soufflé dish. (The dish should hold 5 to 6 cups). Set the dish in a baking pan and pour boiling water to halfway up the side of the dish. Bake in a 350°F oven for 45 to 50 minutes. Serve it warm or cold. Elizabeth David suggests "fresh thin pouring cream to which has been added a little sherry, rum or brandy."

Hot Chocolate

And here's a good way to make "American style" hot chocolate: Use 1 teaspoon of cocoa, 2 to 3 teaspoons sugar, and a drop of vanilla for each cup of milk. Mix the cocoa, sugar, vanilla and a little water to a thick syrup in the pan. Heat it gently until the sugar dissolves and then add the milk. Heat until it's as hot as you like your cocoa, stirring from time to time.

A Weakness for Chocolate

Gnocchi

The Guide
May 1977

GNOCCHI COME FROM ITALY and are similar to dumplings. They are delicious, inexpensive, filling, and easy to prepare. These recipes will feed two very hungry people or four as a first course. They are fine as they come out of the oven with butter and cheese. You can also vary the dish and feed more people if you serve them with a well-flavored tomato or meat sauce (a few dried mushrooms in either sauce goes well with gnocchi). Another variation is to substitute Swiss cheese for the parmesan or use a mixture of Swiss and parmesan to sprinkle on top before the final browning.

Spinach & Ricotta Gnocchi

1 pound fresh spinach or
    10 ounces frozen spinach
1 tablespoon butter
8 ounces ricotta cheese
1½ ounces grated parmesan cheese
2 eggs
4 tablespoons flour
salt and pepper
nutmeg
butter and parmesan cheese

Cook the spinach and drain it well. Add the salt, pepper, a pinch of nutmeg, one tablespoon butter and the cheeses. Stir this mixture over a low heat for five minutes to dry it out. Add the eggs and flour and mix well. Refrigerate for several hours or overnight. Form the mixture into balls about ¾ inch in diameter and roll them in flour. Poach in simmering water; when they rise to the top (5-8 minutes) they are done. Layer them in a buttered dish and sprinkle with butter and cheese. Heat in a hot oven or under the broiler until the cheese melts.

Semolina or Polenta Gnocchi

3 cups milk
1 cup polenta (cornmeal)
    or
1 cup semolina (farina)
3 ounces grated parmesan cheese
2 eggs
salt and pepper
nutmeg
butter and more cheese

Polenta is cornmeal; I have had good results with this dish using stone-ground yellow cornmeal. Semolina is also called farina (available in some health food stores); cream of wheat may be substituted, although it is unevenly ground and may be lumpy.

Bring the milk to a boil. Stir in the polenta or semolina. Reduce the heat to a simmer and stir frequently. When the mixture is thick enough so that the spoon stands up, take it off the heat and stir in the parmesan, eggs, a pinch of nutmeg and salt and pepper to taste. Spread the mixture in a buttered shallow pan or on a wet board or piece of marble. Let it cool until firm (several hours in the refrigerator or overnight). When you are ready to serve the gnocchi, cut the mixture into circles, squares, diamonds or whatever shape you like and layer these pieces with butter and more cheese in an ovenproof dish. Heat in a hot (425°F) oven or under the broiler until the cheese is warm and bubbling.

Mediterranean Mealtime

The Guide
July 1977

EVERY SUMMER I FIND MYSELF wishing that I were somewhere on the Mediterranean. Once I did manage to spend a nearly perfect week in the south of France. My pleasures were simple: the company of good friends, the ocean, hot sun, exotic drinks, learning to play boule (similar to the Italian bolla), inexpensive good wine and some of the best food I've ever eaten.

Shopping for food was a delight — green-grocers with huge piles of ripe tomatoes, strong garlic, little courgettes (zucchini); fishmongers with beautiful fresh bass, mussels, tuna, mullet; butchers who cut everything to order; bakeries full of French bread and pastries.

The two dishes this month — ratatouille and salad niçoise — come from the south of France and are made using my favorite summer ingredients. They don't have to be made in the summer but that's when the ingredients are at their best and they are fine hot-weather eating.

Ratatouille

Some friends of mine have a "ratatouille garden" this summer: eggplant, tomatoes, zucchini, onions, basil, garlic, and green peppers. These are stewed together in olive oil to make this rich-tasting dish. Ratatouille goes very well with lamb, pork and chicken.

> ½ cup olive oil
> 2 large onions
> 2 green (or yellow or red) peppers
> 1 medium eggplant
> 2 small zucchini
> 4 tomatoes
> 1 to 3 cloves of garlic, smashed
> salt and pepper
> basil
> thyme
> rosemary

About one hour before you plan to start cooking the ratatouille, cut up the eggplant and zucchini. Slice them into strips, then into bite-sized pieces. Sprinkle them with salt and leave them in a colander. This draws out juices, which can sometimes be bitter, and makes the final product less watery.

Slice the onions thinly. Heat the olive oil in a large iron skillet and let the onions start to soften. Remove the seeds from the green peppers (red or yellow sweet peppers are also delicious in this dish) and slice them thinly. Add them to the skillet and let them soften, too. Now add the eggplant and in a few minutes the zucchini. If the mixture seems dry, add a little more olive oil. Cover and cook on a low heat for 30 minutes, stirring occasionally.

Pour boiling water over the tomatoes and skin them. Cut them in half along their equators and discard the seeds. Chop them roughly. Squash the cloves of garlic. Add the tomatoes, garlic and a big pinch of basil, a smaller pinch of thyme and an even smaller pinch of rosemary. Salt and pepper to taste. Cook slowly uncovered for about 10 to 15 minutes more. Serve hot, warm or cold.

Salad Niçoise

> Per person:
> 1 small boiling potato
> 2 ounces green beans
> ½ or whole egg
> ¼ to ½ green pepper
> 1 green onion
> ½ tomato

a few anchovies
a few black olives
¼ to ½ small can of tuna
lettuce
vinaigrette made with 3 to 6 parts olive oil,
    1 part red wine vinegar, pinch dry mustard,
    and salt and pepper

Scrub the potatoes, and boil them until they are just done. You should not use mealy, baking potatoes for this dish. Slice them thickly and mix with enough vinaigrette to coat them.

Top and tail the green beans and boil them in lots of water until they are just done. This will take from five to eight minutes, depending on the size of the beans. They should be slightly crunchy. Drain them and mix with vinaigrette.

Boil the eggs for 7 to 10 minutes (any longer and you end up with that unappetizing green around the yolk). Shell them and cut into quarters.

Remove the seeds from the peppers, and slice them thinly. Slice the green onion thinly. Cut the tomato into wedges. Drain the anchovies and tuna.

Assemble each salad on a small plate: lettuce, potatoes, green beans, peppers, tomatoes, eggs, tuna, anchovies, olives and then onions. Pour a little vinaigrette on each, serve with French bread and butter and imagine that you are in a small seaside cafe in Nice.

The Common Lemon

The Guide
August 1977

IT'S HOT AS I WRITE THIS — so hot that it's hard to think about eating, much less cooking. To avoid heating up a non-air-conditioned house* even further, try cooking during the hours when your house is its coolest. Cook a lot of food at one time and serve it cold at the appropriate hour. Cook out on a grill; it's already hot out there, and the heat your grill puts out won't make much of a difference.

The recipes this month all have lemons in common. Their sharp tang is refreshing and may make you feel cooler.

Old Fashioned Make-It-Yourself Lemonade

Take six lemons and a potato peeler; peel off the yellow skin, leaving as much of the white attached to the lemon as possible. The yellow skin contains delicious lemon oil; the white is very bitter tasting. Pour some boiling water over the yellow skins as if you were making tea (a few sprigs of mint are a good addition), and let this cool. Squeeze the juice from the lemons and add this to the strained lemon water. Add sugar and water (or

*More than 20 years later, it's not hard to remember those wicked Durham summers because they come around every year. What's a bit harder to remember is how common the absence of air conditioning was back then. Trying not to heat up her kitchen in the summer and early fall was a theme Helen would return to time and again in her writing, even after AC became more commonplace around town. – ed.

soda water) to taste. Or put the whole thing in the blender using ice cubes instead of water and make a lemon freeze. Or add beer (about half beer and half lemonade) and have a shandy. Oranges and limes work equally well.

Avgolemono Soup

> 5 cups stock – chicken or fish
> ⅓ cup rice
> 2 eggs
> juice of 1 lemon

This soup, though hot, is refreshing; it comes from Greece where eggs and lemons are a frequent combination.

Cook the rice in the stock for 20 minutes or so. Beat the eggs and lemon juice well. Add a ladleful of the stock and beat again. Add the egg and lemon juice mixture to the stock (off the stove) and heat it up over a *low* heat, stirring all the while until it thickens *slightly*. Be careful; if the stock comes to a boil you will have scrambled egg soup which is not nearly as nice as avgolemono.

A recipe from Helen's card file:

Mediterranean Vegetable Salad

> ¼ long cucumber, diced small
> 4 plum or 2 medium tomatoes, diced small
> 1 green onion, chopped
> 2 tablespoons Italian parsley or cilantro, chopped
> 1 tablespoon olive oil
> 1 teaspoon lemon juice
> salt and pepper
> Optional: radishes, bell peppers, jicama, feta, black olives

Mix all ingredients. Can let stand. Serve cool. Serves two.

A Moveable Feast

The Guide
October 1977

ONE WAY TO KEEP AN UNRULY cookbook collection under control and still satisfy a taste for new recipes is to see what's at the local library. My local library is on Duke University's East Campus, and I was recently delighted by my first look at their collection. It ranges from comforting standards to books I'd heard about but never seen (several eminent Victorians) with some fascinating unknowns in between.

Several of the library books had been donated by Mrs. May W. Pohl in 1938, including a loose-leaf mimeographed volume, *Recipes By Request,* which she edited. The long list of participants on the cover included a few famous names: presidential wives and "Amelia Earhart Putnam." Being a big fan of the first lady of the air, I checked the book out, only to find when I got home, that Amelia Earhart's recipes were not there.

Were the pages lost? Or were the recipes too good to return to the library? I don't think they were taken by someone after the recipes of the famous, because while Mrs. Franklin Roosevelt's was also missing, Mrs. Herbert Hoover's and Mrs. Theodore Roosevelt's were not. (Admittedly they looked like real dogs, so my hypothesis may be wrong.)

I'm now intrigued. What was Amelia's recipe? A sensible recipe from a working woman? A lighter-than-air dessert? A dish guaranteed to disappear? Maybe a box lunch suitable for a long flight?

The last would be useful nowadays, with "no frills" foodless airline flights. If I were going to fly around the world, I'd take a thermos full of Potage Bonne Femme, a Ham, Spinach Pie and a bottle of Alsatian white wine. These provisions are also suitable for shorter outings.

Potage Bonne Femme

> **3 tablespoons butter**
> **2 large leeks**
> **1 pound potatoes**
> **2½ cups water**
> **salt and pepper**
> **¼ cup cream**
> **chives, parsley or chervil**
> **Optional: up to ¼ cup chopped carrots,**
> **   celery, tomato, or onion**

Chop the leeks coarsely and wash them. Melt the butter and put in the leeks and any optional vegetables you choose (The optionals are not necessary, merely add a little color and flavor). Let them cook gently until they soften and are absorbing the butter (about 5 to 10 minutes). Peel and dice the potatoes. Add the potatoes and water to the pan. Salt and pepper to taste. Bring to a boil, then turn down the heat and simmer until the vegetables are soft (30-45 minutes). Puree the soup (through a food mill or lightly in the blender). Return the soup to the pan, reheat, and add the cream. Taste for salt. Sprinkle with the herb of your choice and serve.

Ham

This recipe is for a four- to eight-pound piece of ham, cured but not cooked (not Smithfield-type, country ham). Cover the ham with water and soak at least four hours, longer if you suspect it's very salty. Pour out the soaking water, cover with new water and bring to a boil. Skim off any scum

that rises, partially cover and simmer. Get out your personal calculator and figure 30 minutes to the pound. Simmer the ham for all but one hour of the cooking time.

Take the ham out of the water (taste the water, if it's not too salty it will be great stock for any dried bean soup). Preheat the oven to 400°F. Using a sharp knife, remove the rind from the fat and score the fat (any design you like). Stick it with cloves. You can glaze it with mustard and brown sugar mixed together. My original English recipe calls for black treacle (a dark cane syrup). Pour over 1-2 cups hard cider, white wine, beer or whatever your fancy. Bake for an hour, basting frequently. Delicious hot or cold it's wonderful for sandwiches and all those recipes that call for little bits of ham.

Spinach Pie

> **shortcrust pastry for bottom crust**
> *(page 46 or 158)*
> **8 ounces cottage cheese**
> **1 package frozen spinach**
> **   (or 10 ounces fresh, well washed)**
> **2 tablespoons butter**
> **small chopped onion**
> **3 eggs**
> **2 ounces freshly grated parmesan**
> **5 tablespoons cream**
> **grated nutmeg**
> **salt and pepper**

This recipe is based on Italian Spinach Pie in Robert Carrier's *Great Dishes of the World*. He always insists on "freshly grated" this and that. Definitely not a book for dieters, however.

Drain the cottage cheese in a colander.

Make the shortcrust pastry and line your pie pan with it. Bake the pie crust "blind." This means put a piece of aluminum foil on top of the crust, fill it with dried beans to weigh it down and bake in a 400°F oven for 10 to 15 minutes. This makes the final crust crisper and, by the way, is also a good idea for quiches.

Soften the onions in the butter and add the spinach. Cook the spinach (if using fresh you may need to add a little water). Cook until all the water has boiled away, stirring so it won't stick. Beat the eggs lightly and add the spinach and onions, cottage cheese, parmesan, cream, a sprinkling of nutmeg, and salt and pepper. Put into the pie crust and bake in a 375°F oven for 30 minutes or until the custard has set. Like all dishes of this sort, I recommend serving it warm, but not hot. Also good cold.

To close, I'd like to say what's left of *Recipes By Request,* though it may not have Amelia Earhart's recipe, would be perfect for anyone looking for delicacies suitable for formal teas. Some fruit mousses from this book may appear here soon, after experiments in the West Pettigrew test kitchen.

Pudding on The Ritz

The Guide
November 1977

HERE ARE SOME RECIPES for the rapidly approaching entertainment season. The two patés are easily made and keep well. They are wonderful for starting a meal, as part of a buffet and just to have around for lunch or supper. The pumpkin pudding is a delicious alternative to the more traditional pumpkin pie for Thanksgiving.

Chicken Liver Paté

> 1 pound chicken livers
> 6 tablespoons butter
> ½ cup brandy
> 1 clove garlic
> salt and pepper
> pinch each: ground cloves, nutmeg,
>   cinnamon, allspice
> pinch each: thyme, basil, marjoram

Clean the livers, cutting off extraneous matter; rinse them lightly and dry them well. Sauté them in two tablespoons butter over a high heat until they are just done (5 to10 minutes). Cut one open to check; a hint of pink is fine.

Remove the livers from the pan and add the brandy (whiskey, or a mixture of brandy and sherry can be substituted). Let the liquid boil rapidly, scraping the bottom of the pan to mix in all the juices. Blend the livers, or mash them, or put them through a vegetable mill until they are a fine paste. Add the liquid from the pan, the remaining four tablespoons of butter, the mashed garlic, the spices and the herbs. Taste for seasonings; it should seem a little too spicy because the flavors tone down when the paté cools. Put the paté into a serving dish and serve cold with hot toast.

Pork Liver Terrine

1 pound pork liver
1 pound belly of pork
¼ cup dry white wine
¼ cup brandy
big pinch each: cloves, nutmeg, cinnamon,
    allspice
big pinch each: thyme, basil, rosemary
1 clove garlic, mashed
salt and pepper
1 egg
2 tablespoons flour
½ to 1 pound bacon
1 bay leaf

Grind the liver and pork together. Mix them with the wine, brandy (whiskey, once again, may be substituted), and seasonings (except for the bay leaf) and leave them to marinate several hours or overnight. Beat the flour and egg together and mix them into the paté. Fry a little patty of the mixture to check the seasonings. Line a loaf pan or small casserole pan with strips of bacon and pack the mixture in. Put the bay leaf on top and lay on strips of bacon (a lattice looks nice). Cover with foil and if your pan has a lid, put that on, too. Stand the pan in a larger pan, fill the larger pan with hot water and bake in a 350°F oven for 1½ to 2½ hours, depending on the size of your pan. It is done when the juices are no longer pink; poke it with a skewer to be sure.

This terrine is nicer if it is weighted down as it cools. Put a clean piece of wood that fits into the pan on the foil and put something heavy on top of that. Leave it sitting in the larger pan because juices will run over the top.

Serve the next day with fresh French bread or hot toast.

Pumpkin Pudding

2 cups cooked pumpkin
1 cup brown sugar
½ cup white sugar
2 cups cream
1 tablespoon melted butter
1 tablespoon molasses
1 tablespoon brandy
1½ teaspoon cinnamon
1½ teaspoon ginger
¾ teaspoon salt
1 teaspoon nutmeg
3 well-beaten eggs

Mix all ingredients together, using only ½ cup of the brown sugar, and adding the eggs last. Butter a casserole dish and spread the bottom and sides with the remaining ½ cup of brown sugar. Pour in the pudding and set the dish in a larger pan, filling the larger pan with hot water. Bake in a 350°F oven for 50 minutes. Serve with whipped cream.

🔲 *Dale Appleman remembers —*

To my huge pleasure, Helen and her husband left London and moved into our rinkydink Virginia suburb of Washington, D.C. As I look back, cooking duets with Helen escalated as our marriages eroded. By the time both of us had our walking papers, we used our bus rides home from work to discuss what we'd cook. We were already deep into making our own paté (de Campagne), requiring trips to Georgetown's French Market to watch the charcuterie grind exact proportions of veal, pork and beef. We skipped no steps. Our patés, thanks to Helen's diligence and Julia Child's tips, were great beauties.

Only the Lonely

The Guide
December 1977

NOT GOING OVER THE RIVER and through the woods to grandmother's house this holiday season? Don't worry about being lonely at dinner time; make a special meal for that special person — yourself — and discover the pleasure of dining alone. The following four courses can be multiplied to serve more than one, and are even better with music, candles, flowers and a good dry white wine.

Mushrooms & Cream on Toast

¼ pound mushrooms
1 slice white bread
½ cup cream
butter
salt and pepper

Clean the mushrooms gently with a damp paper towel (never wash them, they absorb water and get mushy). Slice them thinly. Fry the bread in butter until golden and put it on a hot plate. Heat the frying pan until very hot, add two tablespoons butter and the mushrooms. Keep the heat on high and stir the mushrooms frequently. When they start to get limp, salt and pepper them and pour in the cream. Keep stirring until the cream thickens, pour the mushrooms and cream onto the toasted bread and serve immediately.

Cornish Hen with Wild Rice Stuffing

2 ounces wild rice
1 very small onion, sliced
1 tablespoon celery, chopped
1 tablespoon mushrooms, chopped
1 tablespoon raisins, soaked in brandy
small pinch thyme
butter
salt and pepper
1 Cornish hen
2 tablespoons brandy
¼ cup chicken stock

To make the stuffing: Cook the wild rice, following the package instructions. Fry the onion, celery and mushrooms in butter until soft. Mix the rice, vegetables, thyme and raisins together. Salt and pepper to taste.

To cook the bird: Fill the bird with the stuffing. Rub the outside with butter and roast at 400°F for 25 minutes, basting a few times. Lower the heat to 350°F and roast for another 25 minutes, continuing to baste. Remove the bird to a serving dish and keep warm.

To make the sauce: Heat the roasting pan on a hot burner until it sizzles. Add the brandy and chicken stock. Stir with a wooden spoon, scraping up all the bits stuck to the pan. Taste for salt and pepper and pour over the bird.

Salad

A salad of romaine lettuce, artichoke hearts and Greek olives, dressed with olive oil and red wine vinegar is recommended.

Caramel Orange

1 orange
¼ cup water
¼ cup sugar

With a sharp knife, pare off some of the orange part of the peel (known as the zest) and cut it into thin slivers. Then carefully cut away the rest of the orange peel and pith completely. Make a syrup of the water and sugar. Let it simmer and dip the orange into it; turning it over for a few minutes so it is coated with the syrup. Remove the orange, turn up the heat a bit and add the slivers of peel. Cook them until the syrup thickens and the peel starts to caramelize. Pour the syrup and peel over the orange and chill well. When you are ready to serve, slice the orange thinly and spoon syrup and candied peel over it. If you expand this recipe you don't need to multiply the water and sugar by the number of oranges; a cup of each will comfortably take care of six oranges.

After dinner, sit back in a comfortable chair with a strong cup of your favorite coffee, a few thin chocolate mints and a glass of brandy.

Culinary Roots, or: What Alex Haley Never Told You

The Guide
January 1978

WHETHER OR NOT YOU'RE INTERESTED in genealogy, there are some roots you shouldn't be ignoring. Finding out about these roots doesn't mean research in libraries, cemeteries or courthouses; you'll be in the foodstore and your kitchen. I ignored root vegetables for years because of a couple of nasty encounters at a tender age, but they are healthy and inexpensive. These recipes take account of each root's distinct taste and are delicious.

You may notice that I ignore beets. The previously mentioned encounters were mostly with them, and I may never recover. I pass on a tip from Edouard de Pomiane — whom I regard so highly that I've almost tried the recipe — bake the beets in a hot oven until just done; peel them, salt and pepper them and smother with cream.

Turnip Soup

This soup is delicious and will amaze those you serve it to. People who think they hate turnips like it, and people who like turnips, love it. It is slightly adapted from a recipe in the *New York Times Cookbook* (with thanks to Keith's Telephone Recipe Service).

2 cups diced turnips
1 quart stock (beef or chicken)
salt and pepper
1 cup heavy cream
2 egg yolks
1 tablespoon butter
chopped parsley

Peel and dice the turnips. Cook them in the stock until tender. Mash or puree them, mix with the stock and bring to a simmer again. Season to taste with salt and freshly ground black pepper. Beat the egg yolks and cream together. Add a cup of the hot soup to the yolks and cream and then carefully add this mixture to the soup off the burner. Heat gently, but don't let it boil or the eggs will scramble. When it's hot and slightly thicker, turn off the heat and add the butter. Sprinkle with parsley and serve.

Rutabaga & Potato Puree

1 pound potatoes
1/4 pound rutabagas
1/2 to 1 stick butter
1/2 cup cream (or milk)
salt and pepper

Boil the potatoes and rutabagas separately in salted water until done. (You can boil them together but they'll probably be done at different times and it's nicer to mix the flavors at the puree stage rather than when boiling.) Peel and mash them or put them through a food mill. Melt the butter in the cream or milk and beat it into the puree. Add salt and pepper to taste.

Leftovers are good mixed with an egg, a little bit of flour and some chopped parsley and shaped into cakes, dusted with flour and fried in butter or bacon fat. The recipe is also good substituting harder-to-find celery root for the rutabagas.

Moving on to Morocco

The Guide
February 1978

THE EXPANSION OF MY COOKBOOK collection this Christmas, while quantitatively modest, was qualitatively extravagant. I now have what promises to be a strange and wonderful collection of tortilla recipes, a very good New Orleans cookbook and Paula Wolfert's *Couscous and Other Good Food from Morocco.* Paula Wolfert obviously loves Moroccan food and has written a comprehensive book that talks about the cuisine in general, where the recipes come from, how they are eaten and much more useful information. Each recipe lists the ingredients and equipment needed, the working time, the cooking time and number served. All the recipes I've had from the book are absolutely delicious, and friends who have eaten in Morocco say they are authentic. The spice combinations are unusual and interesting.

The following recipe for chicken with lemon and olives is adapted from this book. You must plan ahead because pickling the lemons takes time. Paula Wolfert gives two methods for preserving the lemons: the first takes a month, but if done properly, the lemons will keep for a year; the one I reproduce here takes five days.

Five Day Preserved Lemon Special

1 lemon
salt water

Make eight fine 2-inch vertical incisions around the peel of the lemon (a razor blade is recommended, as you should not cut any deeper than the membrane that protects the pulp). Simmer in a stainless steel pan with plenty of salt and enough water to cover until the peel becomes very soft. Put the lemon in a clean jar, cover with the cooled cooking liquid, and leave to pickle for five days.

Chicken with Lemon & Olives

1 chicken, with 2 chicken livers
6 to 7 cloves of garlic
salt
1 teaspoon ground ginger
¼ teaspoon freshly ground black pepper
1 preserved lemon
¼ cup salad oil
¼ teaspoon pulverized saffron
  (mixed with a pinch of turmeric)
½ cup grated onion, drained
6 sprigs cilantro, tied together
½ cup red-brown olives

The day before, wash the chicken in salted water and drain. Pound four peeled cloves of garlic with two tablespoons of salt and rub it into the cavity and flesh of the chicken, pulling out excess fat. Rinse well in running water until it no longer smells of garlic. Using a blender, combine the ginger, a little salt, the pepper, two to three peeled cloves of garlic, the pulp of the preserved lemon (save the peel) and the oil into a sauce. Cut the chicken into six pieces and rub with the sauce. Marinate overnight.

The next day, place, the chicken, livers and sauce in a casserole. Add the saffron, onion, coriander and 2½ cups of water. Stir and bring to a boil. Partially cover and simmer gently for 30 minutes. Turn and baste the chicken often.

Remove the livers and mash, then return to the sauce. Rinse the olives (pit them if you like). Quarter the preserved lemon peel and add it and the olives and simmer for 15 minutes. Put the

chicken on a fireproof serving dish and into a hot oven (400°F) to brown. Reduce the sauce to a thick gravy by boiling rapidly and stirring often. Remove the coriander and spoon the sauce over the chicken. Serves four.

Holly McDonough remembers —

Helen definitely had presence. In a large household with a variety of people constantly coming and going, Helen's first appearance on the scene made an indelible impression on me. A sprightly figure with a mane of curly black hair, she wore a navy blue t-shirt with "Child's Hymn 876" across the front. What was that all about? So, I asked. Helen, in typical style, matter-of-factly and succinctly briefed me on English folk music and on this artist in particular. The simple words on her t-shirt spoke volumes to people "in the know." I felt as though a window had been opened on a world that I did not know existed and that inherent in the opening was the invitation, "Go ahead, climb out!"

This first encounter was so typical of times spent with Helen. One continually learned that Helen knew vast amounts about subjects that were totally foreign to the rest of us. Yet Helen's manner of sharing her knowledge made these subjects seem accessible and not intimidating.

So it was with her cooking. When I first learned that Helen was writing a cooking column for the WDBS program guide I thought, "Oh, so Helen knows how to cook?" Then, I read her columns. Yes, Helen knew how to cook. And, once again I was impressed by how accessible Helen made the world of gourmet cooking. Nothing to be afraid of, nothing to be intimidated by, you can do this too! That's what I remember most about Helen and cooking. She was able to make you truly feel that good and interesting food was something everyone could have and should have as part of their daily lives.

Quick Breads

The Guide
March 1978

HERE ARE TWO QUICK BREAD RECIPES. The first is an unusually good Irish soda bread. It is delicious hot, and unlike many soda breads, it keeps well. As it cools, it firms up and can be sliced for sandwiches. It's a good recipe for bread emergencies. The second is a very good banana nut bread.

Irish Soda Bread

- 1½ cups milk
- 1 to 2 tablespoons vinegar
- 2 cups unbleached white flour
- 2 cups whole-wheat flour
- ½ teaspoon baking powder
- 1 teaspoon baking soda
- 1 teaspoon sugar
- ½ teaspoon salt
- 2 tablespoons butter
- 1 egg, lightly beaten

This bread will be better if you use a whole wheat flour with a slightly flaky texture (grind it yourself, or visit your local health food store).

Add the vinegar to the milk and set aside or use buttermilk. (Omit the vinegar and egg if you do use buttermilk.)

Mix the flours, baking powder, baking soda, sugar and salt together. Pinch in the butter as if you were making pastry.

Add the egg and the now-curdled milk. Mix well and shape into a flat round loaf. Wet a sharp knife and cut a deep cross in the top of the loaf.

Place the loaf on a lightly greased baking sheet and bake in a preheated hot oven (425-450°F) for about 30 minutes. When it's done, the loaf will sound hollow when thumped on the bottom.

Banana Nut Bread

- 8 tablespoons butter (1 stick)
- 1 cup sugar
- 1 teaspoon vanilla
- 3 eggs
- 2 cups flour
- ¼ teaspoon salt
- 1 teaspoon baking soda
- 4 medium mashed bananas
- 1 cup sour cream
- ½ to 1 cup chopped nuts
    (pecans or walnuts are good)

Cream the butter and sugar together. Add the vanilla. Add one egg at a time, beating well after each.

Sift the flour, salt and soda together. Add this to the butter, egg and sugar mixture, Mix in the bananas and sour cream. Add the nuts.

Grease one large loaf pan lightly. Pour in the mixture and bake for one hour in a preheated 300°F oven. You can also make two small to medium loaves that will only take 45 minutes to bake.

This recipe comes from my very good friend, Dale Appleman. The sour cream gives it a distinctive taste. It keeps well, but tastes so good I've never known exactly how long it will keep.

Thanks to the Eggplant

The Guide
April 1978

NOW THAT IT'S SPRING, I'd like to thank the eggplant for helping me through another winter. It's one of those vegetables available year 'round at your supermarket and, unlike some, it doesn't seem to suffer much in storage or in transit. All it takes is a little care when selecting: Choose firm, shiny eggplants; when they get ripe and soft, they are usually very bitter. In fact, even a perfectly good eggplant can be bitter, which is why many recipes recommend slicing, salting, leaving for an hour, rinsing and drying before cooking.

I like to cook eggplants in olive oil (or part olive oil). The combination of the two flavors is one of those culinary marriages made in heaven. Pre-cholesterol obsession recipes call for frying the eggplant in oil. They absorb amazing amounts of oil, which can be wonderful in certain recipes, but brushing the eggplant slices with oil and broiling or baking in a very hot oven achieves the desired result with more moderate amounts of oil.

Baba Ghanoush

Baba Ghanoush is a Middle Eastern appetizer, closely related to hummus. I agree wholeheartedly with the writer who described it as "vulgarly seductive." It's delicious with pita bread.

2 large eggplants
2 to 4 cloves garlic
¼ cup tahini (sesame seed paste)
juice of 2 lemons
2 tablespoons finely chopped parsley
a few ripe black olives or a thinly sliced tomato
for garnishing

Cook the whole eggplant until soft, either by baking in a hot oven or, for a special flavor, over coals. Peel away the blackened skin, slice in half and squeeze out the juices. Mash the garlic and eggplant together or use a blender. Alternate additions of tahini and lemon juice, to taste. Mix in the parsley (and a pinch of cumin, if you like). Put it into a serving bowl and garnish with olives or tomato.

Moussaka

Moussaka is a traditional Greek dish and is very hearty. I gather the Greeks often alter it by using veal or beef instead of lamb or adding potatoes with the eggplants; I've even read a version that uses artichokes instead of eggplants. The following recipe will serve four amply and can be expanded by adding more eggplant.

3 eggplants
olive oil
1 pound minced lamb
1 small finely chopped onion
2 ripe tomatoes, skinned and chopped
4 tablespoons butter
1 tablespoon chopped parsley
½ teaspoon cinnamon
¼ teaspoon nutmeg
½ cup red wine
½ pound grated parmesan cheese
2 cups thinnish béchamel sauce
   (see page 124 for traditional Béchamel;
   see page 169 for Microwave Béchamel.)
1 egg

Slice the eggplant, salt it and let it drain for at least a half-hour. Rinse and pat dry. Fry as many pieces as will fit flat in your skillet in hot olive oil until brown, or brush with oil and cook in a hot oven until brown.

Sauté the meat, onions and tomatoes in butter. Add the parsley, cinnamon, nutmeg and wine and simmer for 20 minutes. Remove the meat mixture from the heat and stir in two tablespoons of the béchamel sauce.

Butter an ovenproof dish and put in layers of eggplant and meat, sprinkling each layer with a bit of the parmesan cheese. Beat the egg well and add it to the béchamel sauce with a pinch of nutmeg. Pour the sauce over the dish and sprinkle with the rest of the cheese. Bake in a 375°F oven for 45 minutes or until the top is golden brown.

Spur-of-the-Moment Meals

The Guide
June 1978*

THE PROBLEM: You want a spur-of-the-moment meal that will feed a couple of hungry people in an out-of-the-ordinary fashion. The Solution: one of these three sauces with the pasta of your choice. The meal can be ready in the time it takes to boil water and cook the pasta. All you have to do is have the ingredients for one of the sauces on hand and work in an orderly fashion. A salad will round out the meal. The recipes will serve two and are presented fastest to slowest in preparation time.

The first step in each case is to put a large pan of water on to boil for the pasta. If you have problems with gummy pasta you are probably not using a large enough pan and may be overcooking the pasta as well. *Al dente* (to the teeth) means that the pasta is not totally soft, but has a little bite left. Start testing a little earlier than the package suggests by tasting — spaghetti on the ceiling is a bit messy. Drain the pasta (if you cook it in enough water you can forget directions to rinse it in hot water), toss with the sauce in a serving dish and serve

June 1978 marked the first time Helen signed her column "H. Hudson Whiting," a rather formal byline that she used in all her food writing and reviews thereafter. Characteristically, we had no idea this was coming. Helen was amused by the etiquette writer, Miss Manners (Judith Martin), and with the name change to "HH" as we sometimes called her, she began to assume the print persona of our faithful and forthright guide in matters of food etiquette — not table manners, but what to eat and how best to select and prepare it. – ed.

immediately. Three to four ounces of pasta per person is an ample serving.

Oil & Garlic Sauce

1 clove garlic, finely chopped
2 tablespoons finely chopped fresh parsley
2 tablespoons butter
2 tablespoons olive oil
salt and pepper
½ to ¾ cup freshly grated parmesan cheese

At the last moment before the pasta is done, cook the garlic and parsley gently in the oil and butter until hot; don't let the garlic take on any color. Drain the spaghetti and toss with the sauce, season with salt and pepper, sprinkle with cheese and serve.

Fresh Tomato Sauce II

2 tablespoons butter
1 tablespoon oil
1 clove garlic (optional)
4 medium *ripe* tomatoes
fresh basil or parsley, finely chopped
salt and pepper

Peel the optional garlic and smash it with the side of your knife. Let it turn brown in the oil and butter as they heat up. Pour boiling water over the tomatoes to loosen their skins. Peel them, cut them open and discard the seeds. Chop them finely. Discard the garlic and add the tomatoes and basil or parsley to the pan. Season with salt and pepper, Stir and cook just long enough for the tomato juices to run and the sauce to heat through. Toss with the cooked pasta. You can add cheese but it may overpower this delicate sauce.

Red Clam Sauce

2 tablespoons olive oil
1 clove garlic
1 small onion
12-ounce can of Italian plum tomatoes
1 small can minced clams
salt and pepper
handful finely chopped parsley

Choose a medium-sized saucepan or a small skillet; the larger the surface area, the faster the sauce thickens. Peel and smash the clove of garlic and let it turn brown in the oil as it heats up. Chop the onion finely, discard the garlic and soften the onion in the oil. When it is becoming transparent, add the tomatoes and their juice and the liquid from the can of clams. Season with salt and pepper. Let the sauce simmer away over a medium high heat to reduce. Stir and smash up the tomatoes from time to time. As the sauce thickens you will need to stir more frequently so it won't stick to the bottom of the pan. Just before your pasta is ready, add the clams. You just want to heat them through; if they cook for more than a couple of minutes, they will get tough. Toss the sauce with the pasta, sprinkle with the parsley and serve. Again, I think this dish is better without cheese.

Pot Luck or Brownies Like Your Mother Never Used to Make

The Guide
July 1978

I'T'S SUMMER. Your garden is doing nicely. You're hoping that the annual drought won't be so bad this year, and your invitations to culinary gatherings have geometrically increased in number. You want to take brownies with something extra, and you check out the Alice B. Toklas cookbook from your local library for a few hints on cooking with special ingredients, only to realize that your library has an old edition from which this vital information has been censored. Relax, these brownies are easy.

Pot Luck Brownies

1 brownie mix
whatever ingredients are called for
on the back of the brownie mix
1 package of real chocolate chips
1 package of nuts
1 amount of special ingredient

You will notice that the exact amounts of the ingredients are not specified. If you use a large brownie mix, use lots of chips and nuts (these ingredients are not absolutely necessary, but make for a much nicer final product). The amount of special ingredient to put in is a trickier question. Keep in mind the strength of your particular brand, the number of people (the whole pan of brownies usually disappears no matter how few people are partaking), and the condition the people are likely to be in when the brownies appear. It is possible to overdo it, and it is easier to eat more

**Helen, 1975,
USA-Pan African
track meet,
Duke University**

photo by Bill Boyarsky

brownies than the alternative. A half-cup will probably be right for a small batch of brownies.

And now the crucial element — technique. Toast your special ingredient. Heat your well-seasoned large iron skillet to medium and toss it in. Stir constantly for a few minutes until it is warm and giving off a pleasant toasted aroma. If it starts smoking, your kitchen will be pleasantly scented but your pan is too hot and something will be lost. Remove from the heat, crush slightly with your fingers, and mix with the dry brownie mix. Follow the directions on the back of the box, adding the nuts and chips last. Bake according to the directions. If you want to approach decadence, ice the brownies with chocolate icing.

I hate to admit to using a mix but I've tried many "from scratch" brownie recipes, and they just don't come out as chewy. Other dishes that take well to special ingredients are gingerbread, banana bread and whatever you think will be good.

Tomato Preservation

The Guide
September 1978

AFTER TOMATO SOUP (hot and cold), tomato sauce, tomato juice, stuffed tomatoes, fried tomatoes (green and red), and everything else I could think of, I still couldn't catch up with the production of juicy, red, perfectly vine-ripened fruits from my garden. I try to get in a lot of tomato-eating when they're in season because I can't stand the pasty things sold in the stores in winter, but I can only eat so many in any one day.

If I had a freezer, I'd make a thick tomato paste and freeze it in ice-cube trays and next winter when I made soups or stews, I'd just pop in the proper number of tomato cubes and remember my garden fondly.

So for my first canning experience, I "put up" tomatoes recently. It wasn't very difficult, though it took a little time. (I must confess the bulk of the time was waiting for a giant pot of water to boil on my less-than-perfect electric stove). *Great Aunt Jane's Cook and Garden Book* by Jane Birchfield was a great source of sensible advice, including home-made tomato juice as a canning liquid.

Here's how I spent a Saturday afternoon:

Tomato Juice

2 quarts tomatoes, cored and cut up
2 cups water
**fresh herbs — basil, marjoram, parsley, mint
   or whatever you might like**
celery seed (optional)
1 onion or 2 to 3 scallions

Put everything in a pot, bring to a boil and simmer until the tomatoes are soft (about 20 minutes or so). Put through a food mill or ricer or force through a sieve. Salt and pepper to taste. Add more water if you think it's too thick. This will make enough to can five quarts of tomatoes, with a quart left over for drinking.

Canned Tomatoes

First, sterilize your jars. They should be completely immersed in boiling water for 15 minutes, Sterilize the !ids and rims by pouring on boiling water and leaving them until you need them.

Blanch the tomatoes in boiling water, briefly, until the skins crack. Peel and core the tomatoes and put them into the sterile jars, cutting up the larger ones into halves or fourths. Fill the jars to one inch from the top. The jars should be full but the tomatoes shouldn't be squashed.

Pour in the tomato juice and run a knife or spatula around the sides of the jar to release air bubbles. Wipe the jar rim with a damp paper towel. Put on the sterilized lid and screw the rim on tightly.

If you have a pressure canner and know how to use it, Great Aunt Jane recommends 10 minutes at five pounds or five minutes at 10 pounds. I neither have a pressure canner, nor know how to use one, so I put the quarts into boiling water — which completely covered them — and boiled for 45 minutes, replenishing with boiling water when necessary.

Cool the jars overnight in a draft-free location. Check the seal before storing. When you tap the tops with a metal spoon they should "ping" and the tops should look slightly concave. Use any jars that haven't sealed properly right away.

Curry Me Back

The Guide
November 1978

CONTRARY TO UNINFORMED OPINION, most likely inherited from the British, curry powder does not turn a dish into Indian food. In fact, curry powder is not even used in Indian cooking. Each dish is individually seasoned with its own combination of herbs and spices, added at a particular stage in the cooking to enhance each particular flavor – the result is a curried dish.

Luckily for us authentic Indian food is now available in Durham at the Sallam Cultural Center* and with two Indian chefs, the Indian portion of the menu is expanding. Suman Kshetrapal, one of the chefs, has contributed two recipes to this month's column.

Suman had never cooked before she married but discovered that she loved it. She likes living in this country because, for one thing, there are foods in our supermarkets that she had never seen before. At home, she cooks a variety of dishes, including Italian and Mexican.

Suman chose the following recipes, Chicken Curry and Pea Pilaf, because she thought they were simple enough to be a good introduction to Indian cooking in your kitchen.

Chicken Curry

4 chicken breasts, skinned and halved
8 fluid ounces plain yogurt
2 teaspoons ginger powder
1½ teaspoons garlic powder
2" stick cinnamon
4 cardamom pods
6 whole cloves
10 peppercorns
2 bay leaves
⅔ cup oil
4 medium onions, chopped and blended with a little water
¾ teaspoon turmeric
2 teaspoons cumin powder
2 teaspoons coriander
1 teaspoon garam masala
red chili powder, to taste

Soak chicken in yogurt. Add ginger, garlic, cinnamon and bay leaf. Marinate for three hours.

Heat the oil and fry the onion until golden brown. Add the chicken and the yogurt marinade. Fry well, until most of the water is gone. Add the turmeric, cumin, coriander, garam masala, chili powder, cardamom, cloves and peppercorns. Stir well and simmer for about ½ hour until the gravy thickens and the oil rises to the top. Add ¼ cup hot water if the mixture sticks to the pan.

*The Sallam Cultural Center not only offered Durham its first authentic Indian food in a restaurant setting, it was also (as its name implies) a pan-cultural center of community activity — a rare and unique setting where peoples of all beliefs and proclivities were welcome and made to feel comfortable. Durham icon and jazz pianist Brother Yusef Saleem was the visionary leader of Sallam, together with Billy Stevens and Suman Kshetrapal, who would later go on to open two more first-rate Indian restaurants in Durham in the 1990s. The Sallam Cultural Center also became a regular stopping point for a wide range of musicians, including Mose Allison, Dexter Gordon, the Nee Ningy Band, and Billie Holiday's old friend and composer, Durham native Bus Brown. — ed.

Rice Pilaf

2 cups rice (Basmati or long grain)
⅔ cup oil
2 medium onions, sliced
2" stick cinnamon
5 whole cloves
4 cardamom pods
10 peppercorns
1 bay leaf
1½ teaspoon cumin seed
1½ cup frozen peas
salt, to taste

Wash and soak the rice in cold water for one hour.

Heat the oil and add the cinnamon, cloves, cardamom, peppercorns, bay leaf and cumin. Add the onion and fry until golden brown. Add the drained rice and fry for a few minutes. Add four cups of water. Boil on a medium heat until most of the water is absorbed. Stir in the peas. Cover and bake in a preheated oven at 325°F for 45 minutes.

Take A Powder

The Guide
December 1978

DID YOU EVER STOP TO THINK about baking powder? Before the 19th century, nobody did, because it didn't exist. Baked goods were either unleavened or lightened with yeast or eggs (beaten, or separated and beaten). Elizabeth David, in her comprehensive new book *English Bread and Yeast Cookery*, says baking powders were first used in "bakestone products" which hadn't been leavened and were usually cooked on griddles (or girdles as they are still known in parts of the United Kingdom). When baking powders began to be manufactured and sold, they were advertised as "yeast powders" and pushed as replacements for yeast.

Baking powder consists of an acid and basic (alkaline) element which, when combined with a liquid, produce carbon dioxide gas and raise the dough or batter. Bicarbonate of soda is the basic element; cream of tartar or tartaric acid, the acid element. Both acids are found in double acting baking powder. Commercial baking powders also contain various things to keep the mixture dry to extend the shelf life.

If I seem a bit scientific, there's a reason. Back when I thought of myself as a chemist-in-the-making rather than a cook-in-the-making, I did a high school science project on baking powder. This is the sort of choice that does not seem as significant at the time as it does later on in one's life. Anyhow, I made up four baking powders and made four cakes. Science was not much advanced, but the cakes were delicious.

Elizabeth David also makes her own baking powder. I wonder if she ever thought of herself as a chemist? You can, too, using the *Joy of Cooking's* formula — for every cup of flour, use two teaspoons of cream of tartar, one teaspoon bicarbonate of soda, and a half-teaspoon salt. This information is especially useful when you discover there's no baking powder one-third of the way into a recipe.

Some recipes call for baking soda, not powder, when they already contain some acid ingredient (sour milk, buttermilk, honey, molasses, etc.).

We didn't completely fall for that early advertising; we still use yeast for breads and the like. However, most fruit cakes and breads are made with baking powder these days. Try a recipe that calls for these items. Yeast breads give a different texture and seem to keep longer. Yeast is a more efficient leaven: less flour and eggs are needed with yeast for an equivalent volume of dough.

You'll have the opportunity to try both leavens if you use this month's recipes for biscuits. I never mind being out of bread at breakfast time because good biscuits are so easy to make. I'm not as patriotic about it as *The Royal Baker and Pastry*

Cook (a publication from an early baking powder manufacturer featuring recipes and endorsements from chefs, chemists, and commissioners of health). The biscuit chapter is designed to "stimulate an interest in and awaken a love for this most healthful and economical of our purely American foods, so that it will be found, as it deserves to be, a prominent part of every day's food in every household."

The first biscuit comes from a collection of recipes by Episcopal women in northern Virginia and it produces light, delicious and quickly made baking powder biscuits.

St. Mary's Biscuits Supreme

> 2 cups flour
> 4 teaspoons baking powder
> ½ teaspoon salt
> 2 teaspoons sugar
> ½ cup shortening
> ⅔ cup milk

Preheat your oven to 450°F. Sift the dry ingredients together. Cut in the shortening and then stir in the milk. Knead the dough on a lightly floured board (Or, as a vaguely remembered recipe from my past advised, "Fold the dough over on itself 12 times.")

Roll or pat out the dough to the desired thickness, somewhere between ¼ and ¾ of an inch. Thin biscuits are crisper, fat ones softer. Cut your biscuits into rounds. The Royal booklet recommends an empty Royal Baking Powder tin, but a glass or cookie cutter works just as well. Dip the cutter into flour between biscuits. It you make the dough softer by adding a little more milk, you can drop the biscuits with a spoon and avoid the rolling and cutting. However formed, put your biscuits onto a lightly greased pan and bake in your 450°F

Take A Powder

oven until brown on top or about 10 to 15 minutes, depending on how thick they are and how hot your oven is when you put them in.

This second recipe is my mother's risen biscuits. They are greatly in demand on all occasions — breakfast through dinner, especially those big family gatherings when a country ham is on hand. The recipe makes four to five dozen. They freeze very well.

Risen Biscuits

> 1 package yeast dissolved in ½ cup
>   lukewarm water
> 4 cups flour, plus some
> 2 tablespoons sugar
> 2 teaspoons baking powder
> ½ teaspoon soda
> 1 teaspoon salt
> ⅔ cup Crisco
> ¾ cup sweet milk (regular milk)
> ¾ cup buttermilk

Warm the liquids. You can use all buttermilk if you wish, or make sour milk by adding two teaspoons vinegar to the milk.

Mix the dry ingredients together. Work in the shortening (as for pastry). Add the liquids and the yeast. Use a fork to mix. Roll fairly thin (about ¼ inch thick) using the extra flour to roll. Cut and dip in oil or melted margarine. Stack one on top of another (double deck) after dipping. Cover with towel and let rise until double (one to two hours). Bake in a 400-425°F oven for 10 to 16 minutes. Do not let them brown very much if you are going to re-heat or freeze them. Use a small cutter because these double in size when baked.

Organ Recital

The Guide
January 1979

ONCE AGAIN I HARK BACK to my childhood when there were certain items I wouldn't touch with a 10-foot fork. These included mushrooms, many root vegetables, tomato aspic,* and any meat from the inside of an animal. Liver was the only such meat I was irregularly expected to eat, and I used every ploy I knew to avoid it. However, I was exposed to lamb's kidneys from time to time. I would watch in horrified fascination as my father split, cleaned and fried them for his breakfast. I put it down to exotic foreign ways (his mother was from Argentina, and I had seen her perform the same operation).

Years later, I moved to England, where it would have been the height of rudeness not to try the Steak and Kidney Pie. I was in Rules, a beautiful old restaurant in the Convent Garden section of London which I hear has been given the English equivalent of urban renewal and has moved. The pie came; I bravely took the first mouthful and *it was delicious.* Years of prejudice fell away as I realized that the main element of the rich, wonderful flavor was the kidney. I was hooked — I found

 *Liz Whiting remembers** —

Helen doesn't quite tell the truth here. Nannie (our Whiting grandmother) was a cook of limited range and interest. When a dish was well received, it was on the menu forever. Our upbringing required us to eat anything presented. It was many years before Nannie learned how much we hated tomato aspic!

myself taking home all sorts of funny looking things from the butcher and ordering dishes in restaurants with names that once would have caused me to move on quickly.

I won't catalog the various innards that have passed through mine, but I will try to tempt you into trying kidney with the following two recipes. Kidney is not something you see every day at your local supermarket, but if you keep your eye out, you will come across it from time to time. I have often found very good calves' kidney. When you see how inexpensive it is, you might be interested in giving it a try. For the following recipes you may use calf kidney, lamb kidney and for the second, even beef kidney will do.

Steak & Kidney Pie

pastry, to cover *(see page 46 or page 156)*
¾ pound calf kidney
2 pounds beef steak (chuck, round)
flour
salt and pepper
4 tablespoons oil
1 small onion
1 cup beef stock
1 bay leaf
chopped parsley
pinch of powdered clove, marjoram

Make enough flaky pastry or shortcrust pastry to cover your pie pan; recipes calling for one cup of flour will cover a small, deep pan; two cups of flour will work for a larger but shallow one.

Rinse the kidney off, then split it and remove the fat and tubes in the middle. Soak it in salted water for 30 minutes to an hour. Dry it off and cut into quarter-inch slices. Cut the beef into large chunks. Mix a little salt, pepper and flour together and coat the beef and kidney with it.

Chop the onion finely. Heat the oil to medium and sauté the onion until golden. Turn the heat to high and add the beef and kidney. Brown these well, turning and stirring constantly. Add the stock (use water if you don't have any good stock around) and seasonings and simmer until the steak is tender (from one to two hours, depending on the cut of meat). Put the meat mixture and all its gravy into your pie pan and allow this to cool down a bit while you roll out the pastry. Place the pastry over the dish, moistening the edges of the dish with water so the pastry will stick firmly. Decorate (if you wish) with any leftover scraps of pastry; make a couple of slits so the steam can escape; and brush with an egg yolk beaten with a little water to give the pie a golden finish. If using flaky pastry bake in a hot oven (425°F) for 10 minutes, then turn down to 350°F for 15 minutes. If using short pastry, bake at 350°F for 30 to 40 minutes.

Kidney & Mushrooms

½ pound calf or beef kidney
flour
salt and pepper
3 tablespoons butter
6 tablespoons red wine
¼ pound mushrooms
mustard

Clean, soak and slice the kidney as above. Mix flour, salt and pepper and coat the kidney slices. Melt the butter in a pan (that has a lid); put in the kidneys and let them cook over a medium heat, stirring often, for about five minutes. Pour in the wine and bring it to a boil. Cover the pan and put into a 300°F oven for a half-hour for calf kidney, or one hour for beef kidney.

Clean the mushrooms with a damp cloth and add them to the kidneys. Put back into the oven for another half-hour. Just before serving, stir in a teaspoon of good mustard (I like Dijon). Serve with mashed potatoes, rice, or fresh bread to sop up the gravy.

Organ Recital

Flaky Pastry &
Medieval Pie

The Guide
February 1979

Here's the flaky pastry I mentioned last month and a Stargazy Pie from Ray Simone* to cover it over. This flaky pastry is the nicest pastry I know how to make. It uses a pound of butter to a pound of flour; the "turns" incorporate the butter into the flour in many layers and the pastry turns out light, crisp and rich. It is the perfect pastry to wrap around Beef Wellington, or to cover savory pies and sweet pies and tarts. It can be started a couple of days ahead of time and kept in the refrigerator until you are ready to use it. This amount will wrap a Beef Wellington or be ample for a two crust pie.

Flaky Pastry

4 cups flour
2 teaspoons salt
7 ounces water
2 sticks (1 cup) unsalted butter

Sift three cups of the flour with the salt. (If you are using salted butter, omit the salt.) Combine with the water (seven liquid ounces, or just under a cup). Don't knead this mixture; you don't want the gluten to develop because this will give you the wrong texture. Roll this dough out on a lightly floured board (or if you're really lucky, a marble slab) to approximately 14 x 16 inches.

Mix the remaining cup of flour with the pound of butter (this is easier if the butter is at room temperature). Form this into a block and place it in the center of your rectangle of dough.

Fold the edges into a package around the block of flour and butter. Wrap the dough in aluminum foil and refrigerate for 30 minutes.

Now you start the "turns." Place your dough package on your lightly floured board and flatten it gently. Roll it out into a strip about 20 x 8 inches. Fold the dough in thirds. Now roll the dough out and fold again, then rewrap in the foil and refrigerate for another 30 minutes.

For the next two turns, fold the dough in fourths, then refrigerate for 30 minutes (or the dough will keep for a couple of days in the refrigerator, if you want to make it ahead of time). The fifth and sixth turns are the last and are done in the same manner as the third and fourth just before the dough is to be used.

To use the dough: Roll it out thinly and wrap or cover whatever you're wrapping or covering. Brush any joints with water and they will stick together. You can decorate the pastry by cutting out little shapes (flowers, leaves, animals, stars, moons, what have you) and sticking them on with a little water. You can also lightly score the pastry in some fanciful design. If you make a small hole or slash, the steam which builds up won't make its own (probably unsightly) hole. Brush the pastry

*Visual artist extraordinare Ray Simone was **The Guide's** cartoonist, creator of "Triangle 1999": a futuristic and satiric look at our area in the then-distant future. With the exception of its emphasis on space travel, many of Ray's future visions have turned out to be remarkably accurate in tone if not detail. Ray remains a leading member of the graphic design industry, working in California's Silicon Valley. He also created the logo for Helen's column and the cover concept for **In Helen's Kitchen.** – ed.

lightly with beaten egg yolk for a golden finish. Your oven should be hot (425-450°F) when the pastry goes in. After 10 minutes, turn the oven down to 350°F. The pastry will be completely cooked in 15 to 30 minutes. If whatever is inside or under the pastry is not cooked, cover the pastry with a piece of aluminum foil, which will prevent its burning.

Stargazy Pie from Ray Simone

Here's a truly spectacular fish pie with which to astound your friends and relatives. For jaw-dropping responses from diners, it is second only to four-and-twenty blackbirds. As amazing as the finished product looks, it is actually quite easy to assemble. You'll find it very forgiving in terms of choice of ingredients and cooking methods.

Fish pies were very popular in the Dark Ages, when the primary ingredients were as close as the local moat. Stargazy is at least five centuries old, and was so celebrated in medieval Cornwall that it became that region's traditional dish.

I committed my first Stargazy under the auspices of the Society for Creative Anachronism in our annual cooking contest. It promptly won the "most unusual" category and, thus encouraged, it scored again at home last Thanksgiving.

Herring or pilchards are the traditional stargazers, as they bake so well they need not be boned. Trout is a reasonable substitute — although it is difficult to bone, it is readily available.

Remove the tails and fins from six to eight herring or pilchards — about 1½ pounds total — but leave the heads attached. Lay a bottom crust (see H.H.W.'s Flaky Crust) in a 9-inch pie pan, preferably metal. Make an egg wash of two yolks and two tablespoons milk (save the whites) and brush half of it over the bottom crust. Bake in a preheated 425°F oven for five minutes to set the crust and seal it against sogginess from the fish juices. Place the fish in the pan after it is cool enough to touch, arranging them with heads in the center and tails equally spaced along the rim. Cover the fish with a mixture of ½ cup of coarsely chopped leeks, ½ cup of chopped fresh spinach, and two chopped hard-cooked eggs. Lay on the top crust, pinching the rim *carefully* to get a good seal (a small amount of water on the rim will help insure airtightness). And now, for the fun part: cut a 2 x 2 inch cross in the center of the top crust, peel back the flaps, and carefully reach in and grab the heads. Gently pull the heads up through the opening until they stick up out of the pie about an inch. Pinch the crust tightly around the heads and recheck the seal around the rim. Apply the other half of the egg wash to the top crust. Beat the egg whites until manageable and brush the heads with them for an attractive glaze. Bake 10 minutes at 425°F to set up the top crust; then reduce to 375°F for an additional 40 minutes.

Serve with a flourish, preferably with a photographer present.

VARIATIONS:

I spent three days in an exhaustive search for fresh whole herring, but all the little buggers were headless; and there wasn't a pilchard to be found anywhere. So I turned to trout. Being basically indolent, I took the path of least activity and asked the fish market for one 1½ pound ocean trout fillet and a half-dozen of their smallest trout heads. They were more than happy to give me the heads free and even gave me several dozen to choose from ("pick of the litter," so to speak). The fillet is cut into bite-sized pieces and spread over the bottom crust, then covered as before. The separate heads are arranged to suit personal aesthetics, and the top crust is draped over them. Cut the crust between the heads and it will fall down around them, ready for sealing. This is much more convenient than pawing around inside your pie.

The separate heads are also much more convenient to deal with when serving and can be left in the pan instead of on some lucky diner's plate. They can even be removed before serving particularly squeamish diners. But their real advantage lies in the flavor they add. The generally bland taste of trout is considerably enhanced by the cooking down of the rich juices from the heads (which some call gore, but I prefer to call "essence"). Note: Never destroy a fish head after the meal is over. Simply stick it under your favorite garden plant; or for a little entertainment, let a cat into the room and stand back.

For extra flavor, you can also try adding ½ cup of parmesan cheese, or exchanging one or both of the hard-cooked eggs for pickled eggs. Be careful that the taste of our friend the fish isn't lost, however, as some of them are pretty shy.

Of course a pie as bizarre-looking as this allows for almost limitless self-expression. There are countless optional arrangements of the heads, lending the pie a more dramatic effect: the "School of Fish," for instance — one large head facing a group of small ones. You might try dressing up the heads with dough ornaments, too: little horns for the "Git Along Little Fishy" pie; or helmets and shoulder pads for the "Shotgun Offense" pie. No personal excrescence can be considered too gauche when you start with a pie that looks back at you.

One last note: You may occasionally be faced with a reluctant diner who refuses to dive into what he sees as a bunch of leering fishes. Before you remove the heads to assuage his queasy stomach, give him one last chance: Offer him the eyes.

Take A Leek

The Guide
March 1979

THIS TIME OF YEAR, gardeners are already at it: reading catalogs, taking soil samples, drawing diagrams, sending for seeds, and starting some of them. They plan to grow some things because they're unavailable fresh (herbs like basil, thyme, tarragon, etc.), others because they're best fresh-picked (beans, corn), some because they can be picked ripe, for eating, not for shipping or storage (tomatoes), others because they're never young enough in the stores (carrots, potatoes) and still others because they're hard to find and/or expensive (sorrel, leeks).

This month's column is a reminder not to overlook the Clark Kent of the onion family: the leek. Their mild-mannered onion flavor is delicious on its own, hot or cold, or in soups, pies, quiches and stuffings.

Leeks are expensive in this area. If you're planning your garden now, you might want to consider a row of leeks. I put one in several years ago but achieved only moderate success; the leeks only got as big as my little finger. They were in the ground for over a year and tasted great but never got any bigger. I started out right, sowing them as early in the spring as possible but missed the next step transplanting them into five-inch furrows when they reached six inches high. Then, as they grow, good gardeners mound loose soil around the stalks to blanch them (i.e., increase the proportion of white). They can be used at any stage in this process but mature between one-half to two inches in diameter. If all goes well, the gardener might end up with offshoots that can be gently separated and planted next year.

Three recipes follow for using your harvest, but don't feel restricted to them. Look in your cookbooks for Cock-a-Leekie soup (from Wales, where the leek is the symbol of the patron saint, St. David), or the two famous versions of leek and potato soup — Potage Parmentier (hot) and Vichysoisse (cold). *Mastering the Art of French Cooking* contains a marvelous leek quiche recipe.

Braised Leeks

> **2 small or one large leek per person**
> **butter**
> **salt and pepper**

First, clean the leeks: Trim off the root end and trim the tops so the leeks will lie flat in your pan. Slice down into the white part, but not all the way through, with two right-angle cuts. Spread the leek open and wash under running water. Lay the leeks in the pan, put in about ½ tablespoon of butter per portion, sprinkle with salt and pepper and barely cover with water. Cook them fairly rapidly until the leeks are very tender (about 30 to 50 minutes, depending on the diameter). Start out with the pan covered, then remove the lid towards the end so the liquid will reduce. When the leeks are tender, if there seems to be too much liquid, remove them and boil down the juices, then put the leeks back in to heat up.

The braised leeks can be served as is or with a little more butter, or you could add a little cream towards the end of the cooking time, or they could be sprinkled with a little mild cheese and put under the broiler until the cheese browns.

Leeks Vinaigrette

> **2 small or one large leek per person**
> **salt and pepper**
> **vinaigrette: 3 to 6 parts oil to 1 part wine**
> **vinegar, salt and pepper, pinch of dry mustard**

Clean the leeks as above, barely cover them with water, sprinkle with salt and pepper and simmer. When they are tender (as above, time varies with diameter of leeks), drain them and while they are still warm, pour the vinaigrette over them. Let them cool, but don't refrigerate because this dish is best at room temperature. This dish is splendid as a first course, or as part of a buffet.

Leek & Sausage Flan

This recipe is adapted from Robert Carrier and is quite rich. Vegetarians who find it interesting can leave out the sausage and ham and make a leek flan.

> **1 medium onion**
> **1 ounce cooked ham**
> **4 small mushrooms**
> **butter**
> **1 tablespoon flour**
> **1 cup milk**
> **salt and pepper**
> **nutmeg**
> **1 egg yolk**
> **2 tablespoons thick cream**
> **4 small pork sausages**
> **4 small poached leeks**
> **4 tablespoons grated parmesan cheese**
> **shortcrust pastry for bottom crust** (see page 156)

The first step is to bake the pastry a bit, so the bottom of the flan won't be soggy. Put the pastry into your pie pan, cover with aluminum foil and fill with beans or something to weight the pastry down. Bake at 400°F for 10 minutes, then remove the beans and give it five minutes more.

Chop the onion, ham and mushrooms finely. Sauté this mixture gently in two tablespoons of the butter until the onion is transparent.

Make a white sauce with the flour, two tablespoons butter and the milk. Season to taste with salt, pepper and nutmeg. Off the stove, beat in the egg yolk; then beat in the cream.

Cook the sausages until they are golden.

Now assemble your flan: Spread the ham, onion and mushroom mixture on the bottom of the crust. Alternate the sausages and leeks in a pleasing pattern; pour over the white sauce and sprinkle with the parmesan cheese. Bake in a 325°F oven for 30 to 40 minutes or until the flan has set and is golden brown. Serve hot.

Herb Today, Tarragon Tomorrow

The Guide
April 1979

THIS MONTH I CONTINUE to encourage gardeners by suggesting some herbs that are easy to grow and delightful to use. There are a lot of people whose only contact with fresh herbs has been parsley or mint. Parsley is a nice finishing touch (and a source of vitamin A) on almost any dish; chopped coarsely, it is a good addition to salads. Mint is available, if you know what it looks like when you see it or smells like when you step on it, almost everywhere.

If you have ever encountered either dried parsley or dried mint, you know there's a big difference between dried and fresh. It is the same with most other herbs no matter how well they've been preserved. Fresh basil has a slight anise flavor that disappears in drying, thyme and tarragon are more intense fresh, and chives and chervil are virtually worthless when dried.

Herbs are easy to grow; most do fine as long as they have good drainage and lots of sun. Any garden of mine is sure to contain basil, parsley, thyme, sage, mint, chives and tarragon. The basil, parsley, thyme, sage and chives are easily started from seed. Tarragon is a little harder. *Never buy tarragon seeds* — you will be getting Russian tarragon which has such a weak flavor that it's not worth space in your garden. *French* tarragon is the one you want. It is a perennial which can only be propagated by cuttings or root division. Luckily we have a local source every year. The herb volunteers at the North Carolina Botanical Garden have an herb sale. They sell, at reasonable prices, everything from common herbs to odd varieties (horse mint, lemon and caraway thyme, scented geraniums, etc.).

And now, in case you're not familiar with tarragon, a few uses. Tarragon's distinctive flavor goes well with eggs; try a pinch in your next omelet or scrambled eggs. Dried tarragon is fine for the following recipes but fresh is exponentially better.

Béarnaise Sauce

Béarnaise sauce is a hollandaise sauce flavored with vinegar and tarragon and is my favorite sauce. It is terrific with poached eggs, lamb, steaks, chicken, and mussels. This version is adapted from *Mastering the Art of French Cooking, Volume I* by Child, Bertholle and Beck which, among other things, contains clear instructions for all kinds of sauces. It makes 1½ cups.

¼ cup wine vinegar
¼ cup dry white wine
1 tablespoon minced shallots or green onions
1 tablespoon minced fresh tarragon or
    ½ tablespoon dried tarragon
⅛ teaspoon pepper
pinch of salt
3 egg yolks
2 tablespoons cold butter
½ to ⅔ cup melted butter
2 tablespoons fresh minced tarragon or parsley

Boil the vinegar, wine, shallots or onions, herbs and seasonings over moderate heat until it has reduced to two tablespoons. Cool.

Then make as a hollandaise sauce. Beat the egg yolks until thick. Strain in the vinegar and beat. Add one tablespoon of cold butter and thicken the egg yolks over low heat. (If you're careful you can do this over direct heat, otherwise use a double boiler.) The egg yolks will thicken to the consistency of light cream. Remove from the heat

instantly, and beat in the rest of the cold butter. Then beat in the melted butter, starting off drop by drop, then a thin stream, making sure the butter is absorbed as you go. Taste for seasoning, and beat in the tarragon or parsley.

Tartare Sauce

2 hard-boiled egg yolks
1 teaspoon vinegar
1 raw egg yolk
1 cup olive oil
1 teaspoon mustard
salt and pepper
1 teaspoon capers
1 teaspoon sharp pickle (optional)
chopped herbs: tarragon, parsley, chives

Make as a mayonnaise: Pound the cooked egg yolks to a smooth paste, add a few drops of vinegar, then beat in the raw egg yolk and a little salt and pepper. Add the olive oil, drop by drop at first, then faster, as it takes.

Add the flavorings, taste and adjust to your liking. This is wonderful with hot or cold poached fish.

Chicken With Tarragon

1 small chicken
1 to 2 tablespoons each, butter and oil
chopped tarragon
2 shallots, finely chopped
1 cup heavy cream
salt and pepper

A simple, delicious dish; good for dinner guests.

I buy a whole chicken and disjoint it. This way I pay less per pound and end up with odds and ends for chicken stock. Use a sharp knife; start by cutting off the wings and legs, then divide the legs at their joint. Separate the breasts from the back and with either kitchen shears or a cleaver (use it decisively, think "samurai butcher") and cut them apart. It they are large, the breasts can be cut in half again. Wash the chicken pieces and pat them dry.

Heat the butter and oil over medium high in a pan that will be large enough to hold all the chicken. Brown the chicken, turning it often; don't let the oils burn. Sprinkle with salt, pepper and (dried) tarragon. When all pieces are nicely browned, turn the heat down to low, cover and cook slowly, turning from time to time. It you have fresh tarragon, add it at this point. The chicken will be tender in 20 to 30 minutes. Remove to a hot platter and keep warm.

To make the sauce, gently cook the shallots in the skillet for a few minutes, then turn up to a high heat and add the cream. Stir constantly, scraping up all the bits stuck to the pan, until the sauce starts to thicken. Add a little more fresh tarragon at this point and pour over the chicken and serve. Boiled or steamed new potatoes with a little parsley and butter are the perfect vegetable.

The Traveling Stomach,
or: What to Nibble While Driving Around the Countryside Listening to the Listed FM Stations*

The Guide
May 1979

EVERYONE HAS HIS OR HER own style of eating on a long trip. Some allow themselves to pull into the very fast food places they avoid at home, others enjoy varying success in a search for "perfect" diners and truckstops, and still others manage gourmet picnics while crossing the country.

My preferred style of traveling, for more than just culinary reasons, is not on the big interstates; I like smaller highways that actually take me through towns where I'm likely to run across more than the usual burger or pizza chains. Asking

*In addition to focusing on seasonal changes and upcoming holidays, H. Hudson often offered subtle support and reference to other **Guide** features. This column, however, makes specific reference to "driving around the countryside, listening to the listed FM stations." Each Spring, **The Guide** published a listing, compiled by Dave "Doc" Searls, of worthwhile FM stations across the US as a service to those who were planning summer vacations that necessitated spending considerable time in cars. Many recommended stations were college and/or NPR affiliated, but most were not. The late '70s were still a time when FM radio was not totally dominated by a half dozen or so rigid formats, and the musical offerings in particular across the country were remarkably varied. – ed.

questions and having an experimental spirit help — that little local bakery might be full of real cream or custard-filled goodies, or on the other hand, the employees might rival the chemists at Hostess. If you're interested in a particular sort of meal, the yellow pages will provide phone numbers, and surely someone at one of the local restaurants can be induced to provide information on other restaurants in town.

I tend to look for a good breakfast about mid-morning. Breakfast is usually good value for money and often the best-cooked meal in a wide variety of eateries. Menu items can include regional dishes. Just think of the number of people who have first encountered grits while traveling in the South, or huevos rancheros in the Southwest.

I highly recommend picnic lunches. There are lots of nice places to stop, picnics are cheap, you get a rest from the road and the food is bound to be better than any coffee, drink or sandwich dispensed by a machine in a gas station. I travel with a cooler to keep perishables from perishing, a good knife (stainless steel so it won't corrode if it doesn't get washed right away) and a thermos. The following recipe is good for filling your thermos because all you need are the ingredients, a source of water (at no particular temperature) and a few ice cubes. It's a refreshing change from overdosing on cola:

Travelin' Iced Tea

⅓ **cup instant tea**
⅓ **cup Tang (or other powdered-citrus-taste-flavored-drink-substance)**
1 package lemonade mix
2 quarts water

Mix. Chill. Drink.

Meat Marinades
The Guide
June 1979

HERE ARE THREE WAYS to deal with four meats before they are cooked out over a grill. None of them is basic southern barbeque sauce. You should have your own secret method for that, perhaps starting with a store-bought sauce to which you add God-knows-what from your pantry and refrigerator. Your pork or chicken is then marinated in, simmered in and/or basted liberally with this amazing mixture. Some concoctions are better than others; the best seem to be inspired by seat-of-the-pants cooking and never come off the printed page.

There are two methods of outdoor grilling: one is to pre-cook the meat in the sauce and finish off on the grill; the second is to marinate the meat in the sauce (overnight or at least two hours) and cook until done (and most likely to some shade of black) over the coals. Both have their charms. Method one gets the sauce flavorings into the meat in a hurry. If you go for method two, remember to take the meat and marinade out of the refrigerator awhile before you are ready to start cooking. The closer to room temperature, the faster and more evenly the meat will cook.

Marinade for Pork

1 tablespoon sugar
½ **cup soy sauce**
3 to 5 crushed cloves garlic
**2 tablespoons hoisin sauce
(Chinese sweet bean sauce)**
½ **teaspoon Chinese 5-spice powder**
2 tablespoons dry sherry
2 tablespoons honey

This marinade is vaguely Chinese and works well for either spareribs or the bigger country-style ribs. Mix everything and use it to marinate about two pounds of pork.

Lamb or Chicken Marinade

 lemon
 garlic
 olive oil
 pepper
 onions
 bay leaf
 oregano or thyme or cumin, turmeric
   and ginger

This marinade has a Middle Eastern flavor. There are many cuts of lamb suitable to cooking out: The leg or shoulder can be cut into big pieces, marinated and threaded on skewers with onions and green peppers; chops or cutlets can be cooked directly on the grill. Chicken should be disjointed. Put the meat in a non-metallic container, squeeze on enough lemon juice and pour on enough olive oil to coat lightly. (Do use olive oil; other oils just don't have enough flavor). Put in seasonings — freshly ground pepper, crushed garlic, bay leaves, chopped onions and the herbs and spices of your choice. Toss it all together and marinate overnight or for several hours.

Marinade for Fish

 onion, sliced
 fennel or dill
 salt and pepper
 lemon juice
 oil

Fish cooked over coals is delicious. Buy a whole fish and have it cleaned (but not filleted). Put some sliced onion and fennel or dill inside the fish and sprinkle with salt and pepper and a little lemon juice. Brush the outside of the fish with lots of oil (for flavor and to reduce sticking). Brush the grill with oil as well. There are special fish grills, which are not necessary but make it easier because you turn the whole contraption instead of the fish itself. Cook your fish until it is just done — the flesh looks opaque and flakes easily with a fork. Overcooked fish disintegrates and is dry and nasty. Large fish steaks can also be grilled, but remember to oil both the steaks and the grill very well.

Vegetables à la Greque

The Guide
July 1979

Here's a french method of cooking vegetables to be served cold as a first course or as part of a buffet. Vegetables à la Greque are good dishes for summer parties because you prepare them in advance and aren't left slaving over a hot stove.

Marinade

> 1 cup water
> 1 cup dry white wine
> 1 cup olive oil
> ½ cup lemon juice
> 1 clove garlic, peeled and crushed
> bay leaf
> thyme
> 12 coriander seeds
> salt and pepper
> fresh parsley or coriander leaves

Simmer everything but the parsley or coriander leaves for 10 to 15 minutes to make a flavorful liquid. The wine is optional; add more water it you leave it out.

Next poach your choice of vegetable(s). (If you are doing more than one vegetable, do each sequentially, using the same poaching liquid.) Cook each vegetable until just done — they should still be slightly crisp. Cool them in the poaching liquid. When you are ready to serve, arrange in a serving dish. Taste the marinade — it may need a bit of sharpening with more lemon, or a bit more olive oil or a little salt and pepper. Moisten the vegetable(s) with the marinade and sprinkle with finely chopped parsley or coriander.

If the dish has been refrigerated, remove before serving; it is more flavorful cool than ice cold.

Vegetable Selection

Onions: Choose small onions. Peel them, which is easier to do it you first dip them into boiling water for 30 seconds. Trim the ends and cut a cross into the root end (this will keep the onion from falling apart when it cooks). Onions will take about 30 minutes to cook. Serve about three onions per person.

Leeks: Trim the ends and wash well, as leeks are apt to be sandy. If they seem very sandy, slice down into the white part and gently spread them apart to wash more thoroughly. They will take 20 to 30 minutes to cook and are best very tender — almost melting. Cook one or two per person.

Mushrooms: Choose mushrooms that are approximately the same size. Leave small ones whole and cut large ones into quarters. Clean them, but don't wash them. You want them to absorb the marinade, not water. They will take about five minutes, and 2 ounces per person is an adequate serving.

Zucchini: Wash them and trim the ends. Leave small ones whole; cut larger ones either into thick strips or one-inch pieces. Cook until they start to go transparent (5 to 12 minutes, depending on their size) but are still firm. Serve one small zucchini per person.

Others: Whatever you think you might like: carrots, cauliflower, celery, etc.

Mill Your Vegetables

The Guide
September 1979

Y OU DON'T OWN a food processor? You are (select one):

(a) waiting for one to appear at the Goodwill
(b) holding down your electricity bill
(c) reading *Consumer Reports* to decide which one you want
(d) hinting for Christmas
(e) reactionary

I confess — I'm reactionary. I actually enjoy the very processes a food processor was designed to perform. I sometimes imagine that if I'd been living back when ovens were first being installed in homes, I'd have refused one, thinking it would do very well for baking but that one couldn't really roast a piece of meat without an open fire and a spit. I don't, however, cook with two rocks over an open pit in my front yard, and I manage to stay on good terms with friends who own food processors so that I can enjoy the fruits of their labors.*

I started cooking seriously while living in London, and I didn't want to acquire a lot of electrical appliances that I couldn't use on this side of the Atlantic. Luckily, electricity is fairly recent in the history of cooking, and there are many good kitchen tools that perform some of the functions of a blender or a food processor without electricity and with considerably less money invested. This month I discuss a few of them. The recipes which follow can, of course, be adapted to a food processor. If you've got one, you'll know what to do.

A decade later, actually, Helen gave up her "reactionary" position on this issue and bought a food processor. – ed.

FOOD MILL: a useful tool for pureeing soups or vegetables. The best ones have interchangeable sieves with different sized openings and are plastic outside for easy cleaning, They are useful for pureeing soups and vegetables, and for some jobs are even better than blenders or food processors. Tough pieces of whatever you're pureeing (like apple or tomato skins, stringy parts of leeks, etc.) stay behind. Because you can choose the size of the opening, it's hard to make the mistake one can so easily make with a blender — over-pureeing to a complete pap. The food mill also purees with less liquid than a blender often needs.

Potato Puree

> 1 pound potatoes
> 4 tablespoons butter
> ½ cup milk, half & half or cream, heated
> salt and pepper

Leaving the potatoes whole and the skins on, bake, steam or boil them until they are done. If you bake or steam, the potatoes absorb less water, which makes a difference in the puree. Peel the potatoes and put them through the food mill. Add the butter and beat with a wooden spoon or a sturdy wire whisk. Add the hot milk or cream gradually and continue beating. Add salt and pepper to taste. Pureed potatoes are lighter and creamier than mashed; it is a difference worth trying. The amounts of butter and liquid can be varied to your taste.

Zucchini Soufflé

> 1 pound zucchini
> 2 eggs, separated
> 2 extra egg whites
> 6 tablespoons Gruyère cheese, grated
>
> **WHITE SAUCE:**
> 2 tablespoons butter

2 tablespoons flour
¾ cup milk
salt and pepper

Wash the zucchini, cut it into rounds, sprinkle with salt and let them drain in a colander for 30 minutes to an hour. Simmer them gently with ¼ to ½ cup water until they are tender and the water has evaporated (10 to 20 minutes). Sieve them through the food mill and mix with the white sauce. Add five tablespoons of the cheese and beat in the two egg yolks. Taste for salt and pepper. Beat the four egg whites until stiff but not dry. Gently fold them into the zucchini mixture. Turn into a buttered soufflé dish and stand the dish in a baking tin filled with water. (Handle this very carefully when removing from the oven to avoid scalding yourself.) Sprinkle the top with the remaining cheese and bake for 40 minutes in a preheated 350°F oven. Serves two as a main course, four as part of a larger meal. It is creamy and delicious — a favorite soufflé.

MANDOLINE: a narrow board with cutting blades attached. Some offer one fixed blade (simple and inexpensive); a more useful version (and more expensive) is wooden, with two blades — one a slanted cutting edge, the other, ridged — and adjustable surfaces so you can change the width of the slice. This is a fabulous kitchen tool. You can slice whatever you want impossibly thin in a very short amount of time. It's good for getting onions sliced thinly enough for onion soup, cucumbers sliced evenly for cucumber salad, apples sliced quickly for pies. Be sure to take the time to read the instructions on how to hold whatever you are slicing or grating (in the palm of your hand with your fingers outstretched) and practice, so that you can use it safely. When I first bought mine, I oiled the wooden parts with warm vegetable oil to season the wood. Now I wash it in cool water as soon as I have finished using it, remembering to loosen the wing nuts so the wood doesn't swell, making it impossible to adjust the blades.

Gratin Dauphinois

1½ pounds boiling potatoes
1 cup milk
½ cup cream
1 clove garlic, finely chopped
½ teaspoon flour
salt and pepper

Peel the potatoes, slice them very thinly, rinse them off and dry well. Put a layer of potatoes in a flattish, ovenproof dish and sprinkle with salt, pepper and garlic. Continue layering until the potatoes are used up. Heat the milk and when it is just about to boil, pour it into the dish. Mix the cream and flour and pour it over the potatoes. Put the dish into a preheated 400°F oven. In 30 to 40 minutes the potatoes will be cooked through; raise the heat to brown the top. Serve piping hot. Some cooks add grated Swiss and/or parmesan cheese to the layers. Cheese is good but not necessary. Try it without at least once and see if you don't agree.

Zucchini with Herbs

1 medium zucchini per person
1 tablespoon butter per zucchini
salt and pepper
fresh herbs, finely chopped (your choice: parsley, tarragon, marjoram, chervil, mint, etc.)

Slice the zucchini into ¼ inch rounds and salt and drain as in the above recipe. Pat dry. Melt the butter in a skillet and put in the zucchini, season with salt and pepper, and stir until coated with the butter. Cook very gently (you don't want them to brown) until tender, stirring from time to time. Just before serving, sprinkle on the herbs and add a small pat of butter. Shake the pan until the butter melts and serve.

Mill Your Vegetables

Filo & Fillings

The Guide
October 1979

I RECENTLY HAD A HALF-POUND of filo pastry
left over from spanakopita (Greek spinach pie)
and used it to make small savory pastries for hors
d'oeuvres. They were fun to make and so delicious
that the recipes follow.

Filo pastry is made from flour and water with
either a very small amount of oil or no oil at all.
The dough is kneaded until it is very elastic, then
allowed to rest for several hours. It is next rolled,
pulled and stretched until it is paper thin, dried
and ready for use. There is a recipe for filo pastry
in the excellent *Home Book of Greek Cooking* by
Joyce M. Stubbs.

I have never made it myself because I can't
imagine rolling it out as thinly as it needs to be.
Also, it is possible to buy excellent filo, usually
frozen, in one pound boxes. It should be thoroughly thawed before use or it will break. Unused
sheets should be covered until you need them
because they will tear easily if they dry out. If you
follow these two simple cautions, the pastry is easy
to use. Any leftover filo can be refrigerated for a
few days or re-frozen according to directions on
the box.

The fillings for the savory pastries are adapted
from Claudia Roden's *A Book of Middle Eastern
Food,* which is available in paperback. The book has
other filling recipes which sound equally delicious.

Savory Filo Pastries

½ pound filo pastry
the fillings given below
1 stick of butter

Melt the butter. Cut the pastry into fourths so
that you have long thin strips 2½ to 3 inches wide.
Brush the entire strip with melted butter. Put a
heaped teaspoon of filling about 1 inch from one
end. Fold the corner over, making a triangle. Keep
folding the triangle over and over. Tuck the loose
end neatly under the triangle and place it on a
greased baking sheet.

When you have formed triangles from all the
pastry and filling, brush the tops with melted butter
and bake at 375°F for 30 to 40 minutes, until they
are crisp and golden. Serve hot or cold. Greek
cooks often use olive oil instead of butter for
brushing the pastry.

Spinach Filling

1 pound fresh spinach or 1 package frozen
1 medium onion
1 tablespoon pine nuts or walnuts
1 to 2 tablespoons raisins
salt and pepper
nutmeg
2 tablespoons olive oil

Chop the onions finely. If you are using fresh
spinach, trim the ends, wash, drain, and chop the
spinach. If you are using frozen, chop it up a bit.
Heat the oil and fry the pine nuts until they turn
golden. Remove them with a slotted spoon.

Soften the onion in the oil. Add the spinach
and cook over a moderately high heat until tender.
You want to evaporate as much of the water as
possible or the pastries will get soggy. Stir often
to keep the spinach from sticking.

Mix the spinach with the pine nuts and add the raisins. Season to taste with salt, pepper and nutmeg.

Eggplant Filling

½ pound eggplant
olive oil
1 medium onion
2 medium tomatoes
rosemary, thyme
salt and pepper

Cube the eggplant, sprinkle with salt and let it drain in a colander for at least a half-hour to drain away bitter juices.

Chop the onion finely. Peel, seed and chop the tomatoes (Dip them in boiling water or pour boiling water over them to make them easier to peel).

Soften the onion in two tablespoons olive oil. Dry the eggplant and add it to the onion. Fry until the eggplant starts to get tender. Add the tomato, a pinch of rosemary and thyme and salt and pepper to taste. Cook over medium heat until the tomato has melted into a sauce. Mash lightly with a fork.

Loving Libya

The Guide
November 1979

THOUGH I FEEL IT SHOULD BE IMPOSSIBLE to like one dish above all others, this couscous from Libya is my favorite recipe. It was given to me by a friend who taught English there for a year before Qaddafi made such occupations obsolete. It consists of three elements: the steamed grain; a spicy, rich lamb and vegetable stew; and an onion and chickpea mixture. (Chickpeas are also known as garbanzos). It's a good recipe for feeding lots of people because, if you're organized, everything can bubble away in advance; the final steaming of the couscous is the only last-minute task. A green salad will complete the meal.

Lamb Stew

¼ to ½ pound stewing lamb per person
1 large or 2 medium onions
olive oil
3 tablespoons tomato puree
2 tablespoons turmeric
3 to 5 hot peppers
1 tablespoon salt
1 tablespoon cumin
2 teaspoons fenugreek seeds
2 teaspoons ground coriander seeds
1 teaspoon ground allspice (or a mixture
    of cinnamon, cloves and nutmeg)
at least four of your choice of the following
    vegetables: carrots, pumpkin, winter
    or summer squash, potatoes, turnips,
    leeks, or what you will

I like to make lamb stews with different cuts of lamb: neck, breast, shoulder (leg is okay, but a little dry and more expensive). The bones and cartilage give more flavor and richness to the broth. Brown the lamb and onions in hot olive oil. Add water to cover, the tomato puree and the spices. Let it simmer for an hour and then start adding your choice of vegetables. They should be peeled and cut into large chunks. The root vegetables will take longest to cook, so add them first. Summer squash will only need about 15 minutes, so add it last. Add more water if necessary. Taste for seasonings and cook until the vegetables are tender.

Couscous

For each person:
2 ounces couscous per person
salt

Put the couscous in a bowl and cover with water. Let it sit for 10 minutes. Turn it out onto a clean tea towel or multi-layered cheese cloth and leave it to swell for an hour. Steam it (uncovered) over boiling water for 20 minutes. Start timing when the steam comes through the couscous. Take the bundle out of the steamer and splash cold, salted water on the couscous, using your fingers or a fork to break apart any clumps. Leave until you are ready to steam it for another 10 minutes just prior to serving.

Onions & Chickpeas

I ounce dried chickpeas per person
I large onion for every two people
olive oil
salt

Soak the chickpeas for several hours (or overnight), then simmer them in plain water until tender — two hours or longer, depending on the peas. An alternate method is to cook them in your oven at its lowest setting for several hours or overnight. You can also substitute canned chickpeas.

Slice the onions thinly, salt them and sauté them gently in olive oil until limp. Add a little of the broth from the lamb stew and simmer, covered, for 20 minutes. Add the drained chickpeas and simmer for 20 more minutes.

TO SERVE:

In a large bowl or deep serving platter, spread and fluff up the hot grain. Pour on broth from the stew until the couscous is lightly coated. Arrange the onion and chickpea mixture evenly over the surface. Then arrange the meat and vegetables and sprinkle lightly with ground cloves or allspice. Serve more broth separately.

Gifts That Cook

The Guide
December 1979

GIVING A COOKBOOK* as a present can be tricky unless the recipient knows so little about cooking that his or her ability to boil an egg properly is in doubt. In that case you give the *Joy of Cooking*. It is *the* basic American cookbook and contains more than anyone will ever need to know about various aspects of cooking ingredients, processes, equipment, timing, storage and so forth.

Beyond this first level, you need to think a little. Will the book actually get used? There are obvious mistakes to avoid - someone who hates lamb probably won't do much Middle Eastern cooking and a vegetarian won't get much use from *Meat at Any Price*. My aim when giving a cookbook as a present is to stimulate or expand the recipient's repertoire — perhaps a specialized or regional Chinese cookbook for someone whose wok is already well broken in; a book of real Mexican food for a chili lover; a good vegetarian cookbook for someone who has commented favorably on vegetarian food in a restaurant but doesn't know how to go about cooking vegetables any way but southern style; or a bread cookbook for someone who has enjoyed making a first few loaves.

You should also consider matching the style of the cookbook to the style of the cook. Scientific

types or those unsure at the range are going to hate the "season-to-taste and cook-until-done" type of book. Others will be put off by a 14-page recipe for french bread. You can see that it's a help to know a little about the cookbook you plan to give. Here's a list of a few of my favorites, with a little information about why I think each book is unique or useful so you can choose a book to give or hint for this Christmas.

French Provincial Cooking by Elizabeth David

This is the first book I ever did much cooking from; therefore I can't be objective. It set me firmly on the road to loving to cook good food. In fact, if I had to cut my collection down to one cookbook, this is the one I would keep. Elizabeth David's instructions give lovely results; her advice is useful and she makes the recipes sound so delicious, you want to cook all of them. I own and love all her cookbooks and also highly recommend *Summer Cooking* and *French Country Cooking* for gift-giving.

Mastering The Art Of French Cooking, Volume I by Julia Child, Louisette Bertholle, Simone Beck and *Volume II* by Julia Child and Simone Beck

Most everyone has heard of Julia Child and has seen her on TV. She exudes a love of good food and a desire to make it possible for others to cook and enjoy it. These two volumes achieve this aim as they contain foolproof recipes for good French food, outlining how things are supposed to work, why they sometimes don't and what can be done about it.

Cooking In 10 Minutes by Edouard de Pomiane translated by Bruno Cassirer

The ultimate real fast-food cookbook, witty and wonderful. Another translation is available; I prefer this one.

---

*All of the cookbooks listed here and elsewhere in this book are referenced in the appendix with the most current editions available. Some are out of print, but the original publication information is also listed in case you want to hunt them down in used book stores or a library. – ed.

Indian Cookery by Dharamjit Singh

This is not a comprehensive book of Indian food but is absolutely authentic. The cook learns a lot about method and every recipe I've ever tried has been absolutely delicious.

A Book Of Middle Eastern Food
by Claudia Roden

This is a survey of Middle Eastern food. Some of the spicing seems a little faint for my taste but that can be corrected. It covers appetizers, breads, main dishes, sweets and so on from many countries.

Couscous & Other Good Food From Morocco
by Paula Wolfert

This book tells you all about Moroccan cooking — from how it's done in Morocco to how to do it in your own kitchen. A few of the recipes call for ingredients that are hard to get in the Research Triangle but this is a minor problem.

Vegetarian Epicure and *Vegetarian Epicure: Book Two*
by Anna Thomas

These two volumes are not for vegetarians only! They are full of delicious recipes that don't use meat. Book Two contains a killer chocolate cheesecake recipe.

The Key To Chinese Cooking by Irene Kuo

This is to Chinese cooking as *Mastering the Art* is to French. Method, utensils, ingredients are very clearly explained and the food is delicious and authentic.

The Good Food Of Szechwan by Robert A. Delfs

This book focuses on the food from one province in China. It is the first Chinese cookbook I ever used that the recipes came out tasting like the food I love in good Chinese restaurants.

The New Orleans Cookbook
by Rima Collin & Richard Collin

Recipes from America's best regional cuisine. The seafood section is especially good. A good present for someone who likes to entertain.

Italian Regional Cooking by Ada Boni

Ada Boni is an Italian cookery writer who has published extensively in Italy and this book starts in the north and works its way south, province by province. The pictures may seem a little strange, but the food isn't. You learn that there is a lot more to Italian food than tomato sauce and parmesan cheese. The seafood recipes are especially good here, too. This book is often found in book stores "on sale" at a good price.

The Complete Book Of Mexican Cooking
by Elisabeth Lambert Ortiz

A good introduction to take someone beyond tacos and chili (though there are good recipes for both).

Great Aunt Jane's Cook and Garden Book
by Jane Birchfield

This delightful book is divided into months of the year with good gardening advice, delicious recipes and amusing anecdotes.

Jerusalem Artichokes

The Guide
February 1980

IT CAN BE FRUSTRATING going into the super-markets around here during the winter to choose a fresh vegetable from the same old selection — limp green beans, year-round squash, hothouse tomatoes, waxed cucumbers, turnips, potatoes, onions, mutilated fresh spinach — so it's nice when there is something different on the shelf. Jerusalem artichokes are one such welcome addition.

They are the small tubers of a native American sunflower and are often sold as "sunchokes" at fancy prices in the gourmet food section. However, they are easy to grow in this area (some friends tell me they are too easy to grow around here; they are taking over a large section of the garden) and you might want to consider planting some in your garden this year.

They taste faintly like artichokes but are more like a nutty water chestnut with a less crisp potato-like texture when cooked. They are delicious with meats or on their own as a salad, soup or vegetable course.

Jerusalem artichokes are thin-skinned and often quite knobby which makes them difficult to peel. The knobbiness seems to be disappearing; it is probably being bred out of the vegetable. To solve the peeling difficulty you can parboil them for a few minutes before peeling or just scrub them well and leave the peel on.

Jerusalem Artichoke & Broccoli Soup

2 tablespoons butter
2 shallots or scallions
½ pound broccoli
¼ pound Jerusalem artichokes
6 cups light stock or water
2 tablespoons cream of wheat (semolina)
salt and pepper
1 cup sour cream
paprika or nutmeg

Chop the shallots or scallions. Trim and wash the broccoli and chop slightly. Scrub or peel the Jerusalem artichokes and quarter them.

Melt the butter and gently fry the shallots or scallions for a few minutes until they soften. Add the broccoli and Jerusalem artichokes and stir them around in the butter. Add the stock. Bring the stock to a boil and sprinkle in the cream of wheat. Stir and turn down the heat to a simmer.

After half an hour the vegetables should be soft. Puree the soup using a food mill or blender (don't overblend to a pap). Reheat and add salt and pepper to taste. Stir in the sour cream and taste for seasonings again. Sprinkle on a little paprika or nutmeg and serve. Serves four.

Jerusalem Artichokes & Cream

1 pound Jerusalem artichokes
2 tablespoons butter
salt and pepper
½ cup cream
finely chopped fresh parsley

Scrub or peel the Jerusalem artichokes and slice them into ¼ inch rounds. Melt the butter in a heavy skillet and add the Jerusalem artichokes, stirring them gently until they start to absorb the butter. Sprinkle with salt and pepper and add enough water to just cover. Cook at a fairly rapid pace, uncovered, until the Jerusalem artichokes are tender and most of the water is gone. Add the cream and let it cook rapidly until it thickens into a sauce. Sprinkle with finely chopped parsley and serve. Serves two.

Jerusalem Artichoke Salad

> 1 pound Jerusalem artichokes
> 2 scallions
> oil and vinegar dressing or mayonnaise

Scrub the Jerusalem artichokes and simmer them in salted water until they are just tender (8 to 18 minutes, depending on their size). Slice them and mix with either mayonnaise or oil and vinegar dressing. A dressing made from walnut oil and red wine vinegar is especially good in this salad. Serves two or three.

Vampires Beware!

The Guide
March 1980

HAVING TROUBLE PEELING GARLIC? Cut off the root end and, using the side of your knife, squash the clove slightly. The peel will slip off easily.

Does your garlic go bad before you've used the entire head? Peel the cloves, put them into a clean jar and cover with olive oil. As a bonus, you get garlic-flavored olive oil.

You don't have a garlic press? Peel the garlic, sprinkle with salt, chop it up a bit and then, using the side of the knife, squash and scrape the garlic along the cutting board. Chop, squash and scrape until the garlic is pulverized. A mortar and pestle makes this job even easier.

Worried about garlic on your breath? Too bad, this month's recipes are not for you. We move beyond the clove of garlic as an invaluable addition to soups, stews, stocks, sauces, vegetables, salads and meats into the world of mega-garlic.

Garlic Soup

> 16 cloves of garlic (1 head)
> 2 quarts of water
> salt and pepper
> 2 cloves
> ½ bay leaf
> 4 sprigs parsley
> 3 tablespoons olive oil
> 3 egg yolks
> 3 or 4 tablespoons olive oil
> hard toasted French bread
> 1 cup grated Swiss or parmesan cheese

Drop the cloves of garlic into boiling water for 30 seconds. Drain, rinse with cold water and peel.

Put the garlic, water, salt, pepper, cloves, bay leaf, parsley and olive oil into a pan. Boil slowly for 30 minutes. Taste for seasonings.

Beat the egg yolks with a whisk in a serving bowl or tureen until they are thick and sticky. Beat in the olive oil, drop by drop, as if you were making mayonnaise.

Just before serving, beat a ladleful of soup into the egg mixture. Gradually strain in the rest of the soup, beating the soup and pressing juices out of the garlic.

Serve with the toasted bread and cheese. This soup is also very nice with a poached egg in each bowl, and is adapted from *Mastering the Art of French Cooking, Volume I* by Julia Child, Louisette Bertholle, and Simone Beck.

Le Poulet Canaille

> **roasting chicken, disjointed**
> **3 tablespoons butter**
> **4 tablespoons olive oil**
> **30 cloves of garlic (2 heads), unpeeled**
> **10 shallots, finely chopped**
> **1 cup dry white wine**

Melt the butter and oil together in a large skillet. Brown the chicken on both sides over medium high heat. Turn down the heat to medium low and add the garlic and shallots and leave for 10 minutes, until lightly browned. Sprinkle with salt and pepper and add the wine. Cover and simmer for 30 minutes or until the chicken is tender.

Uncover, raise the heat and let the juices bubble until they evaporate and the chicken browns again.

Give each diner a portion of the chicken and several cloves of garlic. Serve with a dry white wine.

This recipe is adapted from the delightful *Cooking with Pomiane* by Edouard de Pomiane, edited and translated by Peggie Benton. Pomiane says you can cut down on the number of garlic cloves if 30 seems outrageous to you, but you will probably use 30 the next time you make the dish.

Aioli

> **2 to 4 cloves garlic**
> **1 egg yolk**
> **1 to 1½ cups olive oil**
> **salt**
> **lemon juice**

Thoroughly crush the cloves of garlic with a mortar and pestle. A light sprinkling of salt will help. Add the egg yolk and mash it around until it is thick and sticky. Now add the olive oil, drop by drop, mixing all the while. When the sauce starts to thicken you can add the olive oil in a thin stream, but be careful not to add more than can be absorbed by the sauce at a given time. When the sauce is quite thick, add one teaspoon lemon juice, then taste and add more lemon juice or salt to your liking.

This sauce is wonderful with boiled potatoes, with baked sweet potatoes, with fish, mixed into hot, drained chickpeas, or spooned over split hard-boiled eggs.

Happy Hollandaise

The Guide
April 1980

This month, I'll answer questions. A Mr. Richard Feydor, of Fort Lee, New Jersey*, writes: "How can I make the perfect hollandaise sauce? Do I have to use a double boiler? Can I use bottled lemon juice? Do I need a pan with a special finish? What about variations on the basic sauce? Can I make it in a blender? What is sweet butter, anyway?"

Mr. Feydor sure asks a lot of questions, but he's asked the right person. Hollandaise is an emulsion of egg yolks and butter, flavored with lemon juice. It is rich and creamy, and superb with many meats and vegetables. It is not tricky but can be ruined if you don't pay attention to a couple of points.

Don't use an aluminum pot — it will interact with the sauce and leave a nasty metallic taste.

Don't scramble the egg yolks. Edouard de Pomiane, in *Cooking with Pomiane,* states that at 145°F egg yolks reach maximum viscosity (i.e., they are as thick as they are going to get) and at 155°F they harden and coagulate (i.e., they're scrambled). You can use your finger as a thermometer — when the yolks are getting too hot for your finger to stand, they're getting hot enough.

*Like so many **Saturday Night Live!** fans of the era, Helen loved the character of Roseann Roseannadanna, played by the late Gilda Radner. This column mimics Radner's skit in which she answers letters from her viewers. — ed.

Don't add more butter than the yolks can absorb — 3 ounces of butter is the maximum that one yolk can absorb. Two ounces (½ stick) is safe and will make a rich sauce.

Hollandaise

Serves two.

**½ stick sweet (unsalted) butter & 1 tablespoon
1 egg yolk
1 teaspoon lemon juice
1 teaspoon water
salt**

Cut the one tablespoon butter in half and set aside. Melt the ½ stick of butter and set aside.

Using a wire whisk, beat the yolk, lemon juice and water together in a pan until they are well blended. Put in one pat (½ tablespoon) of butter and heat up over a medium low heat. Stir constantly with the whisk. The mixture will steam as it heats up and then thicken slightly. It is thick enough when it clings to the whisk and the whisk leaves a path in the bottom of the pan.

You can use a double boiler to be absolutely safe, but this takes a long time, dirties more pans and is not necessary. All you need to do is pay attention to the egg yolks and remove the pan from the heat when they thicken. If you are nervous, have a bowl of cold water handy and you can put the bottom of the pan into it if things seem to be moving too quickly.

Remove the pan from the heat when the yolks have thickened and add the second pat (½ tablespoon) of butter. Whisk until it has melted and is incorporated. Now add the melted butter, pouring it in a thin stream, beating all the while. If the butter and egg yolk fail to emulsify, you probably added the butter too fast. Beat another egg yolk in a clean bowl until it thickens slightly, then beat in the failed sauce very slowly.

Taste the sauce and add salt and more lemon juice to taste. Don't try to reheat hollandaise — it will separate. If you make it in advance, it will keep for quite a while in a warm place (over the pilot light, on top of the water heater, etc.). It will also warm up some when you put it on the hot food.

You can make hollandaise in a blender, but I'm not going to tell you how (*Mastering the Art of French Cooking, Volume I* has clear directions). You can't incorporate as much butter so the sauce isn't as rich and wonderful.

Here are a few variations:

Béarnaise

Heat ¼ cup wine vinegar, ¼ cup dry white wine or vermouth, 1 teaspoon minced shallot, and a pinch of fresh tarragon or a smaller pinch of dried, and reduce this down to 1 teaspoon. Strain out the solid bits and follow the basic hollandaise recipe, using the reduced flavorings instead of the lemon juice. You can add a bit of chopped fresh tarragon to the finished sauce. It is especially good with lamb.

Mousseline

When you have finished the basic hollandaise fold in whipped cream (up to ⅓ of the amount of hollandaise). This is delicious with fish, brains or sweetbreads.

Maltaise

Beat 1 tablespoon orange juice into the finished hollandaise. Good with fish, broccoli, asparagus and artichokes.

As for Mr. Feydor's last question: sweet butter is unsalted butter. It is not absolutely necessary to use unsalted butter to make hollandaise but you have control over the amount of salt in the sauce if you do. As for bottled lemon juice, I don't understand why anyone uses it for anything.

Ossobuco & Risotto

The Guide
June 1980

I RECENTLY DISCOVERED A STORE in Durham that carries just the cut of veal necessary to make one of my favorite Italian dishes — Ossobuco ("hollow bones"). The cut is shin of veal sliced into crosswise cuts about two inches thick. The marrow in the center of the bone is an important part of this dish, both for flavoring and eating. The Italians even have a special long narrow spoon so they can get the marrow out.

Ossobuco is delicious, one of those dishes where the sum of the parts is even more tasty than imagined. I include a recipe for the perfect accompaniment — Risotto Milanese. A green salad and a bottle of hearty red wine will round out the meal.

Ossobuco Milanese

3 pounds shin of veal, cut into crosswise cuts
flour
2 tablespoons butter
2 tablespoons oil
½ cup dry white wine
14-ounce can Italian peeled tomatoes
    or
1 pound fresh tomatoes, peeled, seeded
    and chopped
salt and pepper
2 cloves garlic
1 small onion, chopped
grated rind of a lemon
parsley
1 or 2 anchovy fillets

Dredge the veal with flour, season with salt and pepper. Brown the veal in the hot butter and oil. Add one clove of garlic and the chopped onion and cook until the onion softens. Add the wine and simmer for 15 minutes or until the wine has almost disappeared. Add the tomatoes. Taste for salt and pepper and simmer for one-and-a-half to two hours. The veal should be very tender. Add stock or water if the veal starts to dry out during the cooking.

Chop the second clove of garlic very finely with the lemon rind, parsley and anchovy fillet(s). Sprinkle over the ossobuco and heat through, turning it once or twice. Serve with risotto or saffron rice.

Don't forget the marrow — scoop it out with a small spoon or a knife and spread it on bread or a bite of the veal.

Risotto Milanese

4 ounces butter (1 stick)
1 small onion, finely chopped
½ cup dry white wine
3 cups rice
6 cups stock
pinch of saffron
¼ cup grated parmesan cheese

Italian rice makes the best risotto because it maintains its shape when it is done. You can use other rices, but take care not to overcook, or you'll end up with rice pudding.

Put the stock on to simmer gently. Steep the saffron in two tablespoons of the hot stock. Melt two ounces of the butter in a large heavy saucepan. Sauté the onion until transparent. Sauté the rice, stirring all the while, until it turns milky. Add the wine and cook at a rapid simmer until the wine is almost gone. Now start adding the stock by cups, maintaining the rapid simmer and adding the next cupful when the last is almost gone. Start testing after 15 minutes, the rice should be tender but still have some bite to it. Add the saffron and its liquid when nearly done. Turn off the heat and gently stir in the rest of the butter and the cheese. Cover and let it settle for two minutes before serving.

Classically, Risotto Milanese has 2 ounces of marrow fried with the onions, but this is not necessary when serving it with ossobuco.

Both recipes will serve six.

A Puff Piece

The Guide
July 1980

I WAS RECENTLY REMINDED of the versatility of choux (puff) pastry when it appeared in two of four courses — Pommes Dauphine with the main course and as two kinds of cream puffs at dessert at a birthday dinner in a fine local restaurant. Several of my friends expressed an interest in making the potato dish. What follows is a basic puff pastry recipe and recipes for Smoked Fish Puffs, a first course; Pommes Dauphine; and Profiteroles, a dessert.

Sweet Puff Pastry

> 1 cup water
> 6 tablespoons butter
> ¼ cup sugar
> pinch salt
> 4 eggs
> 1 cup flour*

Bring the water, butter, sugar and salt to a boil in a medium-sized saucepan. Remove from the fire and add all the flour at once. Beat with a wooden spoon until the flour is thoroughly mixed in. Return to a moderate heat and keep stirring. The pastry will form into a ball and begin to glisten. When it starts to leave a thin film on the bottom of the pan remove it from the heat again. Add the eggs, one at a time, and beat well until each egg is thoroughly incorporated (this beats the egg and

Helen accidentally omitted this ingredient when the article appeared, inspiring her next column in August 1980. – ed.

adds air; both are essential to the puffing.) The dough is now ready to use.

Pommes Dauphine

PUFF PASTRY:
I cup water
I cup flour
I teaspoon salt
6 tablespoons butter
I cup flour
3 eggs

Make the dough according to the directions for sweet puff pastry above, using this proportion of ingredients, omitting the sugar.

POTATO PUREE:
3 baking (floury) potatoes
6 tablespoons butter
salt and pepper

Boil the potatoes until tender. Peel and puree them. Mix in the butter, and salt and pepper, to taste.

Combine the pastry dough and the potato puree. Fry in deep fat at 350°F until they are puffed and golden brown. Drain on paper towels and serve. If you need to wait, they can be kept warm in a 300°F oven for a short while. Serves six.

Smoked Fish Puffs

PUFF PASTRY:
4 ounces water
3 tablespoons butter
pinch of salt
½ cup flour
2 eggs

Make dough according to the basic recipe above.

FISH PUREE:
½ pound smoked fish
½ ounce butter
salt and pepper

Use a strongly-flavored smoked fish. Pour boiling water over the fish and leave for 10 minutes. Remove the skin and any bones. Coarsely puree the fish, using a food mill, blender or food processor. If the puree seems very moist, dry it out in a pan over medium heat. Mix in the butter. Combine with the puff pastry dough. Deep fry at 350°F until puffed and golden.

This amount serves four as a first course, or two as a main course and is delicious with Sauce Mousseline — hollandaise sauce with whipped cream folded into it. *(See Mousseline recipe, page 67.)*

Profiteroles

CREAM PUFFS:

Make the basic sweet puff pastry above and bake it as cream puffs: Preheat the oven to 425°F and lightly grease some baking sheets. Use a pastry bag, if you have one, or a teaspoon and a finger to shape the puffs. Place one-inch mounds two inches apart on the sheets. Bake for 20 minutes or until the puffs are crisp and golden brown. You will have about three dozen small puffs.

To keep them from getting soggy, poke a small hole in the side of the puff to release steam. Larger puffs can be slit and have their soggy inner parts removed.

WHIPPED CREAM FILLING:
2 cups whipping cream
¼ cup confectioner's sugar
½ teaspoon vanilla extract

Whip the cream with sugar and vanilla extract. Split the puffs and fill the inside with the whipped cream. Don't do this too far in advance or the cream puffs will be soggy. You can use a thin pastry cream or custard, but I think whipped cream is lighter.

CHOCOLATE SAUCE:
½ **cup semi-sweet chocolate**
¼ **cup sugar**
2 **teaspoons cocoa (powder)**
5 **ounces water**
2 **teaspoons corn starch, blended with**
   1 **tablespoon cold water**

Simmer everything but the corn starch for 10 minutes. Add the corn starch and simmer for two minutes. Dribble the sauce over the filled cream puffs and serve.

Missing Ingredients

The Guide
August 1980

THE FIRST MISSING INGREDIENT is one cup of flour from the Sweet Puff Pastry recipe last month. The typesetter has been suitably punished.* This omission led me to contemplate other missing ingredients. Some are inspired cooking, others are dismal failures. Turtle soup without turtles (Mock Turtle Soup) works, while apple pie without apples (Ritz crackers cleverly disguised as apples) doesn't.

I have a copy of *The Cavalry School Cookbook* probably put out in the late 1920s or early '30s at Fort Riley, Kansas. You know the sort — a collection of recipes with the donor's name at the end of each. Reading through the book inspired the hypothesis that Army wives were responsible for the spread of "Mexican" cooking throughout America. Back in those days when Army wives cooked Mexican outside the Southwest, they had to deal with a variety of missing ingredients. They had no "gourmet" or "international" section in their grocery stores. From the Mexican recipes in this book corn meal seemed to be an adequate substitute for masa harina but I can't help suspecting that a combination of tabasco and worcestershire sauce did not give that authentic south-of-the-border flavor.

Here are some recipes designed to defy common expectations:

*The typesetter of **The Guide** at this time was none other than Helen herself. — ed.*

Bouillabaisse Without Fish

¼ cup olive oil
2 teaspoon tomato paste
4 cloves of garlic
2 chopped onions
pinch of saffron
salt and pepper
6 cups water
4 eggs
4 to 8 slices of bread

Dry the bread out in a medium oven (300°F) for 10 to15 minutes.

Chop the garlic finely. If you squash the unpeeled clove with the side of your knife, the skin will slip off easily and it will be easier to chop the garlic finely.

Put everything but the eggs and the bread into a saucepan and bring to the boil. Let it simmer briskly for 15 minutes.

Turn the heat down to a slow simmer and poach the eggs one by one in the broth: Take a spoon and swirl the broth until you get a whirlpool effect and crack each egg directly into the middle of the swirl. If you aren't feeling steady, use a cup as intermediary between the shell and the water. In a minute or two the egg will set. Remove it with a slotted spoon and place it on a piece or two of the bread in an individual serving bowl.

When all the eggs are poached, pour the broth into the bowls and serve. If you happen to have some aioli (garlic mayonnaise) around, it is an admirable addition.

Apple Pie Without Cinnamon

SWEET SHORT CRUST:
2 cups flour
3 tablespoons sugar
pinch of salt
¼ pound butter
3 tablespoons vegetable shortening
5 or 6 tablespoons cold water
    (1 to 2 tablespoons could be lemon juice)

The secret to a good short crust is a light touch. You don't want to do anything that resembles kneading because you don't want the gluten in the flour to develop.

Mix the flour, sugar and salt together. Cut the fats into this mixture using a pastry cutter, two knives, or your fingers. Work quickly in hot weather so the fats don't melt. Mix in most of the water (or water and lemon juice), then add the rest of the water until the pastry just holds together. Wrap up the pastry and refrigerate it while you prepare the apples.

FILLING:
6 apples
2 tablespoons sugar
lemon juice
small pinch of salt

In an apple pie, everything depends on the apples. You want apples that have a good flavor when they are cooked. MacIntosh and Winesaps are good, but even better are Granny Smiths. They are very tart and are excellent cooking apples. They have so much flavor you won't even miss the cinnamon. (You could experiment with, say, cardamom, coriander, nutmeg or whatever you fancy.) Core and peel the apples, then slice them into apple pie-sized pieces. Sprinkle with lemon juice, sugar and salt.

Roll out a little more than half of the pastry for the bottom crust. If you turn the pastry between each roll it won't stick to the board. Put the pastry into your pie pan, poke it a few times with a fork and place the apples on top. Roll out a top crust from the remaining pastry. Moisten the edge of the bottom crust with cold water and lay the top crust over the pie. Press down on the edges to seal the crust and crimp the edges or press decoratively with a fork. If you are feeling fancy decorate with leftover pastry scraps. Cut a slit or two in the top to allow steam to escape. You can brush the top crust with a little milk or egg yolk beaten with water for a shiny crust.

Bake for 40 minutes at 350°F. If the crust is getting too dark, put a piece of aluminum foil over it. Serve hot, warm or cold. Thick cream is a nice garnish.

Carrot Salad Without Raisins

Always.

Stalking Celery

The Guide
September 1980

SEVERAL YEARS AGO I grew celery in my garden. Two plants did well enough to keep me supplied with all the stalks I needed until Thanksgiving, when I dug them up and used them in the turkey stuffing. This year I decided to try growing celeriac (also known as celery root) and persuaded several friends to include it in their gardens as well. The plants seem to be doing fine and now my friends are wondering when to harvest and how to use their celeriac.

I'm wondering about harvesting myself. As near as I can tell they should be dug up when the bulbous root is big enough to be useful and before the first frost. As for using them, here are some recipes from my days lived where supermarkets (or even greengrocers) carried celeriac.

Potato/Celeriac Puree

I celeriac
I potato
butter
cream or milk
parsley, chives or lemon thyme

Peel, rinse and cut a celeriac into chunks and boil until tender. Meanwhile boil an equal amount of potatoes. Puree both and beat with butter and a bit of cream or milk. Sprinkle with finely chopped parsley, chives, or lemon thyme (also good with baked potatoes) and serve.

Cream of Celeriac Soup

1 large onion or 2 medium leeks
2 tablespoons butter
1 celeriac
4 cups water or chicken stock
salt and pepper
1 cup cream

Chop the onions or leeks roughly and soften in the butter over a low heat. Peel, rinse and chop the celeriac. Add celeriac and water to leeks or onions and bring to the boil. Salt and pepper to taste and simmer to 20 minutes or until vegetables are tender. Puree (in a food mill, blender or food processor) add the cream and reheat. Taste for seasoning and sprinkle with finely chopped parsley.

An aside on finely chopped parsley: Just chop the leaves (not the stems — use them to flavor soups or stocks) using a sharp knife and chop until your patience runs out. Stop before you produce a puree.

Shredded Celeriac

1 medium celeriac
2 tablespoons butter
1 tablespoon oil
salt and pepper
1 teaspoon Dijon-type mustard
Optional: $\frac{1}{2}$ cup cream

Peel, rinse and shred the celeriac (use a grater, mandoline, food processor or sharp knife). Melt the butter and oil in a frying pan and add the celeriac. Fry gently until just done (10 minutes). Salt and pepper to taste and stir in the mustard. If you are using the optional cream, turn up the heat, add the cream and stir until the cream thickens slightly.

Celeriac Remoulade

1 celeriac
$\frac{1}{2}$ teaspoon salt
$1\frac{1}{2}$ teaspoons lemon juice
4 tablespoons Dijon-type mustard
3 tablespoons boiling water
$\frac{1}{3}$ to $\frac{1}{2}$ cup olive oil
2 tablespoons wine vinegar
salt and pepper
2 to 3 tablespoons parsley

This recipe is from *Mastering the Art of French Cooking, Volume I* and is a delicious first course or salad. Peel the celeriac and shred it. Toss with salt and lemon juice. Let it sit for 30 minutes then rinse, drain and pat dry.

Put the mustard into a warm bowl and beat in the boiling water, drop by drop. Then beat in the oil, drop by drop, to make a thick creamy sauce. Beat in vinegar, and season to taste.

Fold the celeriac into the sauce and let it marinate for two to three hours or overnight. Sprinkle with parsley before serving.

Garlic, Part 2

The Guide
October 1980

AFTER THE PUBLICATION of my first column on garlic earlier this year *(see page 64)*, a friend pointed out that it wouldn't be difficult to do a year's series featuring garlic.

The reason I bring up garlic this month is that in this area, autumn is the time for planting garlic so that it will mature before the really hot weather next summer. Plant individual cloves, fat base downward, one to two inches deep, two to three inches apart, and if you're enthusiastic, the rows should be a foot apart. Harvest your garlic bulbs when the leaves die down after they bloom and store in a cool dry place.

Here are two more recipes where garlic is crucial. The first is adapted from *The Cuisine of the Sun* by Mireille Johnston (for those readers who pay attention to graphic design, the illustrations are by Milton Glaser). It's a wonderful book of classic French cooking from Nice and Provence.

Sauceaux Noix

½ cup walnuts
1 clove garlic, crushed
2 tablespoons olive oil
2 tablespoons warm water
salt

Pound the garlic and walnuts to a smooth paste in a mortar. Stirring constantly, add the olive oil slowly and steadily. Add the salt (to taste) and warm water. The result should be a smooth sauce that is delicious with pasta or plain boiled rice.

Chicken with Garlic Cream

1 whole chicken
pinch tarragon or thyme
salt and pepper
4 cloves garlic
1 lemon
2 cups cream

Remove the giblets (to your stockpot), rinse and dry the chicken and sprinkle the cavity with salt, pepper and tarragon. Put in one of the cloves of garlic and a little piece of the zest (yellow) of the lemon peel. Rub the outside of the chicken with lemon juice and steam the chicken until done (put it on a plate on a rack in a large pot if you don't have a steamer large enough). Check the water level several times during the steaming and add boiling water if necessary. The timing will vary with the size of the bird from 50 to 90 minutes. The chicken is done when the leg moves easily in its socket and the juices are clear.

Near the end of the cooking time, crush the remaining three cloves of garlic, add them to the cream and boil the cream down until it thickens slightly and is fragrant with the scent of garlic.

Place the chicken on a platter and remove the skin (add it to the stockpot). Take the garlic out of the cream and pour some over the chicken. Serve with plain rice, kasha (buckwheat groats) or noodles and a salad.

Full of Beans

The Guide
November 1980

> *"The Navy gets the gravy, and the Army gets the beans."*
>
> – Old song often heard from the back of the bus on elementary school field trips*

JUDGING FROM MY COPY of *Cooking and Baking on Shipboard,* published in 1945 by the War Shipping Administration-Food Control Division, the Navy also got its share of beans. Judging from the rise in meat prices due to inflation and the drought this summer, we'll be seeing a few beans this winter, ourselves.

That's fine — beans can be inexpensive, nutritious and delicious. They are a good source of protein alone and even better if the meal includes corn, wheat, rice or milk. For more information on complementary proteins, see Lappes' *Diet for a Small Planet* or Robertson, Flinders and Godfrey's *Laurel's Kitchen.*

Mexican Beans (Frijoles)

This is an authentic Mexican recipe for beans which may surprise you because it's so simple. Frijoles (and most beans) are much better the next day because the liquid thickens and the flavors intermingle. The method can be applied to all sorts of beans.

dried pinto beans
lard
small onion
salt

Dried beans will approximately double in volume when cooked. One-half to one cup of dried beans will serve two people depending on what else is being served and how hungry they are. Beans also keep well, either refrigerated or frozen, so don't worry about cooking too many.

Pick through the beans, discarding any that are discolored and any extraneous stuff you may find. Wash them in cold water. Soaking is not necessary (in fact some sources recommend not soaking), but may reduce cooking time by a half hour. If you choose to soak and the weather is warm, do so in the refrigerator to avoid fermentation.

When you're ready to cook, put the beans in a pot and add a little more than twice as much water as beans. Add one tablespoon lard (you may substitute oil, but the flavor will not be authentic) and a cut-up onion, Bring to the boil and reduce the heat until the liquid is simmering. Cooking time varies with the type of bean and how long ago it was dried. The pinto beans available in this area start getting tender after 1 to 1½ hours. Add salt at that point (but not before, it may toughen the beans) and cook until completely tender. Check the liquid level every so often and add boiling water if necessary. You can stir in cheese or chili peppers before serving.

An alternate cooking method is to follow the above directions until you bring the beans to a boil on the top of the stove. Then place the beans in your oven at its lowest setting for six to eight hours (overnight).

*Helen was an "Army brat," growing up on military bases where songs like this really were sung on the school bus. – ed.

"Refried" Beans
(Frijoles Refritos)

Also simple. The beans are actually "fried," not "refried." (Reminds me of the distinction between "iterate" and "reiterate"; one does not reiterate until one says whatever for the third time.) Diana Kennedy, in her excellent *Cuisines of Mexico*, solves the mystery and translates the name as "well-fried beans." Anyhow, you know what I mean.

2 tablespoons lard
small onion, chopped
4 cups cooked pinto beans

Melt the lard in a large iron skillet and soften the onion. Turn the heat up high and add a ladleful of beans. Mash and stir the beans until they are broken up and the liquid is disappearing. Add more beans and repeat the mashing and stirring. Keep going until all the beans are in the pan and the liquid is almost gone.

Black Beans

I'm not sure where this recipe evolved from; I suspect that it is the application of an Italian method to a New World bean, and it's different every time I cook it. Other sorts of beans (white, red, chickpeas) respond well to this treatment, and the tomato sauce is limited only by your imagination. Sprinkling on a little cheese (sharp cheddar, Monterey jack or a good cream cheese, crumbled) never hurts. Certain combinations (this one, for instance) make dynamite burritos with tortillas and sour cream.

2 cups black beans
2 tablespoons oil

Follow the method outlined for Mexican beans. Black beans will take longer to start getting tender (2 to 2½ hours).

Tomato Sauce

2 tablespoons olive oil
1 small onion chopped
1 green pepper, diced
Optional: celery
Optional: chopped chili pepper, paprika
1 or 2 tomatoes, peeled and skinned; or
**   a small can of plum tomatoes, drained**
1 clove garlic, crushed
large pinch basil or marjoram
salt and pepper
chopped parsley

Heat the olive oil and soften the onion, green pepper and optional celery. Add the tomatoes, garlic, optional chili, paprika, salt and pepper, basil or marjoram and cook rapidly until you have a thick sauce. Stir often so it doesn't stick and burn. Add the parsley. When the black beans are getting tender, mix in the sauce for the last half-hour of cooking.

Full of Beans

Hot Competition

The Guide
January 1981

"The only safe generalization to make about chili con carne is that each chiliphile considers him/herself to be an expert and a purist, and his/her own particular version of the dish is 'the authentic one.'"

– Jane Birchfield, in *Great Aunt Jane's Cook & Garden Book*

THE UNMISTAKABLE AROMA of chili drifts out of the kitchen. Fourteen cooks drift in and out, stirring up fourteen pots from time to time, eyeing the competition, wondering when the judging will begin. Whiskey flows like beer; beer flows like water. The Terlingua Chili Cook-Off? No — it's Chili Wars II, mid-December, Durham. But you won't have to wait until next year to taste winning chili because here — in their own words, secret ingredients and all — are the three winners' "authentic" recipes.

Kim Anderson's Chili

- 1 six pack of **Schlitz Malt Liquor**
- 1 bottle of **Dos Equis Dark Mexican Beer**
- 1 bottle of **vino tinto**
- 1 pound **ground beef**
- ½ pound **hot country or Italian sausage**
- ½ head (6 to 8 cloves) **fresh garlic**, minced
- 3 large **green bell peppers**, diced
- 4 medium **yellow onions**, diced
- 15-ounce can **pinto beans** or **"Mexe-hot beans"**
- 15-ounce can **kidney beans**
- 15-ounce can **red beans**
- 1¼-ounce can **ground cumin**
- 3½-ounce can **chili powder**
- 3 15-ounce cans **whole tomatoes**
- 8-ounce can **jalapeño peppers**
- whole **red cayenne peppers**
- crushed **red pepper**
- **cayenne**
- **olive oil**

Drink three cans of the SML. This is absolutely necessary in order to be at the proper altitude for communing with the necessary fire gods.

In a large cast iron frying pan sauté the garlic and fresh vegetables in olive oil. Add about a third of the chili powder and cumin. When partly sautéed, add the sausage and burger, and a little later about a half cup wine and half of the Dos Equis. Sauté until the meat is brown.

In a large (3 to 4 quart) cast iron Dutch oven combine the beans, tomatoes, and another third of the cumin and chili powder. Add some cayenne, crushed red pepper, and a few jalapeños. Heat until it bubbles, and cut up the tomatoes so that the pieces fit well into the matrix.

While both pot and pan are simmering gently, drink a glass of wine and meditate upon the aroma. You are now ready to combine the two pots into one (presumably the larger, since the pan is probably already overflowing).

Drink another SML or two, and let matters simmer gently for about 2 hours, during which time you "adjust the seasonings." To do this you soak and simmer half a dozen of the whole red peppers, a jalapeño, and any other hot items you wish, in about a cup of wine and a few tablespoons of olive oil until cooked down to about a third of a cup. Add this to the mess. Now go to the cupboard and refrigerator, and get out anything that seems appropriate to the taste of the chili. Likely candidates — any leftover wine or beer (flat champagne is great), Texas Pete, a bit of cocoa or coffee, a touch of curry powder, any Indian aromatic spices in moderation, a touch of corn meal, chicory, leftover barbecue sauce, green chilies, hominy, etc. By this time the chili powder, cumin

Helen and Kim Anderson judging at Chili Wars photo by Bill Boyarsky

and hot items will so dominate the flavor that these items should add only the nuances required to make your chili uniquely you. Taste often in conjunction with the remaining wine and beer until it's "correct." The only ingredients considered truly out-of-form are Drano and petroleum distillates. Remove from the heat and let it sit overnight. Heat for about an hour or two before serving. If it's not truly hot, don't make it.

Allen Mason's Chili

1 pound chuck
1 pound pork shoulder, meat should be cut into bite-sized pieces

MARINADE:
garlic (several cloves diced, or generous amount of powdered)
4 large jalapeño peppers, diced
4 yellow chilies, diced
juice from peppers
⅓ cup red wine
several dashes Worcestershire sauce

Soak meat overnight in marinade.

SAUCE:
1 large can whole tomatoes (fresh ones when available, but these are sweeter)
2 large onions, diced; or 1 large Spanish onion, diced
1 large can tomato paste (small one may serve to thicken, use size that seems appropriate)
½ teaspoon crushed red peppers
1 teaspoon oregano
1 teaspoon salt
3 to 4 tablespoons hot chili powder (should contain cumin, other spices, if not, add these; cumin is mandatory)
3 large jalapeño peppers, diced
3 yellow chilies, diced
garlic (to taste)
1 tablespoon molasses (or honey or sugar)
½ to 1 pound hot country sausage (sauté and add to thicken)
water (as necessary)

After soaking the meat overnight, prepare tomatoes with onions, peppers, spices. Do not remove seeds from the peppers unless you don't want hot chili. However, in this case you might as well buy canned chili.

Add marinated meat and allow mixture to simmer on low heat for three hours. You may need to add liquid at the beginning to get the right consistency. I put water on the ingredient list, but beer is excellent in the chili, and better in the cook.

Sauté the sausage toward the end of this period and add to chili for thickness and simmer about 30 minutes.

You may wish to adjust the recipe for heat. I like mine hot, but molasses tempers this, as does the sweetness of the tomatoes. Adding sour cream or cheese when serving also cools the heat.

Please note the absence of beans. I love beans, and I love them in chili. However, real chili has no beans. This would be making chili con carne con frijoles. For this recipe, soak pinto, kidney and black beans overnight, then cook and add to the sauce.

H. Hudson Whiting's Chili*

2 cups pinto beans
1 tablespoon lard
1 small onion, chopped
1 teaspoon salt

Cover the beans to twice their height with water. Add the lard and chopped onion. Simmer, partially covered. When the beans begin to soften (1½ to 2 hours) add salt. Cook until completely soft (a half to one hour).

2½ pounds beef, chuck or round, coarsely
    ground
2 tablespoon lard
1 cup finely chopped onion
2 to 3 cloves garlic, finely chopped
1 large green pepper (sweet), finely chopped
1 bay leaf
1 teaspoon oregano
4 tablespoons or more chili powder
1 teaspoon toasted, ground cumin
1 teaspoon or more very hot dried peppers
    (crushed Thai peppers available in local
    Chinese food stores have an excellent
    taste as well as heat level)
freshly ground black pepper
1 tablespoon paprika
2 tablespoon masa harina or flour
1 quart beef or chicken stock
1 small can "green chilies," blended until smooth
salt
½ square bitter chocolate
3 tablespoons tomato paste
pinch sugar
Optional secret ingredient:
    1 teaspoon anchovy paste

Brown the meat lightly in lard. Add the onion, garlic, green pepper, bay leaf, oregano, chili powder,

cumin (toast cumin seeds in a hot skillet: shake them around until they smell good; then crush), hot pepper, black pepper, and paprika. Sauté and stir for a few minutes, then stir in the masa harina or flour. Add the stock and bring to a boil. Turn down to a brisk simmer and add the canned green chilies and salt lightly (adjust salt later). Add the chocolate, tomato paste, sugar and (can you believe it?) anchovy paste. The listed amounts are just suggestions, as these ingredients are used to adjust the flavor, texture and color. Simmer for a couple of hours uncovered. Cook fast if it seems too liquid, stir often. Add water, beer or coffee if it seems to be getting too thick. Add the beans, adjust salt and other seasonings and cook for another hour. This is much better when heated for an hour or so the next day.

🔳 *Holly McDonough remembers —*

In regard to the chili wars — I happened to be one of the judges the year that Helen entered and won the contest. The experience was unique. Hungry faces pressed up against the kitchen windows hoping to encourage the judges to hurry up so that the eating could begin! We proceeded around the kitchen from coolest to hottest chili. One thing that might not be evident from the winning recipes in this book is the following. The judges had settled on the final three and we were then trying to rank them. All three were delicious, but Helen's nudged out the other two based on two criteria. First, as we let our noses and mouths be sent to sensual heaven, we noticed that there were more layers of flavor and aroma in Helen's chili. But the aspect that really put hers on top: It was definitely the prettiest.

---

*The best recipe as selected by the Chili Wars judges was saved for last in this column. H. Hudson won first prize, though she didn't admit it in print. As her editors, we honored her modesty until now. – ed.

Belgian Endive

The Guide
February 1981

I WAS DELIGHTED TO SEE "Belgian endive," also known as chicory (not the coffee additive of the same name), in a local supermarket recently. It's a welcome addition to our winter selection of fresh vegetables. Belgian endive is elegant and delicious in a salad, either as the main green or with lettuce, or as a bed for a chicken salad, or braised in butter.

Choose smooth, pale green endive. The outer leaves may be slightly wilted but should not be brown. They should not need washing unless dirty or buggy. If you trim the root end, use a stainless knife to avoid discoloration.

Belgian Endive Salad with Walnuts

1 endive
¼ cup walnuts
Optional: orange

DRESSING:
5 parts olive oil
1 part freshly squeezed lemon juice
salt and pepper
    or
5 parts walnut oil
1 part red wine vinegar
salt and pepper

Either separate the endive into individual leaves or cut into one-inch pieces. Mix with the walnuts and dress just before serving. Serves two.

Orange slices are a nice addition. With a sharp knife, cut down to the fruit at the top and bottom ends of an orange; then cut away all the peel and pith around the outside. Slice thinly and add to the salad just before the dressing.

I first had this salad when French friends took me to a steak house in Paris — the equivalent would be my taking French friends to a French restaurant instead of a barbecue place here in Durham.

Belgian Endive Braised in Butter

2 to 4 endive, depending on size
2 tablespoons butter
salt and pepper
1 teaspoon freshly squeezed lemon juice

Melt the butter in a fireproof dish just large enough for the endive. Turn them over in the butter, coating them all over. Cover the dish tightly (use buttered paper or foil under the lid if it doesn't fit tightly). Bake in a 350°F oven for 1½ hours. They should be absolutely tender and browned when done. If necessary, turn up the heat and uncover for a few minutes. Sprinkle with lemon juice just before serving.

They may also be cooked on a burner at a low heat, for 1½ hours. Check and turn them over a couple of times during the cooking time. Serves two.

Belgian Endive with Ham

2 endive
1 tablespoon butter
1 tablespoon freshly squeezed lemon juice
½ cup water
salt and pepper
2 large, thin slices of ham (country ham is good)
¼ cup grated Swiss cheese

Put the endive into a small pan with the butter, water, lemon juice, salt and pepper (take account of the saltiness of the ham when salting the endive). Simmer rapidly for about 20 minutes, turning over once or twice until they are tender and have absorbed most of the water.

Wrap each endive in a slice of ham, lay in a dish and sprinkle with the cheese. Cook in a hot 400–450°F oven for 20 minutes or until brown. Serves two.

Why Not the Best? A Philosophy of Food*

The Guide
March 1981

BECAUSE MY FATHER was in the Army, I never lived in any one place for very long, and I did a lot of thinking the year Durham replaced London as the place I've lived the longest. The positive aspects include knowing some *amazing* shortcuts around town and having friends I've seen nearly every day for years. It makes a difference on my table as well, because I know what's available and where to find it.

We eat every day; why not do it well? I can understand not wanting to make a big fuss all the time or to spend a fortune, both of which are often mistakenly believed to be necessary in order to eat well. What I can't understand is not caring or settling for the clearly inferior. This month's column

*This single column, appearing at approximately the halfway mark of H. Hudson's career with **The Guide**, succinctly presents her "Philosophy of Food" and represents the sure footing she earned in earlier columns to establish her own fully-formed editorial and personal voice. The opinions and recommendations are timeless.*

An interesting historical note: The owners of a new grocery store that had not yet opened asked us if they could run a display advertisement adjacent to this month's "Oral Gratification." Although we seldom guaranteed specific page placement, we agreed to see what we could do. The ad appeared as requested. It read, simply: "WELLSPRING GROCERY is coming . . . 9th at W. Knox, Durham." – ed.

consists of an incomplete list of staples, items likely to be on hand in any kitchen, with recommendations for selecting the best available. It is concerned with matters of taste as well as fact. One group's saint may be another group's witch (remember Joan of Arc?). For example, it's a fact that Velveeta is different from American cheese; but taste-wise, who cares?

This list is not my final word. I'm still learning, and what's available is changing. Remember when you had to make tortillas every time you wanted tacos, or pasta every time you wanted fresh linguine?

BACON

Buy slab bacon that has been sliced by the grocery store. It's usually a bit thicker and less watery. Also, the packaging displays more and you will have an easier time choosing the meatiest bacon.

BREAD

When buying whole wheat breads, go for the closest-to-homemade-type loaves. I like to slice bread myself because then I can match the thickness to the use.

BUTTER

Buy unsalted butter; it has to be treated more carefully when shipped and stored than the salted types and is likely to be in better condition.

COOKING OILS

Look for the ones with the least preservatives. They taste best. Try different ones to see which flavor you like. I can't stand the heavy taste of corn oil and like to use safflower or peanut oil for general use. (Read the label on peanut oil — the ones with preservatives taste funny.) Certain foods will taste better when cooked with the appropriate oil or fat — eggplant with olive oil or parsnips with bacon fat, for example.

CREAM

It's refreshing to read the label on some of the half-and-half sold around here. "Ingredients: milk and cream." Avoid the "ultra-pasteurized" or "sterilized" varieties when possible. They don't taste as good and the regular stuff should last as long as is necessary.

LETTUCE

My salad philosophy (Simple salad. Simple dressing.) doesn't work with iceberg lettuce, but there are so many greens with a far better texture and flavor, who needs it? Romaine is my favorite.

MAYONNAISE

I suspect many people are shocked by the heavy, rich taste of homemade mayonnaise, especially when it's made with olive oil. Potato salad, among other things, is remarkable when made with homemade mayonnaise. Of the store brands, Dukes tastes best and has the fewest additives, including *no* sugar.

MUSTARD

Dijon mustards are more interesting than the regular types.

PARMESAN CHEESE

Always buy a piece of cheese and grate your own. It will be fresher and taste much better than pre-ground types. Real Italian is the best, but very expensive; South American is good and less expensive; the Danish is not good at all.

PEPPER

Have you ever considered how exotic this spice is that we use every day? Grind pepper yourself for fresher flavor. I often add a few whole allspice when filling the grinder.

Why Not the Best? A Philosophy of Food

SALAD DRESSING

Make your own; it is better both for what you put in as well as leave out. Use four to six parts good quality oil (olive is my preference), one part wine vinegar, one pinch of dried mustard, salt and freshly ground pepper. This is simple and delicious.

SOUPS AND STOCKS

Don't bother with the canned and dried varieties; their flavor is so "enhanced" — no matter what price you pay — that many good dishes fail to be great or are ruined by their use. Any simple soup or stock that you make will be better than any store-bought variety.

TOMATOES

Don't bother with fresh tomatoes in the winter. I use canned, Italian, plum tomatoes for cooking when there are no good fresh ones.

VEGETABLES

It's always better to select each item individually, so shop at stores where you can rummage through loose vegetables rather than places that package them for you. This way you can avoid nasty surprises at the bottom of the packages and can buy the exact amount you need.

All-American

The Guide
May 1981

As American as:
   a. apple pie
   b. the flag
   c. Mom
   d. cole slaw
   e. deviled eggs
   f. potato salad

The best potato salad in the world
   a. is just like Mom's
   b. is not like Mom's

Potato salad should never contain:
   a. hard boiled eggs
   b. pickle juice
   c. sour cream
   d. celery
   e. anchovies

A Freudian analyst could, no doubt, make a great deal of your answers to the above questions. I wouldn't attempt to be objective about such matters. While I am unprejudiced enough to appreciate your mother's potato salad, I like my mother's, or rather, *my* version of *my* mother's potato salad, best.

So here are some basic summer recipes: my version of Mom's potato salad and deviled eggs. However, Mom was not my role model for cole slaw; Aunt Carmen was, though it was Roger Tygard who taught me what must have been her secrets. The recipes are vague as to quantities, because that's how they're most often made. If my recipes are missing that certain indefinable something that your mother's has, either check with her or add pickle juice.

Potato Salad

- potatoes
- eggs
- onions
- salt and pepper
- mayonnaise
- pimientos
- finely chopped parsley and/or paprika

First, select the right kind of potato. I prefer waxy, boiling potatoes to the flaky, baking kind for potato salad. My mother can succeed with either; her secret is to chill the potatoes after cooking them. I like to mix everything together while the potatoes are still warm; they will absorb more flavor from the dressing. Therefore I like potatoes that won't fall apart if I peel or slice them when they're hot. When in doubt, chill the potatoes.

Scrub your potatoes, but don't peel or cut them. Cover them with water and bring to a boil. Turn down to a simmer and cook until just done. If there are different sized potatoes, test them and remove each as it is cooked.

Hard boil one egg for every three medium-sized potatoes. Start counting when the water comes to a boil and cook for seven (if you like a slight dampness to the center of the yolk) to 10 minutes (never more than 10, unless you like a green ring around the yolk). Run cold water over the eggs when they are done, then crack the shell all over and peel them. Cut them in half length-wise and then into thick slices.

Peel the potatoes, if you prefer them peeled, and slice thickly. Mix with the eggs, sliced pimientos, a small amount of finely chopped onion, and enough mayonnaise to bind it all together. Taste for seasoning, keeping in mind that the onion flavor

will increase as time passes, and chill, preferably overnight. Potato salad is much better the next day when all the flavors have mingled. Sprinkle with paprika and/or parsley and serve.

Coleslaw

- one medium cabbage
- 2 small carrots
- juice of a half or whole lemon
- mayonnaise
- salt and pepper

This will make enough cole slaw for four to six people depending on what else they're eating and how hungry they are. Slice or shred the cabbage finely, using your preferred method of fine shred-ding/slicing. Grate the carrots. Mix the cabbage, carrots, juice of a half lemon, and enough mayon-naise to coat everything lightly. Add salt and pepper to taste and more lemon, if necessary. This is also better when chilled for several hours or overnight.

Deviled Eggs

- eggs
- mayonnaise
- mustard
- cayenne pepper
- salt and pepper
- paprika

Hard boil the eggs (one or two per person, or however many you think they'll eat), following the instructions above. Peel and cut each egg in half lengthwise. Remove the yolks and mash with mayonnaise, a small amount of mustard, a scrap of cayenne pepper, salt and pepper. Taste and adjust seasonings (an interesting variation is curry pow-der). Fill the whites with the yolk mixture, arrange artfully on a serving dish, sprinkle with paprika, and serve.

Summer Soups

The Guide
June-July 1981

I AM A FIRM BELIEVER in appreciating the seasonal quality of life. I was quite young when I noticed that my grandmother sent her wool rugs to be cleaned and stored and put down straw rugs for the summer. She also started serving cold soups at the first sign of warm weather — usually jellied consommé or vichyssoise. Serving cold soups in the summer is a good idea for several reasons: It's a refreshing way to start a meal (or a refreshing center to a meal with good bread and perhaps some fruit and cheese); it means you're not slaving away over a hot stove because you can choose a cooler part of the day to do your cooking; and you can use seasonal vegetables at their peak, preferably from your garden. Here are my two current favorite cold summer soup recipes.

Gazpacho

    4 medium tomatoes, peeled and seeded
    1 cucumber, peeled and seeded
       (if you're feeling refined)
    1 to 3 cloves garlic
    1 to 2 sweet peppers, green or red
    3 tablespoons olive oil
    ¼ cup wine vinegar
    1 medium onion (optional)
    ½ cup fine breadcrumbs
    salt and pepper
    crushed ice
    Optional extras: chopped, pitted black olives;
       chopped hard-boiled eggs; chopped green
       onions; bread croutons; pinch of cayenne
       or paprika; marjoram, mint or parsley

As in the case of bouillabaisse, there are many methods for preparing gazpacho, and many heated arguments as to which is *the* authentic version. Most of the versions I've ever had were good, so I don't argue, and I advise you to just mess around in the kitchen until you find a version you like.

Gazpacho can be simple or refined. For the simple version, just throw everything in the blender and stop blending when it reaches a consistency you like. Add up to ½ cup of fine, dry breadcrumbs to make it thicker. Thin it down with water, if necessary. Sprinkle in any of the optional extras and serve with crushed ice.

For the refined version you chop up everything as finely as you can, make a puree of the garlic, salt, breadcrumbs, and olive oil in a mortar and pestle. Then mix everything together, thin with water and serve with ice.

My preferred method is to blend three of the tomatoes, half of the cucumber, the garlic, one sweet pepper, olive oil, vinegar, onion, salt and pepper to a rough puree in the blender. I then chop the remaining vegetables finely, mix everything, thin with water if necessary, chill, and serve with crushed ice and maybe a few of the optional extras. I like it better without the bread crumbs, but don't mind a few croutons (freshly made, the boxed ones can be stale, and you are likely to be using better bread and fewer "flavor enhancers" at home). Parsley is the only herb I regularly use because I like the unadorned, fresh, clean taste of the vegetables.

Creamed Pea Soup

    2 pounds green peas
    4 cups water
    a couple of lettuce leaves
    small chopped onion
    salt and pepper
    sprig or two of mint
    ½ cup cream

If you have a food mill, don't shell the peas; the pods will be left behind when you puree the soup. If you are going to use a blender, food processor or potato masher to puree the soup, shell the peas and simmer the pods in the water for half an hour for a more flavorful soup. Strain this stock, pressing the pods, and add water if this is less than four cups.

Put everything but the cream in a sauce pan and simmer until the peas are very tender (about 30 minutes, depending on the age of the peas). Puree the soup, add the cream and some fresh, finely chopped mint. Taste for seasoning, remembering that the seasonings recede as the soup cools. The soup will also thicken as it chills, so you can add a little water now if you are afraid it will be too thick, or a little more cream just before serving. Chill for several hours or overnight.

This is a loose recipe; substitutions are encouraged. Yogurt is a tangy substitute for cream. If you don't have enough peas, add a small potato for thickness and flavor. I've also thrown in some spinach to good effect. If you're growing sugar snap peas, don't worry about the pods; if the peas are young enough to eat whole, use the whole pea. Do use fresh peas, however; the soup is not worth making with either canned or frozen peas.

Homemade Pasta

The Guide
September 1981

ORDINARY STORE-BOUGHT PASTA is good; expensive, Italian brands can be better; but homemade is best of all. It can be time consuming, and rolling out a large quantity can be tedious, but it is worth every bit of effort; the texture and flavor are superb. If you find that you like homemade pasta, a pasta machine is a good investment. It makes pasta-making almost sinfully easy.

Egg Pasta

1 egg
1 cup unbleached white flour

Sift the flour, make a well in the center and break the egg into the well. Mix together and knead energetically. It will seem stiff at first but after 10-15 minutes will become smooth and pliable with little air bubbles forming on the surface. Cover the dough and let it rest for 20 minutes.

Sprinkling lightly with flour, roll the dough out as thinly as you can — if you can see the grain of the wood or marble slab through the pasta, you are getting there. Hang the sheet of dough over the back of a chair, a broomstick between two chairs, a wooden clothes dryer, or whatever arrangement you come up with, to dry for 30 minutes before cutting it to the desired shape or size.

To cut the dough, sprinkle with flour, fold into a loose jelly roll and cut crosswise to the desired width. Separate the pieces and lay on a floured board or cloth until ready to cook.

To cook, bring a *large* pot of salted water to a vigorous boil. Sprinkle in the noodles. They will take about five minutes to cook and will float on the surface when ready. Drain them, toss with sauce or melted butter, and serve immediately. Home-made pasta is especially good with simple sauces: melted butter and parmesan cheese with perhaps a sprinkling of nutmeg; cream, heated with a smashed clove of garlic, sprinkled with cheese; a homemade fresh tomato sauce; good fresh tomatoes, peeled, seeded and chopped very finely with basic and garlic; pesto (garlic, basil, pine nut and olive oil sauce from Genoa); the possibilities are endless.

If you have a pasta machine, prepare the dough as above. Pass the dough through the widest opening of the machine several times, until it is smooth and pliable, to knead it. Roll the dough out by passing it through the machine, narrowing the opening with each pass until it is as thin as you want. This is the step where the machine proves its worth — you end up with impossibly thin pasta in an impossibly short amount of time. The machine has various cutters that you pass the sheet of dough through to achieve the desired width. Some even come with ravioli stuffers to make perfectly stuffed and shaped ravioli.

If you have a food processor you can make the dough in it. Put the egg in the bowl, mix it lightly and add the flour. Mix for about a minute, until smooth and pliable. Then proceed as above to roll out, cut, and cook the pasta.

You will note that no salt is called for in this recipe adapted from Ada Boni's *Italian Regional Cooking*. The salt from the cooking water gets incorporated when the pasta is cooked. If this is not enough salt for you, add a pinch to the flour at the start of the recipe. This makes enough for one or two people, depending on how hungry they are and what else is being served.

Spinach Pasta

1¾ cups flour
1 egg
¾ cup cooked spinach

Squeeze the cooked spinach as dry as possible, add to the flour, break in the eggs and proceed as above.

Whole Wheat Pasta

I have successfully made pasta with up to three-quarters of the amount of flour being whole wheat flour, though I prefer using only one-half. The higher proportions of whole wheat tends to make the pasta softer and it tears more easily if you are trying to stuff it.

Spinach-Stuffed Ravioli

1½ pounds fresh spinach or 1 package frozen
2 cups ricotta cheese
½ cup freshly grated parmesan cheese
2 eggs, lightly beaten
½ teaspoon freshly grated nutmeg
salt and pepper
melted butter and freshly grated parmesan
    for serving

If you are using fresh spinach, wash it and remove the stems. Cook it gently in a large, covered pan, using no extra water. Stir it down a few times at the beginning, until it has wilted. It will take 5 to 10 minutes to cook, depending on the amount of spinach and the size of your pan. Drain the spinach and when it is cool, squeeze out the extra water and chop it up a bit.

If using frozen spinach, cook in a minimum amount of water until done. When cool, squeeze and chop.

Mix the spinach, ricotta, parmesan and lightly beaten eggs together. Season to taste with salt, pepper and nutmeg.

Make egg pasta, using six eggs and six cups of flour. Don't dry the dough after rolling it out; stuff it immediately. Lay out one teaspoon mounds about 1½ to 2 inches apart on the sheet of dough. Moisten with water between the mounds and lay on a second sheet of dough. Press well between the mounds to seal the pasta and cut apart. Leave the ravioli to dry out a bit on a floured cloth.

Another way of shaping the pasta is to cut it into rounds with a cookie cutter, stuff the rounds, and fold them in half to make "tortelli."

If you have a pasta machine with a ravioli attachment, follow the directions.

Bring a large pan of salted water to a boil, drop in the pasta and cook until done (about five minutes). Drain and serve immediately with lots of melted butter and freshly grated parmesan cheese. If you need to cook the ravioli in several batches, toss the earlier batches with melted butter and keep warm in a low oven until all are done. A simple, fresh tomato sauce is also good; meat sauce is okay, but may hide some of the simple, delicious taste of the stuffing.

Holiday Punches

The Guide
December 1981 - January 1982

THAT FAMOUS VICTORIAN, Isabella Beeton, in her *Book of Household Management,* defined "punch" as: "a beverage made of various spirituous liquors or wine, hot water, the acid juice of fruits, and sugar. It is considered to be very intoxicating; but this is probably because the spirit being partly sheathed by the mucilaginous juice and the sugar, its strength does not appear to the taste so great as it really is. Punch, which was almost universally drunk among the middle classes about 50 or 60 years ago, has almost disappeared from our domestic tables, being superseded by wine. There are many different varieties of punch. It is sometimes kept cold in bottles, and makes a most agreeable summer drink. In Scotland, instead of Madeira or sherry generally used in its manufacture, whiskey is substituted, and then its insidious properties are more than usually felt." Punches may have changed a bit over the years, but those Scots understood what Mark Twain was saying when he said something along the lines of: "Too much whiskey is just enough."

I live in a small house, so when I have a large party, I like to serve punch. This eliminates the need for a bar and enables the potential bartender to enjoy the party as much as everyone else.

A nice touch for punches that call for ice is to freeze large pieces of ice, as they don't dilute the punch as quickly as small cubes. If you boil the water and let it cool, or stir it several times before freezing, the air bubbles will be eliminated and the ice will be clearer.

Here are three punches, each of which has been subjected to rigorous trials in the West Pettigrew test kitchen.

Nona McKee's Egg Nog

12 eggs separated
1 cup sugar
1 quart milk
2 cups (1 pint) bourbon
1 cup rum
1 pint whipping cream, whipped
nutmeg

I present this recipe for those who have relied on Nona McKee* for egg nog in Christmases past and don't know what they're going to do this year, now that she's moved to Nashville.

Beat the yolks and sugar until the sugar is dissolved completely. Add the milk, bourbon and rum. Beat the whites until they stand in peaks (not as stiffly as for meringue). Fold the whites and the whipped cream, gently but firmly, into the yolk mixture. Serve cold, sprinkled with nutmeg.

Successful variations have included whiskeys other than bourbon (though bourbon's woody, cinnamon-like taste is especially delicious in egg nog) or two cups rum and one cup brandy.

*Nona McKee was a founder of Durham's Bluebird Cafe, the first restaurant to serve sprouts and yogurt in a town of steak houses, fish camps and barbecue. The Bluebird eventually became Somethyme Restaurant, Mary and David Bacon's first natural foods restaurant, followed in the 1980s by Anotherthyme in Durham and Pyewacket in Chapel Hill. – ed.

Tequila Punch

½ gallon tequila
juice of 6 lemons or limes
½ gallon grapefruit juice
1 quart strong (cold) tea
2 sticks cinnamon
1 thinly sliced lime

Pour the liquid ingredients over ice in a punch bowl; stir and decorate with the cinnamon and the sliced lime. The original recipe calls for sweetening with sugar. I happen to like unsweetened grapefruit juice and like this punch without any sugar; if you find it bitter, by all means add some sweetening.

Rum Punch

1 cup coconut cream
1 quart pineapple juice
3 cups dark rum
3 cups light rum
1 cup orange liqueur
   (Cointreau is my favorite)
1 cup lime juice

Blend everything until frothy (you may need to do it two or three batches) and serve on ice. Freshly squeezed lime juice is best because it has no additives. If not available, try a frozen daiquiri mix, which has much less sugar than the limeade found in grocery stores.

Wok Around the Clock

The Guide
February 1982

IF YOU HAVE BEEN A FAITHFUL READER of this column, you may have noticed a lack of Chinese recipes. Although I have happily eaten in Chinese restaurants around the world and have successfully cooked a number of Chinese dishes over the years, I have never really felt on top it, in spite of my belief that Chinese cooking is the wave of the future (it conserves both energy and meat protein and is infinitely delicious).

My hesitancy is being overcome; the first big breakthrough was sesame oil. It provided an absolutely necessary authentic flavor that I had never been able to achieve. Getting a gas stove and a good wok are more recent improvements. I have an awesome (and I'm not using awesome as defined by Official Prep) Chinese cleaver which I'm sure I'll be wielding easily and confidently someday, but now only comes into play when I'm sure I can't use my smaller Japanese cleaver, the big French knife or even the kitchen shears. Perhaps I need a month or two on a Chinese desert isle confined with a wok, a cleaver, a steamer, a pair of chopsticks and all the right ingredients.

There are three cookbooks I recommend for help: Henry Chung's *Hunan Style Chinese Cookbook,* Robert A. Delfs' *The Good Food of Szechuan,* and Irene Kuo's *The Key to Chinese Cooking.* The last is especially good on technique.

The first recipe, Home Style Bean Curd, is adapted from Mrs. Kuo's book and is the best Chinese dish I've ever cooked. (Bean curd is also known as tofu.) I learned the second from "the

singing chef" of the French restaurant of the same name near Marble Arch in London and later adapted it to a wok. It is simple and delicious.

Home Style Bean Curd (Tofu)

4 squares bean curd (tofu)
¼ pound lean pork

MARINADE:
1 teaspoon soy sauce
1 teaspoon dry white wine or sherry
1 teaspoon cornstarch
1 medium whole scallion, finely chopped
2 quarter-sized pieces peeled ginger, minced
2 cloves garlic, minced
1 teaspoon fermented black beans, rinsed briefly and chopped

SEASONINGS:
2 tablespoons soy sauce
1 teaspoon dry white wine or sherry
½ teaspoon sugar
1 cup chicken or meat stock
1 tablespoon cornstarch dissolved in 1 tablespoon water
1 cup oil
1 tablespoon hot bean paste
2 teaspoons sesame oil

Cut each square of bean curd in half, then into crosswise quarters. Slice the pork loin against the grain into thin slices about the same dimensions as the bean curd pieces. Mix the pork with the marinade. Prepare the scallion, ginger, garlic and fermented black beans. Combine the seasonings and stir until the sugar has dissolved. Make the cornstarch mixture and place everything within reach of the stove.

Heat a wok (or heavy skillet) over high heat until hot. Add the oil and heat until quite hot. Add the bean curd pieces, turn the heat to medium, and deep-fry for about two minutes until they are light brown. Drain well.

Pour out all but three tablespoons oil and heat over a high heat. Add the marinated pork and stir briskly, turning it over for about a minute, until the slices are firm. Toss in the scallion, ginger, garlic and black beans; stir rapidly until they give off a strong aroma, then add the hot bean paste and mix well. Add the fried bean curd pieces and the seasonings; stir, cover and simmer for about four minutes. Gently stir in the cornstarch mixture until the sauce is thick and smooth. Add the sesame oil, stir and serve hot.

Stir-Fried Cabbage (French Style)

½ medium cabbage
½ small onion
1 shallot or scallion
4 pieces of bacon
½ cup white wine
salt and pepper

Choose the cabbage carefully; you want a fresh one, with crisp leaves, not discolored. Cut it into quarters or other manageable pieces and slice it very thinly. Rinse and drain. Finely chop whichever member of the onion family you have selected.

Cut the bacon into bite-sized pieces and put into a wok over medium-high heat. Stir it often and when the fat begins to run out of the bacon and coat the pan, add the onion. Stir it around until it is wilting and add the cabbage. Stir until the cabbage is beginning to soften and is coated with the fat. Add the wine and salt and pepper to taste (you may need no salt because of the bacon), bring to a boil, cover and turn the heat down low. Simmer for 2 to 7 minutes depending on how full the pan is and how you like your cabbage. I recommend "al dente." Serve hot.

The Chicken

The Guide
March 1982

SERVING CHICKEN solves several problems for the cook. It is an inexpensive source of low fat protein, thus confronting worries in the economic as well as the medical science realm. It is available everywhere, year 'round. Almost any method of cooking can be successfully applied and most chickens are quickly cooked. Here are two easy and delicious recipes that are a little more interesting than baked or fried chicken.

I usually buy a whole chicken and disjoint it myself, using the pieces I might not want for a particular dish for stock (neck, back, all innards except the liver, which makes stock cloudy). Cutting it up applies a certain logic to the chicken's form and requires a sharp knife and maybe kitchen shears. Start with the wings: straighten them out and bend them away from the body; find the joint next to the body and cut through it. Next tackle the legs: cut through the skin next to the body, bend the leg out, and cut through the joint. Find the joint between the drumstick and the thigh by bending and feeling and cut through that. The wider end of the carcass is the front of the chicken; cut through on both sides at a slant down to the back. This front piece of back will break away if you bend it back and cut it off. Now cut the breast off the rest of the back: look inside to where the ribs come together in a "V" and cut down the center of the "V"; bend, twist and hack and the pieces will separate. Cut the breasts apart with scissors or a good smack with a cleaver or heavy knife (minding where your fingers are all the while). If you suspect the diners will want both white and dark meat, cut each breast in half. The first time you disjoint a chicken, it might be a little ragged but it gets easier and makes more sense with very little practice. Look the pieces over for hairs and feathers; then rinse and dry them.

Try to buy chickens that have never been frozen because freezing is very hard on the flesh and results in a loss of texture, moisture and flavor. If you are ever offered a "free range" chicken, snap it up. The flavor is stronger and the meat is moister.

Mediterranean Chicken

3 to 4 pound chicken, disjointed
2 to 4 tablespoons olive oil
medium onion, roughly chopped
green or red sweet pepper, seeded and sliced
I cup dry white wine
3 to 4 medium tomatoes, peeled and seeded;
**   or small can tomatoes**
½ to I pound sliced mushrooms
I cup sliced black olives
I clove garlic, peeled and squashed
salt and pepper
basil, bay leaf, thyme

Brown the chicken over high heat in the olive oil in a large skillet. Sprinkle with salt and pepper as you turn it. Remove the chicken, turn down the heat and soften the onion and pepper. Return the chicken and stir it all together. Add the wine, turn up the heat and when it's bubbling, add the tomatoes, garlic and herbs. Stir again. The liquid should cover about two-thirds of the chicken; add water or chicken stock, if necessary.

Cover the pan, but not completely, and cook at a fast simmer. It will take about 30 minutes for the chicken to cook, depending on its size and how well you browned it. Stir everything up a couple of times. After 20 minutes, add the mushrooms and olives. If the sauce seems too thin when the chicken is done, remove the chicken and cook the sauce down rapidly. It shouldn't be watery but should be thinner than a tomato sauce. This is good with rice or pasta and reheats easily. Serves four.

Sautéed Chicken with Mushrooms & Cream

3 to 4 pound chicken, disjointed
I tablespoon butter
I tablespoon oil
I clove garlic, peeled and squashed
salt and pepper
basil, thyme, rosemary, tarragon —
**   your choice or combination**
½ to I pound mushrooms
½ to I pint cream

Brown the chicken and garlic in hot oil and butter in a large skillet (it should fit in one layer). Sprinkle with salt, pepper and herbs as you turn it. Take out the garlic when it gets brown.

Turn the heat down low and cover the pan. Turn the chicken a few times during the cooking, which will again be about 30 minutes. When the chicken is done, remove it to a hot serving dish. Turn the heat up high and sauté the mushrooms. They may be whole, quartered or sliced (thinly or thickly). They will absorb the oil and then appear to be sweating. Keep the heat high and add the cream. Stir and scrape while the cream reduces and thickens. Pour the sauce over the chicken and serve. The quantities of cream and mushrooms are variable depending on how much sauce you want or how extravagant you are feeling. A chopped shallot added with the mushrooms never hurts. This is an adaptation of a recipe in *Mastering the Art of French Cooking* which is very useful when you want something elegant, quickly. Serves four.

The Chicken

The Well-Seasoned Gardener

The Guide
May 1982

DID YOU GET CAUGHT with your tomatoes out during our last cold spell? In the North Carolina piedmont, seasoned gardeners usually restrain themselves until the first couple of weeks in May to plant tender seeds and set out tomatoes, peppers and the like. But if you have perennial herbs in your garden, you don't have to wait for your first harvest. Thyme, chives, parsley, marjoram, tarragon, mint, and sage are already doing quite well. Here are some ideas for using these fresh herbs to season your meals right now.

Herb Butter

    1 stick butter
    1 to 3 teaspoons lemon juice
    2 teaspoons fresh herb (or herbs)
        of your choice, chopped

Let the butter sit out until it is soft enough to work. Mix in the lemon juice and herbs. Fancy equipment is not necessary; a fork works just fine. Store in the refrigerator and use on fish, steamed vegetables (such as potatoes, beans, carrots, or onions), meats, or in an omelet. Try different combinations; a hint of rosemary mixes very well with many other herbs.

Olives with Herbs

    1 pound olives
    1 cup olive oil
    2 sprigs thyme
    3 teaspoons oregano
    1 teaspoon crushed peppercorns

Prick the olives with a fork (the original recipe calls for a "silver fork"; I imagine stainless steel would work just as well). Put everything in a jar, shake up well, add more oil if the olives are not covered, and leave for a week. You now have two products — flavored olives and flavored olive oil — to use as you see fit.

Grilled Fish with Fennel

    whole fish, scaled and gutted; bass is good
    salt and pepper
    2 to 3-inch piece of fennel
    olive oil

Season the inside of the fish with salt, pepper and a few drops of olive oil. Stuff with the fennel and close. Brush the outside of the fish with oil to keep it from sticking and grill over hot coals for 10 to 30 minutes, depending on the thickness of the fish. Turning the fish only once during the cooking saves on wear and tear. When fish is done it flakes easily with a fork. You can also bake the fish at a high temperature (400°F) or grill it in your oven.

Cream Cheese with Herbs

    16 ounces cream cheese
    8 ounces unsalted whipped butter
    2 cloves garlic
    ¼ teaspoon each: thyme, cracked black pepper
    1 teaspoon dill weed (not seed)
    ½ teaspoon each: salt, basil, marjoram, chives

Use a blender, mixer, food processor or plenty of elbow grease and blend everything together until smooth. Use a garlic press to smash the garlic or blend it first so you don't end up with big chunks of it. Taste for seasoning and adjust to your liking, remembering that the garlic flavor will be stronger as time, passes. This mixture keeps well in the refrigerator, but take it out ½ to 1 hour before serving with crackers. These amounts are for dried herbs; you can double or triple the amount when using fresh herbs. You can also experiment with your own combinations of herbs.

Supply-Side Zucchini

The Guide
June-July 1982

FACE IT. If you have put in more than one plant, you are going to have too many zucchini before the summer is over. Several years ago some friends' chickens even got sick of eating it before the harvest was through, although my friends learned the interesting but trivial fact that the chickens liked zucchini better cooked than raw.

To get ready now you could start reading zucchini recipes (they are known as courgettes in your French and English cookbooks). Try to cope when the harvest starts by picking them when they are small — *very* small — and eating them whole (the courgettes a la greque recipe below is better when made with whole zucchini). My mother copes by freezing them for soups and casseroles in the winter.

In order to help you out, I've gathered some favorite zucchini recipes here. I'm planning to help my friends out this summer in a more direct manner — I haven't planted any zucchini.

Zucchini with Pasta

Very simple — grate the zucchini, sauté gently in butter until just done, sprinkle with fresh herbs (parsley, tarragon, rosemary or whatever) and toss with hot pasta with a little grated cheese.

French Fried Zucchini

Cut the zucchini into strips 2 inches long and a quarter-inch thick. Salt lightly and let them drain in a colander for $\frac{1}{2}$ to 1 hour. Dry them gently but well, toss with seasoned flour and deep fry at 350°F until the outsides are crisp and lightly brown and the insides melt in your mouth.

Courgettes à la Greque

1 cup water
1 cup dry white wine
1 cup olive oil
½ cup lemon juice
1 clove garlic, peeled and crushed
bay leaf
thyme
12 coriander seeds
salt and pepper
fresh parsley or coriander leaves
6 to 18 zucchini (the smaller the better)

Make a marinade by simmering everything but the parsley or coriander leaves and zucchini for 10 to 15 minutes. The wine is optional.

Poach the zucchini in this marinade until *just* done — they should still be *slightly* crisp. Let them cool in the liquid. When you are ready to serve, arrange the zucchini in a serving dish. Taste the marinade — it may need sharpening with a squeeze of lemon juice or more seasonings. Moisten the zucchini with marinade, sprinkle with finely chopped parsley or coriander. This dish is nicer cool, rather than cold right from the refrigerator.

Ways With Curds

The Guide
September 1982

THIS SORT OF "ORAL GRATIFICATION" is probably my most typical column — a plea for you to try cooking with some ingredient you may never have used before. Usually I describe it as delicious, nutritious and inexpensive; sometimes, as exotic. This month the ingredient you may be overlooking is bean curd, which I always enjoyed in Chinese restaurants, but didn't use much in my own cooking due to lackluster results. As I hate to give up in the kitchen, I've been investigating bean curd for a while now. In its purchased state, I find it fairly bland. This is fine because it absorbs flavors very well and is delicious when cooked or served in a highly seasoned sauce.

The single most important key to success is to start with good, fresh bean curd (also known as tofu). Buy the type of bean curd that is refrigerated, covered with water. Take it home, change the water daily and keep refrigerated; it should be fine for up to a week.

Cold Bean Curd (Tofu) with Sesame Paste

½ pound bean curd (tofu)
1 tablespoon soy sauce
1 tablespoon oil
1 tablespoon sesame paste (or tahini)
1 teaspoon sesame oil
Optional: 1 teaspoon chili oil or hot bean paste

Mix the soy sauce, oil, sesame paste and sesame oil together.

Cut the bean curd into largish bite-sized pieces. Simmer them in water for three minutes. Drain well and gently mix with the sauce.

Serve cool but not directly out of the refrigerator. Peanut butter is a good substitute for the sesame paste. Serves two.

This is adapted from Kenneth Lo's *Chinese Vegetarian Cooking* which is an interesting book even though Lo does not appear to be a true vegetarian as his recipes often have non-vegetarian optional ingredients. He has several bean curd recipes I have not seen elsewhere.

Spicy Green Beans with Bean Curd (Tofu)

1 pound green beans
1 teaspoon minced fresh ginger
1 scallion, finely chopped
½ pound bean curd (tofu)
1 clove garlic, minced
2 cups oil
¼ cup liquid — water, vegetable stock, or chicken stock
1 teaspoon hot bean paste
1 tablespoon soy sauce
1 tablespoon dry sherry or dry white wine
1 teaspoon vinegar
1 teaspoon sesame oil

Top and tail the beans and break in half. Rinse well and let them drain.

Cut the bean curd into small, bite-sized pieces. Let them drain on paper towels to get rid of excess moisture. Put ginger, garlic and scallions together. Mix the hot bean paste, soy sauce, sherry or wine, and stock or water together.

Heat the oil in a wok or heavy skillet until hot (375°F) but not smoking (smoke indicates the oil is breaking down rapidly). Scatter in the beans and deep fry for about three minutes — they will wrinkle and change color. Drain (you can pour the contents of the wok or skillet into a strainer over a container). Save the oil for other cooking.

Heat the wok or skillet until hot, add two tablespoons oil. Over a medium heat, add the ginger, garlic and scallions, and stir. Add the bean paste, soy sauce, sherry or wine, and stock or water. Stir well until blended and bubbling. Add the bean curd and stir gently until it is hot and absorbing liquid. Add the green beans, stir and cover. Simmer for two minutes or until all is hot. Add the vinegar, stir; then sprinkle in the sesame oil. Stir until mixed and serve. Serves three.

Adapted from Irene Kuo's *The Key to Chinese Cooking,* the best Chinese cookbook I've ever used.

Hazelnuts

The Guide
October 1982

A S A CHILD I NEVER MUCH LIKED other mothers' chocolate chip cookies or brownies. My mother nearly always baked with pecans; I was used to them and thought other nuts tasted "funny." Like most children I was very conservative about food, and I'm glad today for some of the things I wasn't exposed to at a tender age. I tolerated the walnut as a lesser pecan and can only imagine what I would have thought had I encountered the hazelnut, with a flavor nearly as distinct from other nuts as that of the almond.

Hazelnuts, also known as filberts, go very well with chocolate or dates. Here are two recipes, each making use of one of these affinities.

When a recipe calls for "ground" nuts, you have several choices of method. If you use them frequently, you might like to acquire a nut grinder, which is an old design that easily grinds nuts finely. I've seen them in local kitchen stores. An electric coffee grinder works fairly well if you grind small batches at a time, shake the grinder the whole while, and check frequently so that you avoid nut butter. A food processor also works; use the metal blade and, as above, watch out for nut butter.

Date & Hazelnut Bread

¼ cup unsalted butter
¾ cup water
½ cup brown sugar
I cup chopped, pitted dates
I egg
I teaspoon soda
1¾ cups flour
½ teaspoon salt
½ to I cup coarsely chopped hazelnuts

Preheat oven to 350°F. Melt the butter and dissolve the sugar in the water. Add the dates and let cool. Beat in the egg and mix in the other ingredients. Pour into a greased loaf pan and bake for 45 minutes. A scant half-cup of honey may be substituted for the brown sugar.

Hazelnut Meringue

THE MERINGUE:
4 egg whites
1⅓ cups brown sugar
½ teaspoon cider vinegar
1¼ cups ground hazelnuts

Preheat the oven to 350°F. Line two 8-inch cake pans with waxed paper, and brush the paper with melted butter.

Beat the egg whites to soft peaks. Add the sugar by thirds and beat well after each addition. Add the vinegar and nuts and beat until the mixture is smooth and stiff.

Divide the mixture equally between the cake pans and bake for 15 minutes; then reduce the temperature to 350°F and bake for an hour. If the tops threaten to become too brown, cover with foil and finish baking. Unmold onto racks and remove the paper.

THE FILLING:
2 squares (2 ounces) semisweet chocolate
2 cups water
1¼ cups whipping cream

Melt the chocolate in the water over a low heat. Stir until smooth and allow to cool. Whip cream until stiff, then stir in chocolate until well mixed.

Spread about three-fourths of the filling over one of the cakes, cover with the other and cover with the remaining filling. Refrigerate for several hours before serving.

Currying Flavor

The Guide
November 1982

FOR THOSE OF YOU WHO HAVEN'T EATEN much Indian food since the Sallam *(see note, page 41)* closed, here are recipes for Lamb Biryani and Cauliflower and Potato Subji. The recipes are adapted from Sipra Das Gupta's *Home Book of Indian Cookery,* published by Faber & Faber, an English publishing house that has published many "Home Books" over the years, some of which have been offered by American publishers. The two I know best — Greek and Indian — are excellent. You can sometimes find these books in used bookshops. Right now I'm on the lookout for *The Home Book of Turkish Cookery.*

Lamb Biryani

2 pounds lamb (leg, shoulder)

MARINADE:
2 onions
4 cloves garlic
1 tablespoons fresh ginger
1 teaspoon coriander
1 teaspoon cumin
½ teaspoon chili peppers
4 tablespoons lemon juice

1 cup yogurt
2 cups basmati rice
½ cup butter
2 or 3 more onions
6 cardamoms
2 sticks cinnamon, broken up
4 bay leaves
2 tablespoons chopped almonds
large pinch saffron
¼ cup milk
salt

Peel and chop the onions, garlic and ginger. Put all marinade ingredients except the yogurt into a blender and blend to a smooth paste. Mix with the yogurt. A food processor also works well.

Cut the lamb into 1-inch pieces, removing the fat. Mix the lamb and marinade together and let it marinate for at least two hours. Do not use a metal container to marinate.

Put the lamb and marinade in a saucepan. Add a half-cup of water and bring to a boil. Simmer for 30 minutes; then turn up the heat and evaporate the liquid. Stir frequently; this will take about 30 minutes and you will need to stir constantly at the end. You will be left with the meat, coated with a thick paste.

Parboil the rice in a large amount of salted water for about 6 minutes. It will not be completely cooked at this stage but should be starting to soften. Drain it.

Slice the two or three remaining onions thinly. Fry them until golden brown and crisp in a half cup of butter with a little cooking oil added. You may need to do this in two batches. Drain the onions but save the butter.

Soak the saffron in warm milk. Preheat the oven to 300°F.

Now assemble the biryani: Use a large casserole; put a half-cup of water on the bottom. Add the meat. Layer the rice, fried onions (use half for the casserole, save the rest for a final garnish) and remaining spices (bay leaves, cardamoms, almonds and cinnamon). Pour on the saffron milk and then the onion cooking butter. If the casserole lid doesn't fit snugly, use a piece of aluminum foil under the lid for a good seal.

Bake for one hour. Mix the meat and rice gently and garnish with the remaining fried onions. Serves four. To serve six, increase the amount of rice to three cups and use a little more of the spices.

Cauliflower & Potato Subji

I medium cauliflower
2 potatoes
¼ cup vegetable oil
½ teaspoon cumin seeds
2 chili peppers, chopped
½ teaspoon grated ginger
I teaspoon turmeric
½ teaspoon garam masala
½ to I teaspoon salt
½ cup water

Separate the cauliflower into flowerets; rinse and drain them. Peel the potatoes, if you wish, and cut them into chunks.

Fry the cauliflower in hot vegetable oil until it starts to brown. You may need to do this in several batches. Fry the potatoes until they start to brown. Add the cumin seeds. Fry for a minute, then add turmeric, garam masala, ginger, and salt. Fry for another minute. Add the cauliflower, chili peppers and water. Bring to a boil. Simmer briskly until the potatoes and cauliflower are cooked (8 to 12 minutes, depending on the size of vegetable pieces).

In Cider

The Guide
December 1982 - January 1983

I HAVE BEEN READING *Eating in America* by Richard de Rochemont and the late Waverly Root, and I'm finding it a bracing corrective to longing for the "good old days." I am not about to argue that things are now culinarily perfect. For example, some may feel we have achieved the long-awaited "chicken in every pot" — but is that really a chicken? Similarly, we have fresh "tomatoes" in the stores during the winter months. But I'll take a judicious selection from what we have available over the usual colonial diet any day.

It was one thing to dine with Thomas Jefferson, gentleman farmer and horticultural experimenter, and quite another to sit at the table of the average town dweller, especially in the winter months. Our national predilection for a high-protein diet is not new. Meat (usually game or pork) seems to have been the main food. And most people avoided drinking water. The upper classes drank whiskey and wine and the masses drank beer and cider — both sweet and hard.

Early settlers brought appleseeds with them and continued the long English tradition of making cider. (In 55 BC, Julius Caesar's troops found the English drinking cider). Cider was a daily beverage in early America and usually a local product. For more information about the history of cider and how to go about making your own — sweet or hard — I highly recommend Vrest Orton's *American Cider Book*.

This is the time of year to buy good, unpasteurized, unpreserved, fresh sweet cider. Keep it in your refrigerator for a few days, and it will start to ferment and get even better — just remember not to cap it too tightly. For reliable hard cider, I usually buy English or French brands in the local stores; I'd buy American, if someone would make and sell it. Of the following recipes, the chicken is my own; the drinks all come, some with minor alterations, from the aforementioned *American Cider Book*.

Chicken with Cider

> 3½ pound chicken, disjointed
> 2 tablespoons butter
> 1 teaspoon oil
> pinch thyme
> salt and pepper
> 1 cup hard cider (very tart sweet cider may be substituted)
> 1 cup heavy cream

Brown the chicken pieces in the butter and oil. Sprinkle with thyme, salt and pepper. Cover, turn the heat down and cook, turning once or twice, for 30 to 40 minutes or until tender. Remove the chicken and keep warm. Turn the heat to high and add the cider to the skillet and reduce rapidly by about a half, stirring and scraping all the while. Add the cream and reduce until thick. Pour the sauce over the chicken and serve. The addition of an apple or two, sautéed until just tender in butter, is a delicious variation.

Michigan Egg Nog

> 1 egg beaten
> 1 teaspoon confectioners sugar
> ½ cup cream
> cracked ice
> sweet cider
> nutmeg

Shake the egg, sugar and cream over cracked ice in a cocktail shaker (or suitable substitute).

Strain into a frosted glass or tankard and fill with cider. Stir, sprinkle with nutmeg and serve.

Hot Spiced Cider

For each quart of hard cider:
½ teaspoon allspice
1 stick cinnamon
½ teaspoon cloves
¼ cup brown sugar or maple sugar or syrup
2 tablespoons grated lemon rind

Crush the allspice, cinnamon and cloves together and mix with the sugar or syrup and lemon rind. Add to the cider and heat slowly (don't use an aluminum or cast iron pan). Let it steep for 20 to 30 minutes, never letting it come to a boil. Strain and serve. You can garnish each cup with a cinnamon stick or freshly grated nutmeg. This can be successfully made with sweet cider, which can be spiked with brandy, rum or applejack.

Artillery Punch

1 quart dark rum
1 quart bourbon
1 gallon hard cider
6 pineapples
12 oranges
1 quart strawberries (optional)
12 bottles champagne

Mix rum, bourbon, and cider. Slice the fruits and add to the liquid. Refrigerate for several hours or overnight. Add a block of ice and the 12 bottles of champagne.

I must confess I've never made this punch although it sounds smashing — maybe a little too smashing. With this quantity, you need a party. But with this much alcohol you need either guests who all live within walking distance or more spare beds than I've got.

Syllabub

1 lemon
½ cup brandy
1 pint hard cider
1 cup sugar
2 cups heavy cream
2 egg whites

Grate lemon peel and squeeze the juice. Mix with brandy, cider and sugar. Let it stand several hours or overnight. Beat the egg whites to soft peaks; whip the cream. Mix all together and serve.

In Cider

Appealing Oranges

The Guide
February 1983

I FIND IT HARD TO RESIST COOKBOOKS: I check them out of the library to read, I rummage through used bookstores, see what's new at other bookstores and am easily distracted by a shelf in someone's kitchen. I aim for restraint by a pact with myself that I will have no more cookbooks than will fit in my dining room bookshelf. So far I have resisted a second bookshelf in that location, but I hardly ever figure in the four to five cookbooks on the bedside table.

All this means I need a pretty good reason to acquire a new cookbook. One of my newest is *Jane Grigson's Fruit Book,* and it's really stimulating, with a scope ranging from common to uncommon fruits (I've never seen a carambola and never eaten a medlar). She includes a bit of history about each fruit and gives sound advice about selection. The recipes come from all over the world and also range from expected to unexpected.

In addition, Grigson has several idiosyncrasies I share — she greatly admires Elizabeth David and hates to waste anything. I'm concentrating on oranges this month. The candied peel and pound cake recipes that follow are adaptations from her book.

Candied Citrus Peel

> peel of 2 grapefruit
> 1¼ cup sugar
> ⅔ cup water
> more sugar

Wash the grapefruit and remove the peel in nicely shaped sections. Boil in plenty of water until tender. Drain and boil again in fresh water for 20 minutes.

Make a syrup of the 1¼ cup sugar and ⅔ cup water. Put in the peel and simmer until the syrup disappears. (Don't cook at too high a temperature or it will caramelize.)

Spread the peel on trays lined with waxed paper and leave to dry (this may take up to three days) in a warm place (above the water heater, in a gas oven with a pilot light or some other suitable location). Cover with cheesecloth if you're worried about dust. Turn the pieces from time to time. When dry, coat the pieces with sugar by shaking in a paper bag.

The peel can be cut with scissors into smaller pieces anytime after the second boiling.

This is much nicer than the slimy, inexpensive candied peel and less expensive than the fancier, better sort.

Use the same technique for other citrus fruits. Buy the thinner-skinned varieties to cut down on the amount of bitter white pith.

Orange Syrup Cake

> rind of an orange
> ¾ cup sugar
> 1 cup soft butter, cut in pieces
> 1 cup flour
> ½ cup candied peel, chopped
> 1 teaspoon baking powder
> pinch salt
> 4 large eggs
> 2 tablespoons orange liqueur or orange juice
>
> **TOPPING:**
> juice of an orange
> ⅔ cup sugar

With a sharp knife, remove the colored portion of the orange peel and chop it fine. Or, you can grate the peel or use an orange zester. Toss the candied peel with one tablespoon flour, until lightly coated.

Put the butter, sugar and orange rind in a bowl. Sift the flour, baking powder and salt into the bowl. Break in the eggs and pour in the liqueur or orange juice. Beat until smooth, then fold in the candied peel.

Bake in a 7 to 8-inch cake pan (greased and floured) at 325°F for 1¼ to 1½ hours (test with a toothpick, icepick, or if you're old fashioned, a kitchen straw).

Mix the topping ingredients — juice of an orange and ⅔ cup water — together until the sugar is dissolved. Pour some of the topping into a shallow dish that will hold the cake. Turn the cake out of the baking pan into the dish so that it absorbs the topping. Spoon the rest of the topping over the cake and leave it to cool. You can poke some holes into cake with the aforementioned tools to increase absorption. Decorate with a slice of orange or candied peel.

Pollo in Padella Con Peperoni

   1 chicken, disjointed
   1 tablespoon olive oil
   2 medium onions, sliced
   3 cloves garlic, squashed and peeled
   salt and pepper
   marjoram, thyme
   4 large green or red sweet peppers
   3 medium tomatoes, skinned, seeded and
      chopped
   basil
   1 orange

Brown the chicken in oil and remove from pan. Soften the onions in the oil. Return the chicken to the pan, add the garlic, salt and pepper to taste, and a pinch of marjoram and thyme. Cover and cook slowly, turning the pieces from time to time. The total cooking time for the chicken should be 40-60 minutes, depending on the size and age of the bird.

Meanwhile, char the peppers, using a broiler or direct gas flame (I have a French stovetop cast iron grill that works well). Turn them as necessary to achieve even charring. Wrap the peppers in an old tea towel or put them into a plastic bag. When they are cool enough to handle (10 minutes or so) remove the charred skin and rinse under running water. Cut into thick strips and add to the chicken with the tomatoes and a pinch of basil. Cook until the tomatoes melt down into a sauce.

Peel the orange with a sharp knife, cutting away both the orange peel and the white pith. Do this by cutting away a slice at the top and bottom of the orange, then cutting the peel away from top to bottom, around the sides. A thin, slightly flexible knife helps in this process. Slice the orange thinly and lay over the top of the chicken. Cover and heat a moment, then serve with plain rice and a green salad.

The Variety of Life

The Guide
April 1983

AT THIS TIME OF YEAR, you're probably in some stage of getting a garden organized. My own organization is getting easier each year as I face the facts about my garden space which just doesn't get enough sun to grow many of the things I'd like to — tomatoes, peppers, squash and so on. Although most herbs are said to do best in sunny, sandy locations, I manage to grow enough to keep my kitchen supplied with what I consider the basics and a few exotics. There are the ones I couldn't do without — basil, thyme, rosemary, marjoram, parsley, chives and mint — as well as some I have only a few uses for — lovage, sorrel, and sage. Others I grow because they are pretty and smell nice — lavender.

The perennials are already coming up — marjoram, rosemary, sorrel, chives, fennel, lovage, sage, thyme, lemon balm and mint. They come up every year (though I seem to have lost tarragon and lavender to winter freezes) and require little attention beyond weeding and, in the case of the mint and balm, vain attempts at space control (in fact, I may have unwittingly started a West Pettigrew mint plantation). There are annuals — basil, parsley, and coriander — that I'll be putting in when it warms up a bit.

I've started herbs from seed, bought them live, and been given cuttings or plants by friends. The gifts tend to do best in the long run, most likely because they have come from local plants that have already — in the Darwinian sense — proved successful in this area. That doesn't stop me from going through the seed and plant catalogs for an addition or two each year.

Scallions

The Guide
May 1983

BEFORE THE DEVELOPMENT of the transportation methods that so radically altered when, where, and what foods were available, spring must have made a very welcome difference to the table. During the winter, meals were limited to what had been preserved or stored. It must have been wonderful when new growth started and one could go out and pick something fresh to eat — like spring onions, instead of the onions one had been eating all winter which turn flabby, watery and start to sprout.

Nowadays, spring onions — also known as green onions and scallions, and in New Orleans as shallots — are available, inexpensively, year 'round in almost every supermarket. These are either young onions, picked before much of a bulb has formed, or special types bred to be eaten at the scallion stage. Young onions are usually more bulbous and a little more strongly flavored, but the two types can be used interchangeably.

The white part of the scallion can be used as a less intensely flavored substitute for the shallot; the green part, finely chopped, as a more onion-flavored substitute for chives.

The mild onion flavor is delicious raw, in salads and sandwiches (cheddar and green onion is especially good), or as a garnish for cooked foods like soups, stews and omelets. I like them on dishes made from dried beans, either hot or cold, and, perhaps inauthentically, on tacos.

Fresh green onions are firm, not slimy and the green parts are very green and not wilted. To use them, trim off the root tip and any discolored green bits and rinse.

Here are some unusual recipes where the green onion is the important flavoring element.

Scallions & Potatoes

1 bunch spring onions
4 medium boiling (not baking) potatoes
¼ teaspoon cumin seeds
1 tablespoon vegetable oil (or a mixture
    of butter and oil)
½ teaspoon salt

Clean the onions and cut into ½-inch pieces. Clean the potatoes and cut them into ½-inch slices.

Heat the oil until medium hot. Add the cumin seeds and fry them until they start to give off an aroma (about a minute). Add the onions and potatoes, sprinkle with salt, stir and cover.

Reduce the heat to very low. You want the onions and potatoes to cook but not to brown. Cook for 10 to 15 minutes, stirring occasionally but very gently, until the potatoes are done.

Scallion Pancakes

3 cups flour
1 cup boiling water
½ cup chopped scallion
1½ teaspoons salt
5 tablespoons vegetable oil

Pour the boiling water onto the flour. Mix it to a dough then knead until smooth (5 to 10 minutes). Cover and let it rest for an hour.

Turn the dough out onto a lightly floured board and knead a bit more. Shape it into a cylinder and cut into six pieces.

Roll out each piece to a 4-inch, squarish shape. Brush with oil, sprinkle lightly with salt and spread

with one-sixth of the scallions. Roll up like jelly roll, then flatten each end and roll up like a snail. Take your rolling pin and roll out to a 5-inch pancake (a quarter-inch thick).

Cook on a griddle or heavy skillet at a medium low heat until cooked through and flecked with brown on both sides. They can also be deep fried for about one minute in 375°F oil.

Cut into four sections, and serve warm. They are good as hors d'oeuvres or accompanying other food (especially beef dishes). This recipe is adapted from *Chinese Meatless Cooking* by Stella Lau Fessler.

Scallion Pie

pastry for a single crust (see page 156)
1 bunch scallions
1 tablespoon butter
8 ounces cottage cheese or cream cheese or
    4 ounces cheese and ½ cup yogurt
4 eggs separated
3 tablespoons cream
salt and pepper

Make the pastry crust and line a tart or pie pan with it.

Clean the scallions and chop them. Wilt them in one tablespoon butter, then spread them on the crust.

If you are using cottage cheese let it drain a bit in a strainer. If you are using cream cheese buy a brand that has little or no gum additives. Blend your choice of cheese or cheese and yogurt until smooth, then mix it well with the egg yolks, cream and salt and pepper to taste. Different cheeses contain different amounts of salt, so you really should taste before adding any extra salt.

Whip the egg whites until they stand in peaks, then fold them into the cheese and yolk mixture.

Scallions

Pour over the onions in the crust and bake for 20 to 30 minutes at 400°F. If the top of the pie seems to be getting too brown, cover it with aluminum foil and continue baking until set. Serve warm or cold.

This is an adaptation from *Jane Grigson's Vegetable Book*.

Green Peas

The Guide
June-July 1983

THOMAS JEFFERSON and his neighbors were not blasé about green peas. Every spring they competed to be the first to serve fresh peas at a dinner party. These days, we don't get too excited about the first fresh green peas of the year. I suspect this is because frozen and canned peas are available year 'round. Neither of these is particularly exciting; frozen peas are dyed to an unnatural green color and canned peas taste, well, canned. Fresh green peas have a better texture and taste than either. They can be fancied up quite easily, as they have an affinity with cream, ham, onions, artichokes, lemon, rice and many herbs such as mint, thyme, summer savory, and rosemary.

When you're buying peas, look for plump, green pods and avoid dried, wrinkled, faint or discolored ones. Older peas will be larger in the pods and while they are not as sweet and tender as younger ones, you can compensate for this.

Fresh Peas, French-Style

2 to 3 pounds of fresh peas, shelled
¼ cup water
4 lettuce leaves
1 small onion, sliced
2 to 4 tablespoons butter
1 sprig parsley
salt and pepper
fresh mint, thyme, savory or rosemary (optional)

Simmer everything together for about 20 to 30 minutes when the peas will be tender and the liquid almost completely absorbed. Older peas might need a little more water and may take

45 minutes before they are tender. Some recipes call for a pinch of sugar if the peas are not sweet enough. I do not find this necessary; you can taste them near the end of the cooking time and judge for yourself.

These are delicious as an accompaniment to plainly roasted or grilled meat (especially good with duck) or with scrambled eggs. A little freshly chopped mint or parsley sprinkled on top before serving is a nice addition.

Variations include: ¼ cup cream added at the very end and cooked down rapidly to thicken it a bit; small thin pieces of ham or bacon added at the beginning; or very small whole onions instead of a sliced onion.

Green Pea Soup

    1 small onion, sliced
    2 tablespoons butter
    1 ounce ham or bacon, finely chopped (optional)
    1 cup shelled peas
    1 tablespoon lemon juice
    4 cups stock (chicken, veal or vegetable) or
        water
    3 sprigs mint
    salt and pepper
    2 egg yolks
    ½ cup cream

Soften the onion in butter. Add peas and ham or bacon (if you so desire) and let them absorb the butter for a few minutes. Season with salt and pepper and lemon juice, add one sprig of mint and the stock or water. Simmer until the peas are tender (30 to 45 minutes, depending on their age).

Puree the soup, using a blender, food processor or vegetable mill (if you use a vegetable mill, you can include some pea pods in the soup for flavor because they will be strained out at this stage).

Beat the cream and egg yolks together. Add a cup of the hot soup and beat again. Pour this into the soup and reheat gently, stirring all the while. The soup will thicken slightly. Do not let it simmer or the egg yolks will scramble. Sprinkle with the rest of the mint, finely chopped, and serve.

Keeping Your Cool

The Guide
August 1983

W E'VE HAD A BRIEF RESPITE from the heat, during which we have come to appreciate just how cool 88°F can really seem. Once again I have been using all the strategies I know to avoid cooking myself while cooking dinner.

Not cooking is one: the food stores and stands are full of good, fresh summer produce just a rinse and a slice away from becoming a refreshing salad. Add a good loaf of bread and some fruit for dessert, and there's dinner without increasing the temperature in your kitchen a bit.

I aim to avoid turning on the oven during hot weather, or if I must, I try to plan and bake during a cool part of the day and cook large quantities of something that will be just as good cold as hot. Stir-frying or steaming seem the best compromises; it doesn't take much time to fix dinner, and the heat dissipates rapidly when you're done.

Here are several recipes I haven't minded cooking during the recent heat wave. All can be made in quantities large enough to ensure leftovers for lunch or dinner the next day.

Scallion-Oil Shrimp

> 1 pound shrimp
> 1-inch piece ginger, minced
> 4 cloves garlic, smashed and peeled
> 8 scallions finely chopped
> 3 tablespoons oil
> ¼ cup soy sauce
> ½ cup dry sherry
> 4 teaspoons sugar

Remove legs from shrimp, but leave the shells on. Rinse and dry well.

Peel the ginger, smash it with the side of a big knife or cleaver and mince. Smash the garlic lightly and peel. Cut off the root ends of the scallions, rinse, chop both the white and green parts finely.

Heat a wok or heavy skillet to moderately hot, add oil. Stir-fry the ginger and garlic for 10 seconds. Turn the heat to high and add the shrimp. Stir until they turn pink-orange (30 to 45 seconds). Scatter in scallions, stir until their color deepens. Add the soy sauce, sherry and sugar. Stir-fry until the sauce condenses.

Serve hot, lukewarm or cold. The Chinese bite into the shell and suck the meat out rather than shell the shrimp before eating. This recipe is adapted from Irene Kuo's *Key to Chinese Cooking*.

Cold Chicken with Sesame & Spice Sauce

> For 1 small chicken (up to 3 pounds):
> ½ teaspoon roasted and ground Szechwan pepper
> 2 to 3 tablespoons finely chopped ginger
> 2 to 3 tablespoons finely chopped garlic
> 4 to 6 tablespoons sesame paste (tahini) or peanut butter
> 2 tablespoons hot bean paste
> 2 teaspoons Chinese vinegar (or half that amount of another type of vinegar)
> 2 to 3 tablespoons soy sauce
> 2 to 3 tablespoons sesame oil

Steam the chicken. If you don't have a steamer large enough for a chicken, you can rig up some kind of rack in a pot where the water doesn't actually touch the chicken, or poach the chicken in water. The chicken is done when the joints move easily and the juices run clear; this takes about half an hour for a 3-pound chicken.

When the chicken has cooled, skin it and remove all the meat from the bones. (Put the skin and bones in the poaching water and make stock.) Cut the chicken into attractive bite-sized pieces. I like pieces approximating the size of my little finger. Slices and shreds are also nice.

To roast the Szechwan pepper: Use a small skillet and shake the pepper over a high heat until it gives off its distinctive aroma. Crush in a mortar and pestle (or use a hammer or a rolling pin or an electric spice grinder or whatever you have).

Mix the sauce ingredients together and just before serving, toss the chicken lightly with the sauce. This recipe started out in Robert A. Delfs' *Good Food of Szechwan*.

Pasta Salad

Pasta salads are all the rage these days. Boiling the quantity of water necessary to cook several portions of pasta may not seem like ideal behavior on a hot day, but pasta cooks rapidly, and covering the pot until the water boils cuts down on the amount of heat thrown into the air.

Cook an appropriate pasta (I like rotelle or shells) until just done — there should be some "bite" to it (*al dente* "to the teeth!"). Two to three ounces is a good portion per person. When it is cooked, put the pasta into a colander and run cold water over it to rinse away starch and cool it down a bit. Drain thoroughly and mix with dressing and additives.

I prefer the simpler pasta salads — made with vinaigrette (four parts or so olive oil, one part red wine vinegar, salt, pepper, and a pinch of dry mustard; a half-cup dresses about a half-pound of pasta), chopped green onions, plenty of finely chopped parsley and one or two other ingredients (steamed snow peas, ripe black olives, one or two finely chopped anchovies, slivered water chestnuts or peeled, seeded and finely chopped tomatoes). Pasta salads are at their best cool but not just-out-of-the-refrigerator cold.

Cauliflower Vinaigrette

1 small cauliflower
vinaigrette dressing (3 to 6 parts olive oil,
   1 part vinegar, salt, pepper, pinch dry
   mustard)
finely chopped scallions or chives
finely chopped parsley

Break and cut apart the cauliflower into small flowerets. Steam or boil them until just done (6-10 minutes, depending on the size of the flowerets; test often, they should be cooked but still crisp).

Toss gently with the dressing while the cauliflower is still warm. This dressing is also good with potatoes, Jerusalem artichokes, and green beans. A little thinly sliced red pepper looks and tastes good with each of these possibilities.

Keeping Your Cool

Go Fish

The Guide
November 1983

WHAT ELSE FOR A LAZY WEEK at the beach but fish? It was so relaxed that the biggest decisions each day were which of those fresh beauties in the fishmonger's case was going home with us and what specific culinary fate awaited them.

The two key points in fish cookery are to get *fresh* fish and to avoid overcooking. Fresh whole fish is firm, not limp, and has moist shiny scales and a pleasant smell, reminiscent of the ocean. The eyes should be clear and shiny, not dull and milky. Fillets should also be firm, moist and pleasant-smelling.

Minimize the amount of time your fish has been separated from its watery home by cooking it the same day you purchase it. Many people are confused about just how long to cook fish, probably because it comes in many shapes and sizes. One method has been developed in Canada and popularized in this country by James Beard: Take a ruler and measure the fish at its thickest point and cook 8 to 10 minutes per inch.

I usually approximate the cooking time and then check a bit before I have estimated it will be done, because it's easier to cook it a little longer than turn the clock back. Fish is done when it flakes easily with a fork and becomes opaque instead of translucent. Overcooked fish is flabby in texture and loses flavor.

Here are a couple of simple ways of dealing with fresh fish.

Broiled Fish

**5 to 8-ounce fish fillets, steaks or
    small whole fish per person
1 scallion or shallot
1 lemon
butter**

Pre-heat your broiler. You might need to make some arrangements so the fish will be the right distance away from the heat source. Thin pieces should be closer than thick pieces.

Cut off several bits of the zest (yellow) of the lemon and slice as thinly as you as you can. Chop the scallion or shallot.

Oil a pan lightly. Lay the fish on it and sprinkle the onion and lemon peel evenly over it. Dot with about 1 teaspoon of butter per portion.

Broil until done. The onions and lemon may char a bit but are delicious. Squeeze lemon juice over the fish when done and serve piping hot.

This method is successful with a wide variety of fish. I've recently enjoyed cod, perch and swordfish cooked this way.

Sea Trout Provençal

**1½ pound sea trout fillets
2 tablespoons olive oil
2 sweet red peppers, thinly sliced
1 small onion, chopped
1 tomato, peeled and chopped
1 clove garlic, peeled and smashed
1 tablespoon paprika
1½ cups dry white wine**

Preheat oven to 400°F.

Heat the olive oil in a skillet over a medium heat. Add the peppers and onions. When they begin to wilt, add the tomato and garlic. Turn the heat up a bit and when the tomato starts to melt, add the paprika and wine. Turn the heat up a bit more and stir until the wine reduces a bit and amalgamates into a sauce.

Oil a baking dish lightly and lay the fish on it. Cover evenly with the sauce and bake at 400°F until done (about 15 minutes). This fish is delicious with plain boiled new potatoes (served with a little butter and finely chopped parsley) or rice and serves three or four.

Festive Fare

The Guide
December 1983 - January 1984

"I feel now that gastronomical perfection can be reached in these combinations: one person dining alone, usually upon a couch or a hillside; two people of no matter what sex or age, dining in a good restaurant; six people, of no matter what sex or age, dining in a good home."

– M.F.K. Fisher

SHARING FOOD WITH FRIENDS is my favorite way to celebrate anything. No event is too slight nor too momentous that it cannot be enhanced by good food and good company. Neither needs to be fancy, though both should be chosen with care. Balance and contrast are the keys.

Here is a dinner party menu for M.F.K. Fisher's felicitous number of six. If you are having more guests (there are some hosts who feel eight is the ideal number) serve two racks of lamb or a roasted shoulder (boned and tied) or leg of lamb. I'd recommend a good dry sherry or dry white wine for aperitifs; anything stronger is likely to stun your palate. Serve a good red wine — zinfandel, bordeaux, beaujolais with the meal. Plan on one bottle for every two to three people and stop with the salad course — the vinegar in the dressing completely overpowers wine. Finish up with small cups of strong coffee and good, thin after-dinner mints.

Toasted Almonds

1½ pounds shelled almonds
6 tablespoons unsalted butter
1 tablespoon salt

Helen was an early and frequent shopper to our first Wellspring Grocery store. Her sparkling eyes and articulate questions are what I remember most, and the way she shopped often, carefully selecting each item, planning her menu or recipe by what she discovered that day.

When it comes to shopping for groceries, there are two camps. The first selects the recipe before leaving home and gathers the necessary ingredients at the store — they ask questions like "are you really out of sour cream?" or "could you help me find the capers?" The second camp shops for what looks good, what appeals to them on that particular day and then builds a recipe or meal around the ingredients they choose — they ask questions that are more interesting, like "do you think the sweet potatoes have cured long enough to be sweet yet" or "tell me what arrived today that's exciting" or even "what are you having for dinner tonight?" Helen was definitely from the second camp.

If only more people had the willingness to try new things, the confidence to be from the second camp, like Helen. As I read Helen's columns, I see she was trying to do just that — infuse folks with just a little bit of her knowledge, confidence and willingness to try, in hopes that they would discover the cook inside of themselves. She seems to be saying "come on, quit making excuses, and get starting cooking — don't be so serious, because time's a wasting!"

Preheat the oven to 350°F. Melt the butter. Toss the almonds with the butter; sprinkle on the salt and toss again. Spread in one layer on a cookie sheet and roast for 15 to 20 minutes, tossing twice. They are ready when they are golden brown. Drain on paper towels and serve warm. Should you have any leftovers (not very likely), they will keep for a few days in an airtight container.

Pecans can be roasted the same way.

Paté de Foie

½ pound pork or calf liver
½ pound fresh pork belly, boned
1 clove garlic
⅓ cup brandy
2 teaspoons salt
1 teaspoon freshly ground pepper
pinch of marjoram, basil
pinch ground clove, cinnamon, nutmeg, allspice
   or 1 teaspoon Chinese five-spice powder
3 strips bacon, cut lengthwise into strips
1 bay leaf

Grind the pork and liver coarsely. Mix everything except the bay leaf and the bacon thoroughly. You can fry a spoonful in order to taste for seasoning. Put into a three-cup baking container (terrine, loaf pan). Lay the bay leaf on top and crisscross with bacon strips.

Cover (with foil) and bake at 325°F for 90 minutes (the juices will be cooked when done). Uncover for the last 10 minutes. If you can put a weight on top as it cools (flat board, tin can) the texture will be denser.

Paté tastes better when made two or three days in advance. Serve with hot toast. Leftovers make fabulous sandwiches.

Roast Rack of Lamb

1 rack of lamb (two cutlets per person)
1 clove garlic
1 cup lamb stock (made with onion, garlic, carrot, salt & pepper)

Rack of lamb is lamb trimmed as if to make cutlets but left whole. (Crown roast of lamb is two racks put together in a circle.) You may have to go to a specialty butcher to assure getting a cut of meat that you can carve into individual cutlets at the table.

Preheat oven to 375°F. Poke some thin holes into the meat next to a bone and insert slivers of garlic. Roast the lamb in a covered roasting dish, basting with lamb stock and pan juices every 15 minutes. (If you don't have the makings for lamb stock, substitute red wine, reduced a bit). It will take about 50 minutes for medium lamb (just the slightest hint of pink). Leave the roast uncovered for the last 10 minutes so it will brown.

When the rack is done, keep it warm while you make a sauce. Pour away most of the fat from the pan juices. Heat the pan on top of the stove. Add the rest of the stock or wine and cook over high heat, stirring all the while to scrape up all the bits on the bottom of the pan. This makes a little bit of concentrated sauce, to be served on the side.

This is one of my favorite recipes for my favorite meat — lamb — and is an adaptation from Elizabeth David's *French Provincial Cooking*, as is the following recipe.

Sautéed Potatoes & Carrots

½ pounds waxy, boiling-type potatoes
½ pound carrots
3 shallots
3 tablespoons butter
salt and pepper
finely chopped parsley

Scrape the carrots. Peel the potatoes. Cook each separately until two-thirds done (10 to 12 minutes for the potatoes, six to eight minutes for the carrots). Cut the potatoes into ¾ inch squares, the carrots into thick, ¾ inch long strips. Chop the shallots. Mix the potatoes, carrots, onions, and parsley together, salt and pepper to taste.

Melt the butter in an iron skillet and cook the vegetable mixture over medium heat for 10 to 15 minutes. Stir frequently and cook until the vegetables are crisp outside and done inside.

Green Salad with Walnuts & Oranges

romaine lettuce, cleaned and dried
handful of walnuts
1 orange
vinaigrette dressing made with 4 parts olive oil, one part red wine vinegar, salt and pepper

Cut the orange peel away using a sharp flexible knife. Cut a piece off the top and bottom of the orange so it will sit flat, then cut away the peel and all the white pith, leaving only the orange beneath. Slice thinly. Toss everything together just before serving. Leave the lettuce in large pieces and eat with a knife and fork.

Mom's Pecan Pie

3 eggs
1 cup white sugar
1 cup white corn syrup
1 stick melted butter
1 teaspoon vanilla
1 cup pecan halves
unbaked pie shell

Beat the eggs well. Add everything else and mix well. Pour into an unbaked pie shell and bake for 45 to 55 minutes at 350°F. Cool before serving.

While she makes great apple pies, when I think "Mom" and "pie," this pecan pie is what comes to mind. You can add a little bourbon if you want to mess around, but it's not necessary. Use good, fresh pecans.

H. Hudson Whiting has the world's smallest test kitchen and wonders what obscure, but wonderful, kitchen gadgets will be under the Christmas tree this year.*

*This was the first appearance of many "mini-bios" that Helen wrote herself. Typically, the editor writes a one- or two-sentence bio for columnists, but Helen was happy to provide her own. — ed.

Introduction: The Indy Years

By Steve Schewel

IN THE SECOND ISSUE of *The Independent,* 29 April 1983, H. Hudson Whiting wrote our first food article. The topic was fried chicken and how to make it — a perfect topic for our Southern-fried alternative newspaper and our do-it-yourself readers, mostly youngsters who wanted to cook like Mom but didn't know how.

The Independent got started in 1982 in Helen's "office," a windowless cinderblock room on Hillsborough Road where she and Dave Birkhead shared a single typesetting machine. It was an old Mergenthaler photo-typesetter they literally held together with tape, Dave punching the keyboard all night before Helen came in for the day shift. As we assembled a newspaper staff and struggled towards our first issue, hours got long, money got short, tempers got shorter. But never Helen's. She was the calm, kind eye of that storm.

Good jokes, long stories, new recipes, mystery books to recommend, ACC basketball predictions, a laugh beginning just behind her front teeth and ending in a deep wheezy chuckle, fingers flying gently, madly all the while — that was Helen then.

Durham then was full of "meat-and-three" joints: Whit's Grill and Morgan's catering to the textile mill crowd on Ninth Street; Parker's on East Main; Carolyn's on the corner of Angier and Driver; Nance's down near the American tobacco factory where the ballpark stands today. Helen bowed to these fried chicken emporia in this first piece, paid mandatory obeisance to barbecue, Brunswick stew and hushpuppies, then wrote her personal cook's mantra: "Don't be intimidated by the fried chicken legends," by memories of Mom in the kitchen or by the local restaurants. "You can aspire to mythic heights in your own kitchen."

For another dozen years she told *Independent* readers that we could do it ourselves, that good cooking wasn't too hard and she would teach us how to do it. For Helen, cooking wasn't a high-stakes artistic endeavor. Nothing too fancy, no culinary gyrations. Just go ahead and do it! she admonished. Enjoy it! That's what all her columns say.

We all know the big names in the development of food culture in the Triangle — people like the Eure family, Tommy Bullock, Mary Bacon, Ben and Karen Barker, Lex and Anne Alexander. Give H. Hudson Whiting a place of honor among those names. She taught the foodie generation that we could cook, too, and have fun doing it.

H. Hudson Whiting's pieces link two eras. When Helen began writing about food, there was exactly one restaurant, a steak house, between Duke University and Franklin Street. As our food culture exploded, Helen was right there trying humorously to get us to take food seriously.

And, yes, Helen was funny. Never a column went by without some clever headline, some gentle wisp of a joke. When *The Independent* started a new food section in 1992, it was Helen who suggested everyone's favorite feature: "Gadget of the Month," she called it, and she soon wrote a fabulous gadget piece. You know that combo bottle-and-can-opener you've got stuck to the fridge? Helen apotheosized it in the story entitled, "The Magnetic Church Key: Not Just a Simple Twist-Off Fate." In the piece she extols the church key's versatility and ends the piece like this: "An argument could be made that this is the only

refrigerator magnet I'll ever really need, but I'm not sure I could give up my guitar-shaped Elvis swizzle stick."

M.F.K. Fisher was one of Helen's favorite food writers and mine, too. So now when I pull out a copy of Fisher's *With Bold Knife and Fork,* I feel Helen's hands and eyes upon it. Or I sit occasionally in Helen's decades-old bright red swivel chair which she bequeathed to *The Independent* when she stopped setting type, and I remember those flying hands, that husky laugh. I look up her advice on how to skin a pearl onion. When I make yeast bread, I follow her published maxim: "Relax." I cook from the recipes she published over the years, invariably named for their progenitors: Holly McDonough's Burgundy Mushrooms, Nona McKee's Eggnog.

Helen wrote more than once about Bill Neal, the legendary author of *Southern Cooking,* creator of some of the Triangle's best restaurants and best food, a man who, like Helen, died way too young. She once compared Neal to the great food critic Elizabeth David in words that remind me of Helen herself: "We are not being urged to travel to a particular location to eat a particular meal that she once enjoyed," Helen wrote, "but to recognize and enjoy those wonderful moments of our own and to create a few of them at our own table."

In Helen's tiny, packed kitchen, she created those moments for all of us.

Don't Count Your Chickens Before They're Fried

The Independent
April 29, 1983

SOUTHERN FRIED CHICKEN may not be the most common topic of food conversation in North Carolina. I imagine the most hours are logged arguing about barbecue (better east or west of Rocky Mount?), with Brunswick stew (authentic without a squirrel?) a close second and hushpuppies (sugar? onion?) third.

But many of these conversations take place in a restaurant where fried chicken is the next most commonly ordered item.

You know the kind of restaurant I mean, decor ranging from unpretentious to none, friendly waitresses who are not necessarily wearing uniforms, a menu from which a wide variety of customers is ordering a "special" with two to three well-done vegetables. Sweetened ice tea and unending basketfuls of hushpuppies come without question.

As does delicious fried chicken.

Many of us grew up on fried chicken and have a mythic standard of reference with which to compare each portion — Mom's fresh, hot off the stove. But don't be intimidated by the fried chicken legends, from down-home restaurants or childhood; you can aspire to mythic heights in your own kitchen.

I learned to fry chicken at my mother's elbow, and there was never a "recipe," there was a method: Shake chicken pieces in a bag with flour, salt and pepper and fry until done. That was gospel.

It wasn't until I did my own shopping and cooked in my own kitchen that I realized there were crucial details beyond the basic method.

Here's a recipe that considers these details one by one. You'll notice that it's for pan-fried chicken; I've had decent deep- and batter-fried chicken, but it's not the real thing.

Fried Chicken

CHICKEN: You'll want one to three pieces per diner, depending on appetite. It's hard to make too much fried chicken, and anyway, cold leftovers are great.

Buy frying chicken; broilers are younger and have less flavor; roasting chickens are older and can be tough when fried.

If you can, get fresh, not frozen, chicken. Freezing damages the cell walls, and some of the moisture you want under the crispy exterior escapes when the chicken thaws. Tell-tale signs of a freezer in your chicken's past are: It is still frozen or it's swimming in liquid in the package. Freshness is more important than whether the chicken's flesh is yellow or white.

You can save money by buying a whole chicken and cutting it up yourself. If you've never cut up a chicken, use a sharp knife and remember that there's a joint you can cut through to separate every piece except the breast halves. These you can separate with kitchen scissors or a courageous chop with a heavy knife or cleaver lengthwise through the center.

Leave the skin on. I mention this because there are some people who can't stand chicken skin. Some of them actually manage to create a reasonable "mock" fried chicken but this is akin to a recent notion of mine that I could make chili without beef — pleasant, but inauthentic. Rinse the pieces and let them drain, but don't dry them.

Put a couple of cups of flour into a small paper bag. Add a tablespoon or so of salt and lots of freshly ground pepper. Some people (and huge fast-food chains) can't resist spices at this stage. They're not necessary, though; my Mom still winces when I add a bit of paprika.

FRYING PAN: At one time, no Southern woman left her family to get married without proper iron skillets. These days, though there are lots of other reasons to leave home, iron skillets are still a necessity for any good cook.

Your skillet should be large enough to hold the chicken in one layer without crowding. If the pieces are packed in too tight, the temperature of the fat will drop, and you'll end up with greasy fried chicken. I use two skillets or fry in batches rather than crowd the pieces in.

FAT: You want plain old frying fat, nothing fancy like butter or olive oil. I personally don't like corn oil but have successfully fried chicken in all vegetable shortenings and peanut, safflower and sunflower oils. Go for the brands with fewer added ingredients; they taste better. Use enough oil to come just over halfway up the thickest chicken pieces so they will cook evenly.

The proper temperature is important. My mother taught me to test with a drop of water. The water will pop rapidly when the fat is hot enough. Do this cautiously; stand back and use only a drop of water to avoid splattering hot fat on yourself. If the fat is smoking, it is too hot and is breaking down.

METHOD: Put each piece of chicken into medium hot fat. Turn them over when the crust sets, sealing in the juices. Don't turn with a fork —

it pierces the chicken and allows juices to escape. Turn the heat down to medium low at this point. Your aim is to cook each piece through without overcooking the outside. Some people cover the pan, trapping steam; this helps the chicken cook evenly but the outside won't be as crisp. If you use the right amount of oil and turn the chicken from time to time, it will cook evenly.

Knowing when the chicken is done takes experience — the flesh stiffens and the juices run clear. The whole frying process takes about half an hour. If you are in doubt, take a piece out and poke it to check. Undercooked chicken is not delicious, and overcooked chicken is dry and lifeless. The flesh will be white throughout, but don't worry about slight redness on the bones. This has to do with the bones, not the flesh of the chicken.

Drain the chicken on something absorbent — paper towels or brown paper bags — and serve. Fried chicken is best right out of the pan but when necessary can be held briefly (10 to 15 minutes in a 275°F oven).

H. Hudson Whiting, who lives in Durham, has been eating for 36 years, cooking for 18, and writing about it for six.*

*In this, her first column for **The Independent**, Helen continued her tradition of writing her own brief bio. Many were to follow during her years writing for "**The Indy**." – ed.*

Dressing Properly

The Independent
June 24, 1983

THE NAVAJO TEACH that most anything is all right, in moderation. There are two routes to this happy state — excess and restraint. Both have their uses, but here I urge an experiment in restraint, going back to square one to discover the true essence of a thing.

But what I'm really doing is writing about salad.

There are salads where lettuce predominates, cooked vegetable salads (potato, leek, jerusalem artichoke, parsnip, beans — both fresh and dried), meat and seafood salads (chicken, cold roast, crab, fish, lobster, shrimp), cold pasta and rice salads, and salads where a single raw vegetable predominates (carrot, cucumber, tomato, mushroom, sweet pepper).

Research reminded me of raitas (Indian yogurt salads) and all those cold Middle Eastern dishes (often featuring eggplant). My American cookbooks (especially the older ones) brought up "wilted" salads, and one sort I'm always ready to forget — gelatin salads.

Clearly the first exercise in restraint is narrowing the topic.

Since it's early summer and the local weather has been kind to lettuce growers so far, I'll concentrate on the simple lettuce salad. Your restraint should come when making and dressing them. At its best, the green salad is a simple matter of a few ingredients; each element must be chosen and treated with care.

I serve such a salad after the main course. It's refreshing between courses and can be a nice way to end a meal.

If you don't like simple lettuce salads, you are probably using iceberg lettuce. There are many better choices in the supermarket. My favorite is romaine, but I also like many others — Boston, bibb, leaf, red leaf and the funny, spiky-leaved ones that are often bitter. If you usually buy just one type of lettuce, try others so you can explore the subtle and delicious differences.

The lettuce should be cleaned and dried carefully. Rinse each leaf separately to get rid of dirt and insects. Drying the lettuce is an important step because the lettuce stays crisp and the dressing doesn't get diluted. You can dry it gently with towels or spin it. Enclosed plastic spinners dry the lettuce thoroughly without splattering water about. Or you can put the lettuce in a clean dish towel and swing it around. This is best done outdoors.

Over the years I have been surprised when people rave about my salad dressing because it is the simplest of all — vinaigrette. I use six parts oil, one part vinegar, a pinch of dry mustard, salt and freshly ground pepper. Bottled dressings are a waste of money; they usually have too many additives and are not as fresh as those you make yourself.

My choice of oil is olive. You don't have to buy the most expensive for the best flavor, though the virgin pressings do taste more like olives. If you worry about polyunsaturated vs. saturated oils, remember that olive oil is monosaturated and is considered a "good" oil.

I am less dogmatic about the vinegar. My usual choice is red wine vinegar, though I enjoy others — white wine, rice wine, sherry and balsamic vinegars. Sometimes I use lemon juice for a delicate flavor.

Vinegars also range in price and quality. There are some good cheap ones. Read the label carefully and avoid all the "wine-flavored" ones. With the possible exception of tarragon, I'd rather add fresh herbs than use a flavored vinegar.

I use dry mustard because it mixes easily. The only additive that might enhance rather than dilute the dressing's flavor is garlic.

Salt can be omitted if you are cutting down, but freshly ground black pepper is a must. Pre-ground pepper quickly goes stale and is less pungent.

You might be surprised at the scanty proportion of vinegar to oil. The classic mixture is one to three. I find this too acid. Experiment until you find the proportion you like best.

A tablespoon or so dresses salad for one; you are using too much if there is a puddle left in the bowl. Because this dressing is best absolutely fresh, there's no need to make and store vast quantities. You can mix it in a jar or make it in the bottom of your bowl when you start the salad.

Stir it up and cross the salad spoons in the bowl to rest the lettuce on (instead of in the dressing) until you are ready to toss.

Toss thoroughly just before serving. I eat my salad on the plate I have just finished dinner on. A little leftover juice or gravy never hurts.

After a spell of restraint in your salad making, you will be ready to consider additives, one or two at a time. I've been successful with olives, grated carrot, thinly sliced oranges (remove all the peel and pith with a sharp knife first), nuts, mushrooms, green peppers, cucumbers, spinach, watercress, artichokes, onions, snow peas, herbs, sprouts, freshly made croutons (rubbed with a little garlic), a few anchovies and seven-minute eggs.

But do use restraint when contemplating cheeses and meats. Some work well but they can easily be cloying or at odds with the simple refreshment you are aiming for in a tossed green salad.

The World of Apples

The Independent
December 23, 1983

All human history attests
That happiness for man — the hungry sinner!
Since Eve ate apples, much depends on dinner.

  – Lord Byron

ONCE AGAIN, MODERN SCIENCE has altered one of our staple edibles. Apple varieties are being bred because they have big yields, ship well and store for long periods of time. But surprisingly, many of the apples found in the supermarket also taste good.

From all accounts, the first Delicious apples lived up to their name; these days they are often the least interesting variety in the fruit bin. I prefer the crisp texture and tart flavor of Staymans, Winesaps, Pippins, Yorks, McIntoshes and Granny Smiths.

Apple season stretches from fall to early spring in the U.S. Varieties such as Granny Smith, which are imported from New Zealand and Australia, are in season there during our summer, so we have good apples available year 'round these days. Check out the apples available from small fruit stands — you may not have heard of the varieties, but many will be pleasant surprises.

Ripe apples give off ethylene gas, which hastens the ripening of other fruits and vegetables — so store them away from potatoes and onions. You can use this property to your advantage if you have some pears or avocados that you want to ripen.

I wash apples with soap and water to remove pesticides if I am planning to use the peels. If not, I use a potato peeler to peel the apples. I also use one of those German gadgets that cores and slices the apple in one operation. This works fairly well, though I have to slice the apples more thinly for most purposes.

Here are some of my favorite sweet and savory recipes for apples. All are best with tart cooking apples. The apple varieties recommended above will work well, though McIntoshes, which collapse when cooked, are better for apple sauce and apple butter than for the other recipes.

Applesauce

apples
liquid (apple cider or water)
seasonings

Applesauce is easy to make in small or large quantities and can be seasoned to suit whatever you plan to serve with it. Here is the method:

Core the apples and cut them into rough chunks. Put them into a saucepan and add enough liquid (cider is the first choice, water is fine) to cover the bottom of the pan so they won't stick before they start giving out their own liquid. Don't bother peeling them if you have a food mill; the peels will stay behind when you puree them. Bring to a boil and simmer until the apples are tender (about half an hour).

Puree the apples, using a food mill or potato masher. Taste the puree and season: a slight pinch of salt, sugar, lemon juice, cinnamon, rosemary or coriander are just a few of the possibilities. Whatever you choose should enhance, not overpower, the apple flavor.

Heat the puree, stirring frequently. If it is too liquid, let it cook down a bit. If you are serving the applesauce hot, stir in a lump of butter.

Sautéed Apples

    I medium apple per person
    I tablespoon butter per apple
    up to I tablespoon sugar per apple

Peel, core and slice the apples and toss them with the sugar. Melt the butter in your trusty iron skillet and cook the apples over a gentle heat until golden and tender. Turn them carefully from time to time. This dish is simple and delicious served alone or with a bit of *creme fraiche* or heavy cream poured on top. If you want to get fancy, flame them in brandy before serving: Heat the brandy, pour over the apples, ignite carefully with a long match, then tilt and shake the pan until the flame goes out.

Cabbage & Apples

    2 pounds red cabbage
    2 medium onions, sliced thinly
    2 cooking apples, peeled, cored, thinly sliced
    I to 2 tablespoons sugar (white or brown)
        or mild honey
    I tablespoon port or other dessert wine
    2 tablespoons red wine vinegar
    parsley, thyme, bay leaf
    salt and pepper

Remove wilted outer leaves and cut the cabbage into quarters, remove the stalk and slice thinly. Arrange the cabbage, onions and apples in layers in a deep oven-proof dish. Season each layer with sugar, herbs, salt and pepper. Pour over the wine and vinegar. Cover tightly and cook for three hours at 300°F.

This dish, which is an adaptation from Elizabeth David's *French Provincial Cooking,* can be made a day in advance and reheated.

Apple Pie

    double-crust pie dough
    5 to 7 apples, cored, peeled and thinly sliced
    up to one-half-cup sugar, white or brown
    grated lemon peel (optional)
    juice of a lemon (if the apples aren't tart)
    your choice of cinnamon, nutmeg or
        Chinese five-spice powder
    I tablespoon butter

Mix the apples with the lemon peel, a light coating of sugar and a scant pinch of spice. Put the bottom crust in your pie pan and add the apples. Dot with butter. Cover with the top crust and, using water, seal the edges tightly. Slash it a couple of times so steam can escape. Brush with a beaten egg yolk, cream or milk to ensure a golden crust and bake at 450°F for 10 minutes, then turn the oven down to 425°F for 30 minutes. You can check to see if the apples are done by poking with a skewer or sharp knife through one of the slits.

All Right, Campers!
No More Excuses!
Into the Kitchen and COOK!

The Independent
March 16, 1984

I RECENTLY OVERHEARD A FRIEND say that if only he could take some time off from work he would become a really good cook. This intelligent adult thought he would have to devote five months away from his usual (admittedly busy) schedule to achieving this goal. But most of his excuses are illusions. Actually, he could start with the next meal he cooks.

If, like my friend, you think good cooking takes more time than you can spare, remember that bad cooking takes time as well. Paying attention while you are in the kitchen is more important than the amount of time you can spend.

You don't need a kitchen full of gadgets; all you really need is a good, sharp knife, a large sturdy cutting board, a big pot to boil things in, a big mixing bowl, a couple of saucepans, an iron skillet, a couple of baking dishes and a stove.

Good food is based on good ingredients. All this means is that you have to learn to recognize and buy them and reject ingredients that aren't up to your standards. It doesn't mean that you have to spend hours in obscure locations depleting your bank account to acquire exotic items.

The last excuse we'll consider is not having the "right" or "enough" cookbooks. If you're completely lost in the kitchen, the *Joy of Cooking* is a good place to start. Otherwise, look for a good cookbook in a cuisine that interests you. Ask the advice of a good cook, or check out a couple from your local library.

Start out with one recipe or concept and get it down right, then explore related dishes to expand your possibilities. A good main dish and a salad can be the basis of an excellent meal.

Italian cooking is a good style for Americans to explore. Most of us are familiar with some dishes, so we have some idea of what we're shooting for and are not intimidated. You'll quickly realize that there is much more to Italian cuisine than you suspected, and that you could happily spend many of your remaining hours in a kitchen exploring it. Ada Boni's *Italian Regional Cooking* or Marcella Hazan's *Classical Italian Cookbook* will show you what I mean.

Here are two recipes to start you out. They use related techniques and ingredients, so when you get the first one down, the other is easy.

Lasagne

> 1 pound lasagne noodles
> salt, water
> 1 recipe meat or tomato sauce (below)
> 1 tablespoon olive oil
> 1 clove garlic, peeled and smashed
> 1½ ounces dried mushrooms
> 2 tablespoons finely chopped parsley
> 1 cup milk or stock
> béchamel sauce (below)
> 4 ounces grated parmesan cheese (about 1 cup)

Cook the lasagne noodles in vast quantities of salted boiling water. (My pot holds 8 quarts of water so I usually only cook one half pound at a time.) Rinse the pasta in cold water and drain thoroughly.

Soak the dried mushrooms in boiling water for half an hour. Drain them, cut away and discard the tough stems and chop the caps finely. Fry the garlic clove gently in two tablespoons of olive oil in a small skillet or saucepan. When it turns golden brown, discard the garlic and add the mushrooms. Add the parsley and milk or stock and simmer for 15 minutes.

Butter a baking dish and assemble the lasagne: a layer of noodles, a thin layer of béchamel sauce, then meat or tomato sauce, then a sprinkling of parmesan cheese. Repeat, substituting the mushrooms for a meat or tomato sauce layer. The last layer should be noodles, meat or tomato sauce, then the rest of the parmesan cheese. Bake for 30 minutes at 375°F. Let the lasagne "settle" for five to ten minutes before cutting and serving.

Bolognese Meat Sauce

4 tablespoons olive oil
1 onion, finely chopped
1 carrot, finely chopped
1 rib of celery, finely chopped
2 slices bacon, finely chopped
12 ounces ground beef (or half beef, half pork)
2 to 3 chicken livers, finely chopped
(if you happen to have them on hand)
½ cup dry white wine
salt and pepper
1 large can Italian plum tomatoes
4 tablespoons cream

In a large skillet, soften the onion, carrot, celery and bacon in the olive oil. Add the meat and livers, turn up the heat and fry, stirring frequently, until the meat turns brown. Add the wine, stir and cook until the wine has nearly evaporated. Season with salt and pepper, add the tomatoes — chopped up a bit — and the liquid from the tomatoes. Let the sauce simmer while you prepare other parts of the recipe (about an hour). Stir from time to time and add the cream about 10 minutes before you are ready to use the sauce.

Tomato Sauce

(See also Fresh Tomato Sauce, page 9)

1 clove garlic, peeled and smashed
3 tablespoons olive oil
1 small onion, finely chopped
1 quart home-canned tomatoes or
**   1 large can Italian plum tomatoes**
basil or Italian parsley or oregano,
**   finely-chopped**

Fry the garlic clove gently in the olive oil until it turns golden brown. Discard the garlic and let the onions soften in the olive oil. Chop the tomatoes up a bit (or blend them lightly) and add to the onions along with their liquid. Let the sauce simmer for about half an hour, stirring from time to time. If you are using a dried herb, add it at the beginning of the simmering; if fresh, towards the end. The sauce is ready when a good deal of the liquid has evaporated and the tomatoes have amalgamated.

Béchamel Sauce

(See also Microwave Béchamel, page 169)

6 tablespoons butter
6 tablespoons flour
5 cups hot milk
½ teaspoon salt
pinch nutmeg

Melt the butter and stir in the flour. Cook gently for three minutes without browning the flour. Using a whisk, stir in the hot milk. Bring this to a boil, stirring constantly. Turn down to a simmer, season with salt and a pinch of nutmeg. Let the sauce cook for 10 minutes.

Eggplant Parmesan

3 pounds eggplant
olive oil
1 recipe tomato sauce (above)
½ pound mozzarella cheese, coarsely grated
¼ pound parmesan cheese, grated

Slice the eggplant into quarter-inch slices sprinkle with salt and let them drain in a colander for half an hour. This removes any bitterness.

Brush each slice of eggplant with olive oil, arrange in one layer on a baking dish and cook in a 400°F oven for 20 minutes, turning about halfway through. More traditionally, the eggplant is fried in olive oil, but it absorbs alarming quantities of the oil this way, and the final dish is quite heavy.

Butter or oil a baking dish and arrange a layer of eggplant slices in it. Cover with a layer of tomato sauce, then mozzarella and parmesan. Continue with these layers until the ingredients are used up, finishing up with a thicker layer of parmesan cheese. Bake at 375°F for half an hour. If the top is not browning, turn the oven up to 450°F for the last five minutes. Let this dish rest for five to 10 minutes before serving.

H. Hudson Whiting lives in Durham and frequently publishes favorite recipes in hopes of encountering these dishes away from home.

The Berry Best, or: Strawberry Fools

The Independent
May 25, 1984

"Doubtless God could have made a better berry, but doubtless God never did."

—William Butler (1553-1618)

RIPE STRAWBERRIES are in a class by themselves. They are tender and juicy and the flavor is a delicate balance of sweet and tart. If you pay attention, it is easy to buy good ones. Look for an even red color — underripe berries are green or white. Avoid signs of mold or wetness — an indication of age or careless handling. Take the time to make sure they smell like ripe strawberries: rich, sharp, warm.

Of course, if you pick your own, you can select just the ones you want and avoid unpleasant surprises in the middle of the container.

When you get the strawberries home, discard any bad ones and store in your refrigerator either wrapped or covered — unless you want everything in there to smell like strawberries. They should keep for a day or two; but the sooner you use them, the fresher they taste.

Wash them gently and quickly — you don't want to bruise them or allow them to absorb water. Just before you use them, remove the green part with a small, sharp knife or a strawberry huller.

Fresh, ripe strawberries are delicious on their own, in a simple fruit salad or with a spoonful of thick cream or yogurt. They can be sliced into halves and marinated with a sprinkling of sugar and orange juice or liqueur (Cointreau is especially good). When you've had your fill of plain berries, you might want to try some of the recipes below.

Strawberry Shortcake

THE BERRIES:
2 pints strawberries
2 to 4 tablespoons of sugar
juice of ½ lemon

Wash and drain the strawberries. Hull and slice them into halves or quarters. Sprinkle with sugar (the amount depends on the sweetness of the berries and your taste) and the lemon juice. You may also use Cointreau or another liqueur as a marinade. The berries should be lightly coated, not sodden.

THE CAKE:
2 cups flour
3 teaspoons baking powder
¼ teaspoon salt
2 tablespoons sugar
6 tablespoons butter
2 egg yolks
5 fluid ounces milk

Preheat the oven to 375°F. Sift the flour before measuring. Resift with the baking powder, salt and sugar. Work the butter in with a pastry cutter, two knives or your fingers until the mixture looks mealy. Beat the egg yolks lightly and add the milk. Working lightly and quickly, mix the liquid into the flour until it holds together. Turn out onto floured board and fold over on itself eight to twelve times. Pat or roll into a round about 1½ inches thick and place on a greased baking sheet. Bake at 375°F for 20 to 25 minutes.

THE TOPPING:
½ pint cream

Whip the cream. If you like, you can sweeten it with a bit of sugar or flavor it with a teaspoon of vanilla.

When the shortcake is done, split into two layers and put half the berries on the bottom layer. Cover with a little less than half the cream. Put the top layer on this and cover with the rest of the berries and cream. Serve warm. You can make four to six individual shortcakes with this amount of dough. They will need only 10 to 15 minutes to cook.

Strawberry Fool

1 pint strawberries
2 to 4 tablespoons sugar
½ pint whipping cream
1 egg white

Wash and drain the strawberries. Hull them and set aside the nicest-looking half of the berries, cut into halves or quarters. Puree the rest using a blender, food mill, food processor or potato masher. Adjust the sweetness with sugar.

Whip the cream until stiff and fold in the strawberry puree and the sliced berries. Whip the egg white until stiff and fold it in as well. Put into a pretty serving dish and chill for several hours. To garnish, put on a few sliced berries or some fresh mint leaves.

You can vary this by pureeing all or none of the berries and proceeding as above. I think you get the best of both worlds by pureeing half.

Jeanie Gamble's Strawberry Pie

Courtesy of Somethyme Restaurant*

2 to 2½ pints strawberries
½ cup Triple Sec, Cointreau, Grand Marnier (optional)

⅓ cup fresh lemon juice
¾ cup sugar
¾ cup water
⅛ teaspoon salt
⅔ cup cornstarch
4 tablespoons butter
¾ cup whipping cream
single crust pie shell

Clean the berries. As you hull them, sort into halves — the best and the rest. Slice the best ones into halves or quarters and, if you choose, marinate them in the liqueur.

Puree the less-than-perfect berries with the lemon juice and sugar. Put into a 4-cup measure and add enough water to make 3½ cups of puree.

In a large saucepan, mix together the water, salt and cornstarch. Add the strawberry puree one tablespoon at a time until you are sure the cornstarch has dissolved without any lumps.

Add the rest of the puree and cook over a medium heat, whisking all the while, until thick and translucent. When the mixture comes to a boil, it has gotten as thick as possible: Don't overcook. Remove from the heat, add the butter and whisk until the butter has melted. Let this cool to room temperature, whisking from time to time to avoid the formation of a skin on the puree.

Bake a single crust. Put the dough into the pan, prick with a fork and crimp the edges. Put in a piece of aluminum foil and fill with dried beans (to weigh the crust down as it bakes so it won't puff up). Bake at 425°F for 15 minutes; remove the foil and beans, put the crust back in for five minutes or so until it is golden and done.

While the crust is cooling, add the sliced berries to the puree. Whip the ¾ cup of cream until stiff and fold in the strawberry mixture. Pour into the crust and chill for several hours or overnight.

Serve cold. You may want to use more whipped cream as a garnish. The texture is best if it's eaten within a day. The flavor is so good I don't think you have to worry about keeping it too long. This is an extraordinary pie, one where all the elements work together to enhance the strawberry flavor.

Strawberry Puree (for freezing)

For each pint of berries:
2-4 tablespoons sugar
juice of ½ lemon

Clean, drain and hull the berries. Freeze only unblemished ripe berries; use damaged or overripe ones for another purpose.

Puree berries with the sugar and lemon juice in a blender, food mill or processor. Adjust the sweetness to your taste. Pour into clean containers, leaving room for expansion, and freeze.

I find whole berries mushy when they have been frozen and prefer to freeze a puree. The puree can be used as a sauce or base for fools, water ices or ice cream when strawberries are no longer in season.

H. Hudson Whiting remembers fondly her first strawberry season in England when she discovered English cream.

*Somethyme Restaurant was Durham, North Carolina's "Home of Fine Natural Foods" for nearly a decade. – ed.

The Berry Best, or: Strawberry Fools

Your Own Simple Fall Festival

The Independent
September 28, 1984

THERE IS SOMETHING MARVELOUS about eating outdoors, especially when the weather is as beautiful as ours has been lately. The picnic can be the sole object of the excursion, or it can accompany some other activity. The menus can be absolutely simple — bread, cheese and a bottle of beer — or several elaborate courses cooked and served on the site.

Here is a suggested menu and recipes for a very simple picnic for four people. All you'll need is a basket or other container large enough to hold everything, a ground cover of some sort to sit on, napkins, a knife or two, a bottle opener or cork puller, some glasses or cups, a citronella candle if biting insects are likely, and good companions.

A Middle Eastern Picnic

hot or cold mint tea or a rough red wine
pita bread
hummus (recipe follows)
sliced tomatoes, onions, crumbled feta cheese and mint, mixed together
dates, pitted and stuffed with cream cheese

No plates are necessary; this menu is designed so that the food can be eaten with your fingers or on the bread. If you wrap chilled bottles of beer, cider or wine in damp newspaper, they will stay pleasantly cool for several hours and you can dispense with a cooler.

Hummus

1 large can chickpeas or 2 cups cooked chickpeas
juice of 1 to 2 lemons
2 cloves garlic
salt
½ cup tahini paste
finely chopped parsley
pita bread

Drain the chickpeas, but save the cooking liquid. Puree the chickpeas and garlic, using a food mill, blender, food processor or mortar and pestle. Add reserved cooking liquid until it is the consistency of a thick mayonnaise.

Add lemon juice, salt and tahini paste and mix well. Taste, and adjust the flavors to your liking. Chill and sprinkle with finely chopped parsley before serving. The hummus can be picked up with the pita bread.

Super Soups for Winter

The Independent
January 18, 1985

MAKING A HEARTY WINTER SOUP, like chopping wood, provides more than one benefit. Your house smells great while it's cooking and, if you are generous with the amounts, you end up with several wonderful meals.

Here are two easy soups that can serve either as substantial first courses or, along with some good bread, as the centers of simple meals for family and friends.

The first, Pistou, comes from the south of France, uses only a few ingredients and takes very little preparation and cooking time. The tomato, garlic and basil paste from which the soup takes its name are added at the very end and make all the difference between a simple vegetable soup and something very special.

The second is that famous Italian peasant soup, Minestrone, a flexible combination of beans, vegetables, pasta and cheese, more often resembling a stew than a soup. When I say flexible, I mean it. You probably can't think of an ingredient — up to and including pigs' ears — that hasn't already appeared in an absolutely "authentic" version.

Pistou* II

> 1 onion
> 4 tomatoes
> 2 boiling potatoes
> 6 cups water

Helen loved pistou. Her recipe for it appears in a similar form on page 21 in her March 1977 column. — ed.

> 1 zucchini
> 1 pound green beans
> salt and pepper
> 2 ounces vermicelli
> 1 to 2 cloves garlic
> 2 tablespoons fresh basil or 1 teaspoon
>   dried basil
> 1 more tomato
> grated Gruyère or other Swiss cheese

Chop the onion. Pour boiling water over all the tomatoes to loosen their skins; peel, seed and chop four of them. You may use canned tomatoes in the winter when it is hard to find good, ripe ones.

Bring the six cups of water to a boil, add the onions and tomatoes, then lower the heat so as to maintain a brisk simmer. Salt and pepper to taste.

Peel and dice the potatoes, then add them to the soup.

After 10 minutes, scrub the zucchini and cut it into quarter-inch slices. String the green beans, if necessary, and cut them into 1-inch pieces. Add the zucchini and beans to the soup.

After five more minutes add the vermicelli, breaking it up a bit if it is very long.

Prepare the pistou by pulverizing the garlic, basil and the last tomato together, using a mortar and pestle, blender or food processor. When all the ingredients of the soup are tender, stir 2 to 3 tablespoons of the soup stock into the pistou, then mix it all into the soup. Serve hot and pass the cheese separately. Serves four.

Minestrone

> ½ cup dried white or red beans, or
>   one small can of beans
> Optional: one-quarter pound salt pork,
>   bacon or good Italian sausage
> 1 large onion, chopped

½ small cabbage, thinly sliced
1 clove garlic, peeled and crushed
1 turnip, peeled and diced
1 large potato, peeled and diced
1 green or red sweet pepper, diced
1 or 2 tomatoes, peeled and chopped, or
    2 to 3 tablespoons tomato paste
1 zucchini, sliced
3 tablespoons parsley, finely chopped
¼ pound pasta (vermicelli, spaghetti, shells,
    stars, alphabets, or whatever you fancy)
parmesan cheese, finely grated
Optional: leftover pesto
Optional vegetable substitutions:
    spinach, peas, leeks, eggplant, pumpkin,
    mushrooms, fennel, Jerusalem artichokes,
    swiss chard, lima beans

This description is more a method than an exact recipe. The amounts given will serve four to six generously. My own constants are beans, cabbage, potatoes, pasta and cheese. Everything else depends on what is in my vegetable bin or looks good at the store.

Look the dried beans over carefully, discarding any foreign matter or odd-looking beans. Rinse them well, put them in your soup pot, cover them with three times their depth in water and bring them to a simmer. The cooking time for dried beans varies, depending on how long ago they were dried, but after 1½ to 2 hours they should be starting to soften.

If you choose to add meat, blanch the salt pork or bacon for 10 minutes in boiling water to reduce saltiness. Drain, discard the water and slice the meat into small pieces. Slice the sausage into ⅜-inch slices. Stirring from time to time, cook the meat over a medium low heat until the fat begins to run. Add the onion and cabbage and cook until they wilt. Mix the contents of this pan into the beans. If there seems to be a lot of fat, use a slotted spoon to remove the solid bits, leaving most of the fat behind.

If you are not using meat, add the onion and cabbage directly to the beans in the soup pot. If necessary, add more water to cover everything.

After 20 minutes add the garlic, turnip, potato, peppers, tomatoes or tomato paste, and salt and pepper to taste.

After 20 more minutes, or when the turnip and potato begin to soften, add the green beans, zucchini, pasta and parsley. When the pasta is done serve the soup, passing grated cheese separately. If you have some leftover pesto, stir in a tablespoon or two just before serving.

Cooking Fresh Vegetables the Classic Way

The Independent
May 10, 1985

THE EXACT NATURE of my summer culinary advice has been determined by two events. The first is that I have moved, and most of my cookbook collection is still in boxes. Foreseeing this, I didn't pack the cookbooks I couldn't live without. These turned out to be the old reliables, the books I learned from and loved 18 years ago when I had my first kitchen — including Elizabeth David's *French Provincial Cooking* and a collection of recipes from engagement calendars, *The Flavour of France in Recipes and Pictures,* compiled by Narcissa G. Chamberlain and Narcisse Chamberlain with photographs by Samuel Chamberlain. It has been a pleasure rediscovering recipes, especially the classic French ways with vegetables.

The second event is beyond my control. It is, after all, vegetable season. Many fresh vegetables are at their best in the late spring and early summer as the new growing season gets underway. Some, like carrots, potatoes and spinach, are available nearly year 'round but are younger and more tender and flavorful at this time of year.

What follows are tips for selecting the choice specimens and some simple, classic recipes for presenting them at their best.

♦ Choose vegetables of the same size so that they will cook in the same amount of time.

♦ Select firm, undamaged, fresh-looking vegetables. Avoid dried-up or discolored ones. The spray attachment in many supermarket vegetable sections keeps them fresh longer but can also disguise less than perfect vegetables if you don't look closely.

♦ Shop where vegetables are loose and you can select just the ones you want in the numbers you will use.

♦ Buy amounts you will use before they go stale. Plan to use those that lose their flavor fastest, first. Peas, asparagus and beans lose flavor quickly; use them within a day. Spinach will keep for a couple of days, if necessary; carrots, potatoes and turnips, longer.

♦ Experiment with the fresh herbs that are widely available, but don't overlook parsley just because it is common. Finely chopped parsley sprinkled on at the last minute gives a flavorful shot of color and is a good source of vitamin A. Tarragon, coriander, mint, chervil or a very small amount of rosemary are also delicious as a garnish with simply cooked and buttered spring vegetables.

Buttered New Potatoes

2 to 3 new potatoes per person
$\frac{1}{2}$ tablespoon butter per person
parsley, finely chopped

This is one of those very simple dishes that is spectacular when right. It's important to choose potatoes all of one size; you want to cook them whole and you don't want any over- or under-cooked ones.

Scrub the potatoes carefully with a brush, under running water. Cut away any parts you wouldn't want to eat; there won't be many since you looked them over carefully in the store.

Cover with water and simmer until tender all the way through, 15 to 30 minutes. If they are small potatoes, start checking after 12 minutes.

When they are done, drain them and return them to the pan with the butter and parsley. Shake until the butter is melted and well distributed. They may be kept warm, covered over the lowest possible heat for about 15 minutes. Serve with extra butter and salt and pepper.

Asparagus & Shrimp Salad

We're at the end of the peak asparagus season. If you've already had plenty of the plain buttered variety, here's a recipe you might also want to try. Look for asparagus with a good color and tight tips.

1 pound asparagus
¾ pound shrimp
¼ cup mayonnaise
finely chopped fresh parsley

Snap off the hard parts of the asparagus stems and clean the spears under running water. Steam or simmer until just done (10 to 18 minutes depending on the size and age of the vegetable). Set aside the eight best-looking stalks; cut the rest into one-inch pieces.

Cook the shrimp in boiling water until done, about five minutes. The shells will turn pink and the flesh opaque. Shell and devein the shrimp.

Thin the mayonnaise with a little water or lemon juice to the consistency of heavy cream and toss the asparagus pieces, the shrimp and the mayonnaise together. Serve, decorated with the whole asparagus spears and sprinkled with parsley. Serves four as a first course or two as a main course.

Sautéed Carrots & Potatoes

1 pound new or boiling potatoes
¼ pound carrots
2 shallots
salt and pepper
4 tablespoons butter
finely chopped parsley

Peel the potatoes and scrape the carrots. Cook them separately in boiling water until two-thirds done — just starting to get tender in the middle when you test with a skewer but still firm.

Cut the potatoes into three-quarter-inch squares and the carrots into thick strips about an inch long. Mix both with finely chopped shallots and sprinkle with salt and pepper. Sauté them in the butter starting out with a high heat, turning them often. When they start to get crisp on the outside, turn the heat down a bit and turn them less often. When they are crisp on the outside and tender on the inside they are done. Sprinkle with parsley and serve. This recipe is adapted from Elizabeth David's *French Provincial Cooking* and is one of my favorite vegetable dishes. It goes with almost any meat dish and is delicious on its own. Serves four.

Green Peas

2 pounds of peas in the pod
½ cup water
4 lettuce leaves
1 small sliced onion
2 tablespoons butter
sprig of parsley
thyme (optional)
salt and pepper

Shell the peas. I know it's work, but how else are you going to get fresh peas? Two pounds of plump pea pods should provide servings for four people unless they are very fond of fresh peas.

Put everything in a sauce pan. If you choose to add thyme, you want merely the barest hint. Simmer briskly, uncovered, until the peas are "melting." This will take about 20 minutes for young ones and up to 45 minutes for older ones. If they are done before the rest of the meal, you can stop cooking and reheat them just before serving.

Carrots Vichy

1 pound carrots
2 tablespoons butter
pinch of sugar (optional)
salt and pepper
about ¾ cup of water
finely chopped fresh parsley, mint or tarragon

Scrape the carrots and cut them into finger-sized pieces a couple of inches long if they are bigger than that. Put everything but the chopped herb of your choice into a saucepan. Bring to a boil and cook, uncovered, at a brisk simmer, for about 15 minutes, when the carrots should be tender and the water nearly gone. Add a little more butter or a tablespoon of cream and the herb and shake over low heat until the butter is melted.

The authentic version is made with Vichy water, a bottled water from France which is naturally carbonated. Some cooks add a pinch of bicarbonate of soda but this is not necessary.

Buttered Spinach

2 pounds fresh spinach
salt and pepper
2 tablespoons butter

Wash the spinach well. If it is gritty, you may need to swirl it around in a bowl of water. Drain and remove the stems. If you tear them away from the leaf, any tough ribs will come away as well.

Cook in a large pan starting out over medium to medium high heat. There should be enough water clinging to the spinach for the cooking. It will "melt" on contact with the heated bottom of the pan so stir it around until it has all collapsed, then turn down the heat and cover the pan. Simmer for five to 10 minutes. Start tasting after five minutes and stop cooking when you think it tastes done. Drain away any water and add the butter and salt and pepper. Stir around over very low heat until the butter is absorbed. Two tablespoons is just a starting suggestion; I usually use twice as much. Serves four.

Having left behind her treasured but tiny kitchen of eight years, H. Hudson Whiting is trying to figure out how to use four times the space in her new Durham home.

Thought for Food:
Two Books That Urge Us to Trust and Please Our Senses

The Independent
October 25, 1985

I EAGERLY AWAITED THE PUBLICATION of Elizabeth David's *An Omelette and a Glass of Wine* and *Bill Neal's Southern Cooking* because each author has given me a good deal of pleasure at the table. With Elizabeth David the pleasure was mostly at my own table; when I set up house and began cooking on a daily basis, her *French Provincial Cooking* was the first cookbook that really inspired me. I enjoyed following the recipes only a little more than I enjoyed reading her lovely prose. I first encountered Bill Neal's imaginative cooking at Restaurant La Residence years ago when it was at Fearrington in Chatham County. I have been interested ever since, following him to Chapel Hill and Crook's Corner, where I have eaten some of my favorite Triangle restaurant meals.

The two books are very different in scope. David's covers a wide range of topics, while Neal's is very specific as to time and place. However, there are very strong elements common to both books: a love of good food and a desire to place it in a meaningful context.

Avoiding Complication and Degradation

Elizabeth David has been a primary inspiration to the wave of interest in good cooking now flourishing in England. But the number of good American food writers who cite her influences, dedicate their books to her or mention her books in their bibliographies provides evidence that the inspiration has traveled across the Atlantic. Perhaps you have not heard of her, but I'll bet you have enjoyed food that owes something to her efforts.

An Omelette and a Glass of Wine is a collection of essays, book reviews and profiles of the famous and not-so-famous in the world of food. (Most of the pieces were published in English periodicals between 1949 and 1979.) David turns her discerning eye to topics both particular and general. She considers individual foods: whiskey in the kitchen, Bramley apples, the differences between Dutch, Welsh and Norman mussels, to mention a few. She examines the customs of the table, encouraging those of which she approves, like drinking sweet wines with the sweet course, and discouraging others, like the presumption of many waiters that "ladies" really want half rather than full bottles of wine when dining out.

She considers the movement of recipes in and out of fashion and from country to country. She is amused to find that the pissaladiere of the south of France has become known these days as pizza. These details are fascinating, and her sense of history can be illuminating, For instance, she points out that there was not some "golden age" of good cooking in the distant past. The culinary art is not declining daily.

The common thread running through the essays is the thoughtful consideration of good food, especially the "primitive and simple," coupled with advice on how to avoid "complicating, altering, travestying and degrading" it. She quotes Norman Douglas to reinforce advice on indulging oneself: "To be miserly towards your friends is not pretty; to be miserly toward yourself is contemptible."

Elizabeth David has been accused of evoking a mythic past of culinary perfection. This is misreading her because what she really does is elucidate standards for food and eating that can be applied here and today, wherever here is and whenever today is. She urges us to reject the inferior, to pay attention to what is set before us and to trust our own senses. We are not being urged to travel to a particular location to eat a particular meal that she once enjoyed, but to recognize and enjoy those wonderful moments of our own and to create a few of them at our own table.

The Interplay of Custom and Cuisine

Bill Neal's *Southern Cooking* is, as its title announces, a personal Southern cookbook, not an encyclopedia of Southern cooking or a collection of recipes from Crook's Corner Restaurant. The 117 useful recipes are grounded in history as filtered through his own heritage.

Bill Neal says he didn't have a particular a audience in mind when he wrote his *Southern Cooking* though he recognized there would be a market for a Southern cookbook because of the trendy interest in American regional cooking. He wrote mainly to please himself and to keep specific recipes from this unique cuisine from being lost. He feels that "things done honestly will find their own market."

Neal defines Southern cooking as a "confluence of cultures — Western European, African and Native American." This confluence took place between 1607 and 1860 when these cultures "accepted and modified each other's agricultural, dietary and social customs and molded them into a distinct regional cuisine." He believes the collapse of the economy after the Civil War killed the cuisine and that thereafter technology became "the major force," replacing "the interplay of culture and custom."

Each chapter clearly takes its place in the book's scheme; each recipe has further information about the dish or a particular ingredient. And it's an interesting collection of recipes, ranging from the simple and homely Dog Bread to the elegant Sweet Potato and Pear Souffle.

He admits that the choice of recipes was governed to an extent by the availability of ingredients (though he couldn't resist including a recipe for Possum with Sweet Potatoes.) He would have liked to have had more game recipes (turtle and dove, for example) and some with mulberries if these were more readily available.

Neal develops a recipe by gathering all the versions he can find from various sources: old cookbooks, manuscripts and directly from good cooks. He says you can often tell if a recipe is going to be any good by reading the list of ingredients. He often finds the explanation of technique is the least useful part of a recipe. Once he has decided on the likely essential elements of a recipe he goes into the kitchen and tries them out. When he's happy with the results, he records exactly how he got them.

Neal is especially good at recognizing and communicating the details that make all the difference to a dish: using a sharp, clean biscuit cutter without twisting your wrist so that you don't seal the edges of the biscuit and hamper its rise. He includes six anchovies in his venison stew — a little trick that the French often use in their stews. Very few people recognize anchovies as the secret ingredient but most do notice the subtle enrichment that they provide.

His recipe for fried chicken starts with a consideration of the chicken itself: whole and fresh. Then he describes dismembering it into appro-

Thought for Food

priate pieces and follows with the selection of the proper pan (cast iron) and instructions on where to buy it and how to care for it. The recipe itself provides clear instructions for producing Southern fried chicken.

Though he has a national reputation and could probably have published with any of several publishers with extensive cookbook lists, he's very pleased with his association with the University of North Carolina Press. They gave him the freedom to write the cookbook he wanted, and he knew he wouldn't be directed by some market research report as to what to include. He felt confident the press would produce a handsome volume — good printing, heavy paper, good binding and good design. It's a bonus that it's a local press — he knows the people there and sees them as friends. Being a university press they were very sympathetic to his scholarly aims.

Neal believes that "a family is defined by its meals," and wanted to record the cuisine of his heritage in its historical context. At the same time — rather than a dry discourse featuring facsimile recipes — he wanted to write a cookbook that would be useful to cooks today. He has fulfilled his aims remarkably well in this beautiful, well-written book.

H. Hudson Whiting especially enjoys cooking from the South — south of France, south of Italy, south of India, south of the border and the Southern states of the U.S.

Last Minute Gifts from the Kitchen

The Independent
December 20, 1985

Here is a selection of last-minute food gifts that are all very easy and take little preparation time. If you have children, they can help make or package them. The selection ranges from lemon-flavored vodka for vodka martini drinkers to a Dundee cake for fans of English-style afternoon tea.

You can find many other great gift ideas in *Gifts of Food* by Susan Costner and *Better Than Store Bought* by Helen Whitty and Elizabeth Schneider Colchie, available at local libraries and bookstores.

Lemon Vodka

1 lemon for each quart of vodka

This is very simple to make. With a very sharp paring knife or swivel peeler, peel a lemon. What you want is a long attractive piece of the yellow part of the peel — not the bitter white pith. Pour vodka into a pretty bottle, drop in the peel and let it steep for a week to impart a citrus flavor and a pale yellow color.

Hot Fudge Sauce

6 tablespoons unsalted butter
6 ounces (squares) unsweetened chocolate
1 cup boiling water
1 cup sugar
⅓ cup light corn syrup
2 teaspoons vanilla extract

This is a delicious bittersweet sauce that hardens slightly on contact with ice cream.

Melt the butter and chocolate completely over a very low heat. Stir to blend well. Add the boiling water, sugar and corn syrup and stir until these ingredients are well blended.

Bring to a boil and boil for 8-10 minutes without stirring. The sauce will be thick and smooth. Remove from the heat and stir in the vanilla. You may add a teaspoon or two of a more spirited seasoning at this point: brandy, bourbon, Cointreau, etc.

Pour into sterilized jars with tight-fitting lids. This makes 1½ cups of sauce — enough for three half-pint jars.

Include serving instructions: Set the opened jar into barely simmering water and stir from time to time until the sauce is warm.

Dundee Cake

1 cup currants
⅔ cup sultanas (golden raisins)
⅔ cup raisins
½ cup halved glacé cherries
1 cup flour
1 cup ground almonds
1 cup almonds
pinch of salt
1½ sticks butter
1 cup brown sugar
3 large eggs
1 tablespoon whiskey
12 blanched almonds

This is an English tea cake, lighter than a traditional fruitcake. The ground nuts and dried fruits mean that it will keep well. The recipe is adapted from Carolina Conran's beautiful new cookbook, *English Country Cooking at Its Best*.

Preheat the oven to 325°F. Butter and flour a 7-inch diameter, deep-cake pan, or a 4 x 8-inch loaf pan.

Toss the currants, sultanas, raisins and cherries in three tablespoons of the flour. Mix the rest of the flour, the almonds and salt together in a large bowl. You can grind blanched (skinned) almonds in a food processor but be careful that you don't end up with almond butter instead of ground almonds.

Thoroughly cream the butter and brown sugar together. Add the eggs and beat well. Add the flour and almond mixture and gently stir until well mixed. Mix in the whiskey and fold in the floured fruits. Pour into the prepared baking tin, decorate the top with a ring of whole almonds and bake for one-and-a-half hours or until a skewer comes out clean after being poked into the middle. If you are using a rectangular loaf pan, test after an hour and 15 minutes. You could bake this in two smaller loaf pans and start checking for doneness after an hour. If the top is in danger of getting too brown, cover loosely with a sheet of foil.

Ginger Preserved in Sherry

fresh ginger root
dry sherry

I've used this method of preserving ginger for years. While not as hot as fresh ginger, it is infinitely preferable to the dried-up bits of ginger that I find lurking in the bottom of my refrigerator when I'm gathering ingredients for a Chinese recipe. Ginger-flavored sherry is a delightful bonus.

Peel the ginger root and slice thinly (⅛ to ¼-inch thick). A food processor is a big help when preparing large quantities. Pack into sterilized jars and cover with sherry. Cover tightly. Ginger in sherry will keep for months.

Bill Neal's Creole Mustard

½ cup white wine vinegar
4 tablespoons of water
4 tablespoons vegetable oil
⅛ teaspoon celery seed
¼ teaspoon ground white pepper
4 whole cloves
2 cloves garlic, sliced
¼ teaspoon salt
½ teaspoon sugar
½ cup whole mustard seed
¼ cup ground mustard

This is a brash, chunky mustard and comes from *Bill Neal's Southern Cooking*. [*Reprinted by permission from University of North Carolina Press. — ed.*]

Combine the vinegar, water, oil, celery seed, white pepper, cloves, garlic, salt and sugar in a saucepan. Cover tightly and bring to a boil. Remove from the heat and let the seasonings steep in the vinegar for 30 minutes. Strain the liquid and discard the solids.

Put the whole mustard and ground mustard into your blender or food processor; activate the blades for one minute. Slowly pour in the liquid and process as long as desired (but the mustard should be "pebbly"). If it seems too dry, add more vinegar.

I filled three spice jars with the amount of mustard produced by this recipe.

Horseradish Mustard

½ cup dry mustard
½ cup hot tap water
½ cup white wine vinegar
1 teaspoon salt
1 tablespoon bottled horseradish
1 clove garlic, peeled and sliced
1 teaspoon sugar
6 black peppercorns, crushed
2 allspice berries, crushed

This is a smooth, creamy and very hot mustard is an adaptation from *Better Than Store Bought*.

Mix the dry mustard and hot water and let them stand for 20 minutes, stirring once or twice.

Combine the vinegar, salt, horseradish, garlic, sugar, pepper and allspice in a blender or food processor. Process until the garlic and horseradish are completely pureed. Strain through a fine strainer and press all the juice you can from the pulp.

In the top of a double-boiler placed over simmering water, combine the juice with the mustard-water mixture. Cook, stirring constantly, for about five minutes, or until the mixture thickens.

Cool and taste. It thickens as cools. Add a little more horseradish if you like. Thin with dry white wine or more vinegar if it seems too thick. This amount also filled three spice jars.

Other Ideas

And finally, here are several other quick ideas for holiday gifts from the kitchen:

♦ Tie up the dry ingredients for your favorite cider or wine mulling recipe in cheese cloth squares and give with a copy of the mulling instructions.

♦ Mix butter, brown sugar, cinnamon, allspice, nutmeg and pack into jars with tight fitting lids. This is suitable as a base for hot buttered rum.

♦ Bake several small loaves of a special bread — cinnamon raisin for instance.

♦ One of the nicest gifts I got last year was a bottle of exotic vinegar and really good olive oil. For weeks afterward at salad time, I thought of those gift-givers.

Ideas for Those Other Holiday Meals

The Independent
December 20, 1985

IF YOU ARE ANTICIPATING a houseful of people for the holidays, you probably have the festive meal all planned to satisfy everyone's craving for traditional favorite recipes. But what about the other meals — the night guests arrive from out of town, or a couple days after the big event when everybody wants something simple?

There are many good possibilities: your favorite vegetable soup (so full of vegetables that it approaches a stew); a thick spaghetti sauce that can be turned into a meal almost as quickly as you can boil water; or, taking a tip from the fast food joints, a big baked potato with a substantial topping. (My current favorite is pimiento cheese: grated cheddar and parmesan cheeses mixed with chopped pimientos and bound together with mayonnaise, then spooned into a baked potato and broiled until it bubbles.)

Mo Ferrell remembers —

In the fall of 1998, the leaves and the weather had turned and my thoughts were aching to crawl out of our typical Thanksgiving menu rut. Thanksgiving holiday has always been a bit of a vegetarian challenge for me. Every year we try to make something new and interesting, but can't seem to forsake the mashed potatoes, gravy and sweet potatoes with pineapple and marshmallows. Helen rescued the family or I should say she rescued our sweet potatoes with a wonderful recipe using toasted pecans. I'm forever grateful.

A one-pot meal — preferably a recipe that can be made ahead of time and will reheat well — is a good solution to staggered arrivals and will leave you plenty of time to catch up on the news. Chili is the perfect holiday dish — warming, substantial and even better the second day. *(See page 79 for Helen's recipe.)* Serve with cornbread or a good fresh bakery loaf and a salad. Beer and cider are good beverage choices.

The Potato and Cheese Supper recipe below is a suggestion for later on in the holidays. It is a simple and comforting contrast to fancy meals and can be a main dish or accompany leftovers.

Potato & Cheese Supper

2 pounds of potatoes
½ pound cheddar cheese, coarsely grated
butter
salt and freshly ground pepper
⅔ cup milk
1 bay leaf
2 or 3 slices onion

Preheat the oven to 350°F. Butter a 10-inch, oval, ovenproof dish. Peel the potatoes and slice them thinly. Cover the bottom with a layer of potatoes, season with salt and pepper and cover with cheese. Repeat these layers until you can use all the ingredients (four layers or so, depending on the size of your baking dish). Cover the dish and bake for 30 minutes.

Meanwhile, heat the milk with the bay leaf and onion. Keep warm to let the flavors infuse into the milk. After 30 minutes remove the potatoes from the oven and strain the milk over them. Bake, uncovered, for 30 to 40 minutes, until the potatoes are cooked and the milk is absorbed.

Serves four. This recipe is adapted from *English Country Cooking,* by Carolina Conran.

Tailgates and Artichoke Hearts: Easier and More Elegant Picnicking

The Independent
September 12, 1986

I WAS QUITE SURPRISED RECENTLY when a friend who had never shown much interest in college football announced that his family had purchased Duke season tickets this year. Then further conversation revealed that this family thinks watching football is a pleasant way to spend some time after the main fall event — the tailgate picnic.

In fact, tailgating doesn't require any football game at all. The main thing you need is a car and, perhaps, an appreciation for picnicking on an elaborate scale. Because you can eat soon after you leave home, and there's no hiking or bicycling involved, you don't have to be concerned about the weight or perishability of your meal. I always admire the more elegant picnickers, their tailgates set with silver candelabra, chafing dishes, flowers and real china. One drawback to this sort of elegance is that everything must be packed and washed up later on. And if that doesn't appeal to you there are plenty of simpler options.

Below are some tips and recipes so you can make your next tailgate party — or any picnic — either easier, more elegant, or just more tasty. For the more ambitious, there are two sample menus and recipes for everything from cold fried rabbit to raspberry tarts.

In all cases, the principles of sensible picnicking are best followed. If you decide on disposable plates, get good heavy ones that won't wilt under the food you plan to serve. When they are necessary, buy plastic knives and forks that won't make you feel like you stumbled into a doll's tea party. Take along wet washcloths and hand towels so everyone can clean up after the meal. If you're planning a hot dish, use a heat source that won't leave you trying to figure out what to do with a bunch of hot coals before you can drive home.

Making a list will help you avoid the frustration of forgetting indispensable items like a corkscrew, bottle opener, can opener, serving utensils, cream and sugar that might be essential to your menu. There are ways of improvising but I, for one, have never been able to open beer bottles using any part of my car.*

You'll be less likely to be in a rush and overlook something if you plan a meal that can be prepared in advance and packed up the day of the event. You want a menu that is pleasing and can be eaten with a minimum of fuss under the prevailing conditions. This means that, if you are going to be eating standing up or using your lap as a table, you want to avoid foods that need cutting or are swimming in sauce. Garnishes are fine — grated cheese or finely chopped herbs can be packed in little plastic bags for freshness and sprinkled on at the time of serving. But things will flow more smoothly if you forget dishes that require elaborate last-minute assemblies.

For tailgaters and more ambitious picnickers, my friend Jeff Ensminger of A Wandering Feast Catering recommended two menus and provided several recipes from these menus. For cool weather, he suggested: Bloody Marys to start, followed by hot Pumpkin Soup, Cold Fried Rabbit with

*This column was written before the widespread popularity of twist-off bottle caps. — ed.

champagne mustard, potato salad, apple turnovers with cheddar cheese (baked in or on the turnovers), oatmeal cookies and mulled cider. And, for warm weather: pizza napolean (cold pizza with gorgonzola cheese, prosciutto ham, olives, basil, thyme and pesto); Artichokes Provençal; calamata olives; Raspberry Tarts with Pine Nut Cream Filling, and Chianti Classico.

Here are the recipes:

Pumpkin Soup

> ¼ to ½ pound bacon
> 4 tablespoons butter
> 6 to 8 cups pumpkin, peeled
>   and cut into chunks
> 6 cups beef stock
> ½ cup marsala
> 1 teaspoon thyme
> salt and pepper

Cook the bacon until crisp. Remove from the pan. Add the butter to the bacon fat and when it has melted, add the pieces of pumpkin. Stir these around and cook over medium heat until they start to get tender. Drain away some of the fat if there seems to be an excessive amount and add the marsala, thyme and salt and pepper to taste.

Add the broth, bring to a boil and then turn down the heat to simmer the soup until the pumpkin is cooked. Puree the soup in a blender or food processor until smooth. Return the soup to the pan and crumble in the reserved bacon. Bring back to a simmer, taste and make any adjustments that might be necessary. If it's too thick, add liquid; if too thin, reduce over high heat.

Pour into a thermos that you have already warmed with hot water. Toasted pumpkin seeds make a nice garnish sprinkled into the cups just before serving.

This soup is designed to be drunk from cups so spoons won't be necessary. The recipe serves four.

Cold Fried Rabbit

> 1 rabbit, cut into 8 pieces
> 3 eggs
> ½ cup champagne mustard
> 2 cups unbleached all-purpose flour
> salt and pepper
> paprika
> 4 tablespoons butter
> ¼ cup vegetable oil

Rinse the rabbit and dry it thoroughly. Beat the eggs with the mustard and put in the pieces of rabbit, turning them around in the mixture until all are thoroughly coated.

Mix the flour with two teaspoons of salt, lots of freshly ground pepper and a big pinch or two of paprika.

Heat the butter and oil over medium high heat in a large skillet. When it gets hot but before it starts to smoke, dip each piece of rabbit in the flour mixture, making sure it is completely coated, and put it into the hot fat. Turn the pieces to lightly brown them and then lower the heat to low. Cover the pan and cook until done, about 30 minutes. Turn the pieces once or twice so they brown and cook evenly.

You can use this technique with other fancy mustards and cook duck or chicken the same way. Delicious hot or cold. Serves four.

Artichokes Provençal

> 2 cans artichokes (or frozen artichokes
>   or 6 fresh artichokes)
> 3 leeks
> ¼ cup olive oil
> 4 to 5 garlic cloves, peeled and crushed

salt and pepper
½ cup dry white wine
juice of ½ lemon
3 tomatoes
¼ pound mild, soft chevre cheese (optional)

Drain the canned artichokes, rinse them and drain again. If you use frozen artichokes, cook them according to the package directions. If you opt for fresh artichokes, follow a recipe to prepare cooked artichoke hearts. Quarter the artichokes.

Trim away the roots and any dried parts of the leeks and chop coarsely. Put into a colander and rinse thoroughly to remove all traces of sand. Heat the olive oil in a skillet and soften the leeks over medium heat. Clean and quarter the mushrooms. Add them to the leeks and cook until they are tender.

Add the garlic, salt and pepper, wine, and lemon juice. Cook until everything has reduced a bit. Remove from the heat and taste for seasonings.

Meanwhile, scald the tomatoes, peel, seed and chop them roughly into small pieces. If you can't find good ripe tomatoes in the stores, use a can of good quality tomatoes.

Add the artichokes, tomatoes and crumbled cheese to the leek and mushroom mixture. Toss until well mixed but be gentle so the cheese stays in discrete pieces. Chill. Serves four to six.

Raspberry Tarts with Pine Nut Cream Filling

short crust pastry (see page 156)
2 to 3 cups fresh or frozen raspberries
jar of apricot jam
kirsch or other liqueur

FILLING:
¾ to 1 cup pine nuts
8 tablespoons (1 stick)butter, softened
½ cup sugar
3 eggs
½ cup unbleached all-purpose flour

Make the filling: chop the nuts finely in a blender or food processor. Add all the other ingredients and blend until smooth.

Make a short crust pastry and fill your tart tin or tins as usual. Bake the pastry "blind" (cover with aluminum foil, then cover the foil with beans to weigh it down) at 425°F for 10 to 15 minutes. Remove the foil and beans, spread the pine nut mixture evenly on the pastry and bake at 375°F for 15 to 20 minutes, until the filling is set.

Heat one jar of apricot jam with a half-cup of water and a tablespoon or so of the kirsch or other liqueur until it is well mixed. Take it off the heat and mix in 2 to 3 cups of fresh or frozen raspberries. Drain frozen berries thoroughly before using them. Spread the berry mixture on top of the cream filling and chill before serving.

Remember that whether you cook up your own raspberry tarts and rabbit, or contract with a caterer, or decide to raid your local gourmet food stores, this is the South, and we have certain standards of hospitality and picnicking to uphold. If you're not sure what I mean by this, go early to a football game this fall and wander around and check out what's being served up on all the various tailgates.

H. Hudson Whiting lives in Durham and is glad that her newish hatchback automobile opens up to a flat surface that is suitable for tailgating.

The Incredible Shrinking Dinner Hour

The Independent
April 27, 1989

WHAT'S FOR DINNER? That's a question somebody in the household has to answer every day. Even those of us who find food preparation soothing therapy after a hard day's work, appreciate recipes that promise a good dinner in a short amount of time. And a cookbook that is full of these recipes lifts us out of our usual quick dinner ruts and keeps us off the frozen food aisle is even better.

Marian Burros' new *20 Minute Menus* is such a book. She promises "freshly cooked meals every day," paying attention not only to the clock but also to recent trends in healthy eating. And she does it without a microwave oven; in fact the only special kitchen item she recommends is a food processor.

Burros' practical strategies for the 20-minute cook, advice for cooking more healthfully, information about deciphering food labels, and suggestions for stocking the pantry are probably worth the price of the book alone. My favorite tip is to freeze ginger and then grate what is needed while it's still frozen, thus eliminating limp, stale, useless ginger lurking somewhere in the refrigerator.

Each menu has two to three recipes, a game plan laying out an efficient order for preparing the recipes to ensure that everything will be ready at the same time and a list of what you'll need from the pantry and the store. Most menus serve two; some will serve three. She warns you that you'll need five to 10 minutes more if you multiply the recipes to serve more people.

With *20 Minute Menus* you can sit down before going to work, choose a menu, make a shopping list, stop by the store on your way home and cook an easy, from-scratch dinner when you get there. Best of all — the dinner will be very good. Many of the recipes make use of Chinese, Middle Eastern and Latin American ideas and ingredients. And if you've been looking for ways to use sun-dried tomatoes, you'll love one of her chicken recipes which uses the tomatoes, low-fat ricotta cheese and white wine to make a delicious sauce.

Emalee Chapman knocks five minutes off the schedule in her *Fresh 15-Minute Meals.* Don't mistakenly buy her earlier *Fifteen Minute Meals* because she obviously perfected her technique between the two books, and the newer version is much the better of the two.

The book is organized into standard cookbook chapters — appetizers, soups, one-dish meals, and so on — rather than a menu format, so producing an actual meal might end up taking more than 15 minutes. The recipes are for two, and Chapman warns you they will take longer if you are cooking for more.

Many of my favorite recipes here are from Italy — Turkey Fillets with Marsala, for example — or feature an imaginative use of unusual ingredients, such as Pork Chops with Fennel, and Turnips in Cream.

There is only one real drawback: if you need to reduce your cholesterol level, the book may not be worth your while as there are many recipes calling for heavy cream. But I enthusiastically recommend it to anyone else who is interested in some very easy, very quickly prepared, absolutely delicious food.

To prove that I'm no culinary Luddite, the last book I recommend is *Microwave Diet Cookery* by Marcia Cone and Thelma Snyder. It offers seasonal menus using fresh ingredients that can be prepared in less than 30 minutes. The recipes serve four, with special instructions for one or two because in microwave cooking the number of servings critically affects the timing.

The fish recipes are especially good. Microwaves do a great job of cooking fish (as well as fresh vegetables). The difference in flavor intensity is almost as great between microwaved and steamed as it is between steamed and boiled.

Cone and Snyder offer several dessert recipes based on pureed frozen fruit with yogurt, a little sugar and perhaps a little liqueur for flavoring. This is a terrific idea, and I have substituted just about every fruit or melon available locally. I have had less success with the cooked desserts — notably a grey, rubbery banana custard.

Don't be misled by the title — *Microwave Diet Cookery* — into thinking you need to be on a diet to get good use out of the book. The recipes produce good food that just happens to be low-calorie and will give you some useful ideas on how best to use a microwave.

So if you're bored cooking the same few quick meals over and over again when you're rushed for dinner, or you're spending too much on convenience foods or restaurants, any of these last three books will broaden your repertoire of good fresh fast food and make dinner at home tonight easier and more interesting. You'll have some time and energy left to enjoy the rest of the evening; perhaps by reading one of the early classics in the dinner-in-minutes genre, Edouard de Pomiane's *French Cooking in 10 Minutes,* published in France not

long after World War II. It is so delightful I read it about once a year.

Chicken with Sun-Dried Tomatoes

> 12 ounces of chicken breast, skinless and
> boneless
> 1½ tablespoons olive oil
> 1 large leek
> ¼ cup sun-dried tomatoes, packed in
> olive oil, drained
> ⅔ cup low-fat ricotta
> ¼ cup dry white wine or dry vermouth
> ¼ teaspoon dried oregano
> freshly ground black pepper to taste

Wash and dry chicken and cut each breast half into three pieces. Heat oil in skillet and brown chicken on both sides. Wash leek and slice; chop in food processor. Add leek to chicken and sauté.

Meanwhile, chop tomatoes in processor. Add ricotta and wine and process until mixture is blended. Add to chicken in pan with oregano and pepper to taste. Cook over low heat just until sauce has been heated through. Do not boil.

Turkey Fillets with Marsala

> 2 turkey fillets (about 6 ounces each)
> from the breast
> 2 tablespoons unsalted butter
> 1 teaspoon dried rosemary, or
> 2 teaspoons chopped fresh rosemary
> 2 tablespoons Marsala
> 4 tablespoons white wine or water
> freshly ground black pepper

Flatten the turkey fillets by whacking them several times with the flat side of a chef's knife. Melt butter in a sauté pan over medium heat and add rosemary. When butter foams add turkey fillets. Cook on both sides until golden, about three minutes per side. Add Marsala, and when it is bubbling add white wine. Cook four to five minutes, until tender. Season to taste with pepper, and serve at once.

Peach "Ice Cream"

16-ounce bag frozen peach slices, or 1 pound
    fresh peaches, pitted, sliced and frozen
2 tablespoons sugar
½ cup low-fat plain yogurt
1 tablespoon Amaretto

If the frozen peaches are too firm to puree, place them, still in the bag, in the microwave. Heat on defrost for one minute to defrost slightly; break the pieces apart. Pour the peaches into the bowl of a food processor and chop them into small pieces. Add the remaining ingredients and puree until smooth. Serve immediately or freeze until later.

A Culinary Caper

The Independent
May 18, 1989

THINK ABOUT THE BEST COOKS you know. What is it that elevates one of their meals from the merely good to the very good, even when it's been a spur-of-the-moment, here-we-are, let's-cook-dinner meal? Part of the answer is in the refrigerator or on the shelf in the pantry — little touches that make all the difference to the final appearance and flavor of a dish. Every cook's collection of little touches is unique, but some likely possibilities include fresh parsley and perhaps other herbs, tomato paste in a tube (so it's easy to get a squeeze when that's all that's needed), fresh lemons, fresh garlic, parmesan cheese, anchovies, interesting hot sauces and, just maybe, capers.

Capers are flower buds from a shrub that grows wild around the Mediterranean which are dried, then pickled in vinegar. Italy, Spain and Algeria are all major producers, but the most desirable capers are the smaller ones — non-pareilles from the south of France. You'll find them in better gourmet shops. A few go a long way, with an agreeable flowery sharpness, so they are not quite as extravagant as they might seem.

The recipes presented here are classics. Tapenade (from the Provençal word tapeno, meaning caper) has a powerful, mysterious flavor and makes an interesting dip for raw vegetables. Caponata is Italian; it is good warm or cool as a first course, a side dish or as a pizza topping. The pork chop dish here is the centerpiece of one of my favorite "automatic pilot" meals, and I usually accompany it with boiled new potatoes, fresh bread, and a green salad when I want something good without going to a lot of trouble.

But don't stop with these recipes. Use capers as a garnish whenever you want a little burst of tartness. The French mix a spoonful with mayonnaise, lemon juice, parsley, tarragon and chives to make Sauce Tartare for fish. The Italians mix mayonnaise (thinned with stock), tuna, anchovies, lemon juice and capers to serve over cold sliced veal as the classic Vitello Tonnato. The same sauce is also quite good with cold chicken or turkey breast and makes a welcome change from chicken or tuna salad on a hot summer's evening.

Tapenade II

½ cup black olives, pitted
1 small clove garlic, peeled and finely chopped
4 anchovy fillets
2 tablespoons capers
pinch of dry mustard or ¼ teaspoon
   Dijon mustard (optional)
4 to 6 fresh basil leaves (optional)
1 tablespoon lemon juice
½ teaspoon brandy (optional)
freshly ground black pepper
¼ to ½ cup olive oil

Puree the olives, garlic, anchovy fillets, capers, mustard, basil, lemon juice, brandy and black pepper as completely as you can in a blender, food processor or mortar and pestle.

With the processor, blender or pestle going, add the olive oil very slowly — drop by drop — as if you were making mayonnaise. As the sauce absorbs the oil, you can up the amount to a thin stream. Use the smaller quantity of oil if you are planning to spread the tapenade on toasted bread or stuff small raw tomatoes; use more oil for a dip for raw vegetables (try fennel bulb in addition to more usual choices), to brush on pizza dough or as a pasta sauce.

This makes about ¾ cup of intensely flavored sauce and is enough to mix with the yolks of a dozen hard-boiled eggs for delicious deviled eggs. It will also sauce one pound of hot pasta (serve with freshly grated parmesan). Tapenade will keep for a couple of weeks in the refrigerator without much loss of flavor.

Caponata

1 small eggplant, cubed
¼ cup olive oil
1 medium onion, chopped
1 large red, yellow or green pepper,
   seeded and sliced
1 clove garlic, finely chopped
2 tomatoes, peeled and chopped
1 tablespoon tomato paste
2 tablespoons red wine vinegar
salt and freshly ground pepper
1 tablespoon fresh oregano, finely chopped
   or ½ teaspoon dried oregano
2 anchovy fillets, finely chopped
¼ cup pitted olives, black or green,
   coarsely chopped
2 tablespoons capers

Place the eggplant in a colander, lightly salt it and leave it for 30 minutes to draw out any bitter juices. Rinse lightly and dry with paper towels.

Heat the olive oil in a large skillet over a medium heat. Add the onions; cook and stir until they begin to soften. Add the peppers and when they begin to soften add the eggplant and garlic. Stir occasionally and cook for 15 minutes.

Add the tomatoes, tomato paste, wine vinegar and oregano. Lightly salt and pepper the mixture (you'll correct the seasonings at the end) and let it simmer slowly for 20 to 30 minutes, stirring every once in a while, until the eggplant is completely cooked but not a mush.

Stir in the chopped anchovy fillets and let the mixture cook for five minutes. Now add the olives and capers and remove from the heat. Taste for seasonings and add more salt, pepper or vinegar if desired. Serve hot or cool to four to six as a first course or side dish or use as a pizza topping.

Pork Chops with Mustard & Capers

4 ¾-inch thick pork chops
small pinch of thyme and/or rosemary
salt and freshly ground pepper
1 clove garlic, crushed and peeled
½ to1 cup dry white wine, vermouth,
   hard cider or water
1 tablespoon capers
2 tablespoons parsley, finely chopped

In a large skillet lightly brown the pork chops on each side over a medium high heat. You may need a small amount of oil to keep them from sticking if they are very lean. Sprinkle with thyme, rosemary, salt and pepper.

Add the garlic and enough liquid to almost cover the chops. Bring to a boil, reduce to a simmer, cover loosely and cook for 30 to 45 minutes, until the chops are tender. Turn them a couple of times and add more liquid if necessary.

Remove the chops and keep them warm while you finish the sauce. Remove and discard the garlic. Turn up the heat to a boil and reduce the sauce slightly, stirring and scraping all the while with a wooden spoon. Add the mustard and continue to stir briskly until the sauce comes together. If the mustard threatens to remain in discrete lumps, use a whisk to smooth things out. Stir in the capers, taste for seasoning, reduce the heat and add the chops. Turn them once or twice until they are heated through. Sprinkle with parsley and serve to four.

Beach Eats

The Independent
June 15, 1989

WHEN YOU STEP INTO THE KITCHEN of a rented beach house you never know if you'll find carefully color-coordinated and matched sets of everything or a haphazard collection of just about anything. The only thing you can count on is that there will be no sharp knives.

If you're going for more than just a weekend, make room for a sharp knife and consider just how much more pleasant cooking will be with a cutting board, a blender, an iron skillet or wok and a wire whisk. (Hollandaise sauce can be made with two forks and a lot of nerve, but it's a scary experience.) Better than squeezing your kitchen into the trunk of your car is to share a beach house with a bunch of avid cooks, who will each show up with at least one essential utensil.

I make room for two cookbooks: a standard with a good seafood section so I can take advantage of the freshest fish in the markets, and a second, more exotic and perhaps ethnic — Mexican, Caribbean, Indian or Cajun/Creole.

Take with you any basic ingredients that might not be so basic in a beach supermarket (in 1987 at Emerald Isle, unflavored yogurt apparently was too exotic to be stocked). You might want good soy sauce, fresh ginger or fermented bean paste for Chinese cooking; tahini for Middle Eastern fare; or your favorite salsa to add Latin American flavor.

Once at the beach, look for a fish market right on the water. If the freshest fish on display is one you don't know, ask how best to cook it; it may cook like a fish you do know. A good generic way to cook fish is to place it on oiled aluminum foil, cover with thinly sliced onion, fresh dill and a lump of butter. Fold up the foil, seal it tightly and bake at 350–400°F until the fish flakes easily with a fork and is just done. This will usually take about 10 minutes per inch of thickness of fish. Squeeze on lemon or lime juice and serve.

If you're using a grill and are worried the fish will stick, put a layer of thinly sliced onions on the grill first. Turn the fish only once, gently, using two spatulas.

You forgot to pack the sharp knife? Take the dull one in the drawer and run each side of its edge over the rough bottom of a ceramic bowl or cup a few times. This will achieve some semblance of sharpness.

Here are some recipes I've successfully cooked or helped to cook on recent beach trips. All take advantage of seasonal, coastal ingredients.

Orzo Salad

3 to 4 pounds of shrimp, boiled and peeled
2 pounds orzo (rice-shaped pasta)
1 cup olive oil
¼ cup vinegar
salt and pepper
2 green peppers, cored and thinly sliced
1 cup black olives
1 bunch green onions, thinly sliced
     on the diagonal
sliced tomatoes
fresh parsley, chives or basil, finely chopped

Cook the orzo following the package its directions. The usual directions tell you to pour the orzo into vast quantities of rapidly boiling water and cook until just done (al dente). Drain it immediately.

While the pasta is still warm, toss with the olive oil, the vinegar and the salt and pepper. The aim is to coat the orzo completely, but lightly. You don't want a puddle in the bottom of the bowl. You may need a little more oil if the first cup is completely absorbed.

Toss in the remaining ingredients except the tomatoes and herb garnish. Taste for seasonings and adjust the salt and pepper. More vinegar will sharpen the flavor.

Just before serving, toss again, arrange the sliced tomatoes on top and sprinkle with the finely chopped herb of your choice.

The dish serves 12 and is best cool rather than cold. No orzo? Use rice, cooking it like pasta in plenty of water. Don't overcook it; start testing for doneness after 10 minutes.

E.D. Whiting's Tuna Salad

This dish relies on leftover grilled tuna — and is so good you'll find yourself buying extra fish the next time you're going to grill.

cooked, cooled tuna, skinned and boned
mayonnaise
salt and pepper
lots of parsley, finely chopped

Flake the leftover tuna and mix gently with just enough mayonnaise to coat lightly. Taste and season with salt and pepper (you may not need salt if the mayonnaise is salty) and mix in the parsley. And I mean *lots* of parsley — a large handful for a medium-sized tuna steak.

Stir-Fried Shrimp with Salsa

2½ to 3 pounds of shrimp
¼ cup olive oil
2 cloves of garlic, peeled and smashed
½ can of beer
½ cup salsa
dash of red wine vinegar
salt and pepper
fresh parsley, finely chopped

Use unshelled shrimp for this recipe; it's messy to eat but more flavorful. (Buy shelled shrimp when Miss Manners comes for dinner.) Rinse and drain it.

Use a wok or large sturdy skillet over a high heat. Add the olive oil and garlic and give it a stir. Toss in the shrimp and stir fry until it turns pink. Add the beer and let it boil rapidly until it is nearly gone (a matter of seconds), stirring all the while. Add the salsa and a splash of vinegar and stir until everything amalgamates. Sprinkle with parsley and serve.

Serves six. The flavor of the dish will be greatly influenced by the salsa, so choose one you like.

Carolina Blues

The Independent
June 29, 1989

THE BROCHURE OFFERED THE prospect of 12-foot blueberry bushes that required very little ado. (They don't need rich soil or much cultivating; you just have keep the shallow roots from drying out during drought season.) I sent in an order and started paying attention to every blueberry recipe that passed my way. I imagined a not-too-distant Christmas when I would please friends and relations with homemade blueberry syrups, cordials, jams, chutneys and the like.

This was a couple of years back. Last year, after a late frost reduced the possible yield, enough fruit ripened at once for a small batch of sparsely berried muffins. This year it looks like a 5-inch tart or just maybe an 8-inch pie. I continue to read blueberry recipes but find myself noting only those that require just a few berries at a time.

Luckily it's nearly blueberry season at the local groceries; the price is going down as the quantity — much of which is grown in North Carolina — increases. Every summer I package the rinsed berries in ½- to 1-cup portions (suitable for adding to pancake or muffin batters all winter long) and stick them in the freezer. For those, I choose recipes that call for cooked or pureed berries because the texture isn't as good after freezing.

If there's a choice, smaller berries usually have a more intense flavor. Avoid berries that are crushed, seeping or moldy. When you are ready to use them, pick through carefully, discarding under- or overripe berries, twigs, leaves and other inedible bits, then rinse and drain them.

Blueberries are delicious in fruit salad; "smoothies" — blended mixtures of yogurt, crushed ice and fruit (bananas, strawberries, peaches and/or blueberries); or pancake batter, as well as the following recipes.

Blueberry Shortcake

½ pound (2 cups) unbleached white flour
2 teaspoons baking powder
pinch of salt
6 or more tablespoons sugar
4 tablespoons butter, cut into pieces
5 fluid ounces milk
2 egg yolks, lightly beaten
2 pints blueberries
lemon juice
1 pint whipping cream

Sift together the flour, baking powder, salt and two to four tablespoons of the sugar. Cut in the butter until the mixture resembles coarse meal. Add the milk and egg yolks, stirring until the mixture holds together.

Turn the dough onto a floured board and fold it over on itself four to six times to knead lightly. Roll or pat out into four to six rounds. Bake at 425°F for 12 to 15 minutes or until golden. Meanwhile, taste the berries. Toss with lemon juice and/or sugar if needed. Whip the cream. Add two tablespoons of sugar if you like it sweetened.

Split the warm shortcakes. Spoon two-thirds of the berries or fruit onto the bottom halves; top with a little of the whipped cream. Put on the top halves of the shortcakes and spoon on the rest of the fruit and whipped cream. Serve right away. This makes either four large or six moderate servings. Or, you can make one large shortcake, which will take 15 to 20 minutes in the oven.

The recipe is adapted from *The Robert Carrier Cookbook*. Carrier, born and raised in America,

has lived in Europe (mostly England) since World War II, and this shortcake is a cross between an American biscuit and an English scone. It is also good made with two pints of strawberries or six peeled, pitted and sliced peaches.

Blueberry Sauce

1 pint blueberries
1 tablespoon or more lemon juice
2 to 4 tablespoons sugar

Toss all the ingredients together in a stainless steel or enameled saucepan. Cook over medium high heat, stirring from time to time, until the berries burst and a sauce forms. This takes just a few minutes. If you want a smooth sauce, cook a little longer and puree in a blender or food processor. Taste and adjust the sweetness or tartness to your liking with sugar and lemon juice.

Serve the sauce hot, warm or cool over ice cream, pancakes, crepes, pound cake or anything else you think you might like it on. When I have been planning shortcake and the blueberries seem a little bland, I make a chunky version of this sauce because the flavor is more intense than raw berries. It is simple, delicious and serves four to six.

Fruit Pie Crumb Topping

1 stick unsalted butter
1 cup brown sugar
¾ cup flour
pinch cinnamon (optional)
pinch salt

Melt the butter; remove from the heat and stir in the other ingredients. Using your hand, crumble the topping onto blueberries (or peaches, apples, or pears) in an unbaked pie shell. Bake at 400°F for 30 to 40 minutes, until the crust and the fruit are cooked and the topping is crisp and brown.

James Beard tops one pie with this quantity in his *American Cookery*. I think just the right proportions are achieved by doubling the recipe and topping three pies. But then, I always want some ice cream or whipped cream with my slice of pie, so moderation with the topping makes me feel less extravagant.

Following are two additional blueberry recipes from Helen's card file:

Blueberry Cornmeal Muffins

1½ cups flour
½ cup yellow corn meal
⅓ cup sugar
1 tablespoon baking powder
1 teaspoon baking soda
¼ teaspoon salt
1 cup buttermilk (or milk with vinegar)
3 eggs
4 tablespoons melted butter
1½ cups (½ pint) blueberries

Preheat oven to 425°F. Butter muffin tins. Sift together flour, cornmeal, sugar, baking powder, baking soda and salt.

Whisk together buttermilk, eggs, melted butter. Combine the wet and dry ingredients (15-20 strokes). Stir in berries. Do not overmix.

Fill each cup ½ full. Reduce oven to 400°F and bake 20-25 minutes, until muffins are light golden brown on top.

Lex's Blueberry Buttermilk Pancakes

1½ cups of flour (whatever mixture of all-purpose and whole wheat you prefer)
½ cup yellow corn meal
2 tablespoons sugar
1½ teaspoons baking powder
1½ teaspoons baking soda
½ teaspoon salt
1½ cups blueberries, picked over, rinsed and rolled on a towel to dry
3 eggs
2 cups buttermilk
2 tablespoons unsalted butter, melted
2 tablespoons milk, or as needed

Sift dry ingredients together in a large bowl. Add blueberries and toss gently.

Separate eggs, adding buttermilk, then melted butter to the yolks. Beat in buttermilk, then melted butter. Add to dry ingredients, mixing quickly and lightly until dry ingredients are moistened — do not overmix. Batter should be thick enough to hold berries in place. Beat egg whites until stiff, then fold in. If too thck, thin batter with up to 2 tablespoons milk.

Heat large heavy skillet or griddle over medium heat. Grease lightly with unsalted butter. Using a ¼ cup measure, ladle batter onto hot skillet. Cook slowly until undersides are golden brown, about 3 minutes. Turn pancakes over and cook second side until cooked through and springy when pressed in center — about another 3 minutes. Transfer pancakes to warm platter. Serve immediately with maple syrup and melted butter.

Carolina Blues

Get Fresh with Herbs

The Independent
July 20, 1989

ONE REASON TO LOVE SUMMER is for its profusion of fresh herbs.

Your first taste of a fresh herb will surprise you if you've only known the dried. Basil and tarragon have slightly anise overtones. Coriander has a clean, almost soapy flavor. Some herbs — coriander, chervil and parsley — are so dull when dried that there's no reason to use them.

Don't be timid. Certain Thai dishes are delightful because of lavish use of coriander or basil. And pesto just isn't the same with a hint rather than a handful of basil. When substituting fresh for dried herbs in a recipe, triple the quantity called for. The flavor of fresh herbs is more delicate than of dried ones, which can be musty and overpowering in large quantities.

Break out of your usual patterns. Bring home an herb you don't often use and go wild. Try rosemary with pork, chicken, green beans, tomato sauce, ratatouille, zucchini; or, a sprinkling of chopped lemon thyme on mashed or baked potatoes.

But, don't ignore the usual. Fresh parsley, for instance, can be found in just about every supermarket year 'round and is relatively inexpensive. Finely chopped, it is a great garnish for almost every dish that comes to the table — stews, vegetable dishes, potatoes, salads — and is a good source of vitamin A. Don't listen to those who sneer at the ordinary variety and think the flat leafed Italian parsley is so much better. The raw flavor and crunchy texture of curly leafed parsley is terrific.

Certain herbs paired with certain foods have become classics because these combinations have pleased many palates over time: tarragon and eggs, chives and potatoes, thyme and mushrooms, basil and tomatoes. My favorite is tarragon, especially in béarnaise sauce, and that, especially with lamb.

The explosion of interest in food in recent years is paying dividends for fresh herb shoppers. These days fresh coriander and basil have joined parsley in supermarkets, and some stores offer other fresh herbs much of the year. High prices and fancy packaging are no guarantee of quality. Look carefully before you buy. Avoid brown, dried up or moldy herbs. If you don't like the looks of what's available, ask when fresh supplies will arrive.

The typical selection ranges from three or four fresh herbs to more than a dozen. An opportunistic attitude is necessary — you can't count on getting a particular herb on a particular day in a particular store. Have an alternative in mind.

Pesto alla Genovese

2 cloves of garlic
4 small bunches fresh basil leaves
    (about 2 cups)
pinch of salt
1 tablespoon of toasted pine nuts
6 to 8 tablespoons freshly grated parmesan
    and/or pecorino cheese
½ to 1 cup olive oil

Pound the garlic, basil leaves, salt and pine nuts to a paste in a mortar and pestle or thoroughly puree in a blender or food processor. Add the cheese and continue pounding or pureeing. When this paste is smooth, gradually blend in enough olive oil to make a thick creamy sauce.

This quantity will generously sauce one pound of hot pasta (and if you're being authentically Genovese, a couple of boiled potatoes), which will serve four to six.

If you have any leftover pesto, consider yourself lucky and drizzle it on pizza dough, boiled or baked potatoes, or stir it into soups. It will keep for a couple of days in a lightly closed container in the refrigerator before the flavor fades. Pesto can be frozen but the texture is better if you don't add the cheese until the sauce has thawed.

This recipe for a simple classic pesto is an adaptation from Ada Boni's *Italian Regional Cooking.*

Green Guacamole

> 4 medium tomatillos (Mexican green tomatoes)
> 2 large ripe avocados
> ½ small while onion, minced
> 2 tablespoons fresh coriander (cilantro),
>   very finely chopped
> 1 or 2 green serrano chiles, seeded and
>   very finely chopped
> salt and pepper
> ¼ cup sour cream

Remove the papery outer covering from the tomatillos and rinse them. Put them in a small saucepan with a tablespoon or two of water and simmer for 10 minutes or until soft. Drain and chop them finely and let them cool to room temperature.

Peel and mash the avocados. Mix in the tomatillos, onion, coriander, chiles, salt, pepper and sour cream. Taste and adjust the ingredients. Sometimes you will need a squeeze of lemon juice to sharpen things up. Serve with tortilla chips. Makes about two cups.

This unusual version of guacamole began in Elisabeth Lambert Ortiz's *Complete Book of Mexican*

Cooking, but I'm grateful to David Birkhead for suggesting the sour cream.

Tarragon Cream Sauce

> 1 cup heavy or whipping cream
> 1 or 2 garlic cloves, crushed
> 2 or 3 tablespoons fresh tarragon, finely chopped

Gently simmer the garlic in the cream five to 10 minutes, until the cream has reduced a bit and is well scented with the garlic. Remove the garlic and stir in the tarragon.

Serve with a roasted or steamed chicken into which you have place a sprig or two of tarragon before cooking. For beauty's sake, remove the skin from a steamed chicken and spoon the sauce over it when you serve.

Red, Ripe & Luscious

The Independent
August 24, 1989

THIS IS THE MOMENT TO EAT the tomatoes you'll remember next winter.

In a few months' time, when you are in a restaurant looking down at a faintly pink slab with all the taste of cardboard and wondering why anyone bothered, you can fondly call up the scent and flavor of the tomato that could be in front of you today.

When you're choosing tomatoes, look for firm but ripe or about-to-be ripe ones. Take a sniff — a good tomato smells like a tomato; the stem often smells like basil. Avoid refrigerated ones; tomatoes, like peaches, never really ripen properly after they've been chilled. And a tomato that hasn't ripened properly isn't really a tomato. It doesn't have the scent, the flavor or the texture of the real thing and, to my mind, just isn't worth it.

The simplest way to enjoy a ripe tomato is to slice it, sprinkle it with salt and freshly ground pepper and dribble on some olive oil and a drop or two of red wine vinegar. Finely chopped fresh basil and a couple of good black olives, or sliced fresh mozzarella and chopped oregano are agreeable variations.

Recipes often specify skinned tomatoes. That's easily accomplished with a ripe, room-temperature tomato dipped briefly into boiling water to loosen the skin. You can keep the kitchen cooler by microwaving the tomatoes briefly: 15 to 45 seconds for one tomato, 1 to 2 minutes for four. The time varies depending on the size, ripeness and quantity of tomatoes. No matter which method you use,

when the skin begins to split that's a good indication that it will come off easily with a sharp knife. In many recipes the next step is to remove the seeds, leaving only the pulp.

A food mill easily separates pulp from seeds and skin. Rinse, cut out and discard the cores, and place the tomatoes in a saucepan. Add a little water to keep things from sticking before the juices start to run. Bring to a boil and simmer until the tomatoes are tender. Put them through the medium screen of the food mill. The skins and seeds miraculously stay behind and the pulp goes into the bowl or pan. Reduce it a bit by simmering and stirring, then freeze the pulp in useful quantities (pints, quarts, tablespoons) for the winter. Specialty stores and catalogs sell gadgets which vaguely resemble old-fashioned meat grinders that also separate the pulp from the skin and seeds, but a food mill has so many other uses (the best mashed potatoes in the world, for instance) that you might consider acquiring one.

Here are some recipes that are especially good with real, fresh, ripe tomatoes. Enjoy them now. The season is almost over and even when ripe, the cherry tomatoes which are available year 'round are not quite the same thing.

Gratin of Sliced Tomatoes

1½ pounds firm ripe tomatoes, peeled and sliced
softened butter
6 teaspoons dry sherry
fresh basil, chopped
salt and pepper
12 tablespoons heavy cream
6 heaped tablespoons grated cheddar
parsley, chopped

Divide the tomatoes between six buttered gratin dishes. Dribble a teaspoon of sherry over each. Scatter on the chopped basil and sprinkle with salt and pepper. Bake for 30 minutes at 300°F.

Remove from the oven and pour two table-spoons of cream over each dish and sprinkle cheese on top. Bake for 15 minutes longer and sprinkle with parsley before serving.

Serves six. You may bake it in one large shallow ovenproof dish. This dish is one of the few that is nearly as good in the winter with ripe cherry tomatoes.

Uncooked Tomato Sauce

> **2 medium tomatoes**
> **½ clove garlic**
> **6 to 10 basil leaves**
> **salt and pepper**
> **onion**

Don't bother with this dish unless you have really good, absolutely ripe tomatoes. Peel and seed them and chop them finely with garlic and basil. Season to taste with salt and pepper. Let the flavors mingle while you cook up some pasta. Toss the cooked pasta with the sauce and serve with a slight sprinkling of freshly grated parmesan.

The quantity of each ingredient is variable, but for a hearty serving for one, two medium tomatoes, one-half clove of garlic, six to 10 big basil leaves and a pinch of salt and pepper will sauce four ounces of uncooked pasta (after it's cooked). You can add a bit of onion and use parsley or chives instead of basil. If you use a food processor or blender to chop things up, stop before the puree is completely homogeneous.

Cheese & Tomato Tart

> **pizza dough**
> **Gruyère or comte cheese, sliced**
> **tomatoes, peeled and sliced thickly**
> **salt and pepper**

Pizza dough is available in local stores either partially baked (which is very breadlike) or in the dairy case (Pillsbury's is pretty good right out of the oven, not so good the next day). If you make your own pizza dough, double or triple the recipe and freeze leftovers in one-pan quantities after the first rising. When you're ready for pizza, let it thaw on top of the stove while the oven preheats and you assemble other ingredients.

Cover the dough with the sliced cheese. Arrange the tomato slices on the cheese, leaving space between each. Sprinkle with salt and pepper.

Cook in a 450°F oven for 15 to 30 minutes, until the dough is cooked. Serve hot. A little thyme, basil, or freshly grated parmesan sprinkled on the top before baking is fine but not necessary.

Tomatoes with Horseradish Sauce

> **4 tomatoes**
> **4 tablespoons whipped cream**
> **1 tablespoon vinegar**
> **3 tablespoons horseradish**
> **salt**
> **cayenne pepper**

Gently combine the whipped cream, vinegar and horseradish. Season to taste with salt and a pinch of cayenne pepper. Spoon over skinned, sliced, ripe tomatoes and serve.

This sauce is equally good with roast beef and is adapted from *The Gentle Art of Cookery* by Mrs. C.F. Leyel and Miss Olga Hartley, originally published in 1925.

Shortcrust Pastry

The Independent
September 14, 1989

IN THE FALL MY CULINARY FANCY turns to thoughts of the warmth and aroma of pies baking in the oven. With this in mind here's the first installment of a mini-series on pastry-making — the foundation of a good pie. First, I'll focus on shortcrust pastry, and in the future I'll offer directions for a couple of unusual crusts as well as some recipes and suggestions for filling them.

It takes longer to explain the hows and whys of making good shortcrust pastry than to actually do it. The goal is to produce a crisp and flavorful container for sweet or savory fillings. There are several important considerations along the way.

+ *The protein content of the flour.* High gluten or bread flour is suitable for yeast-raised baked goods because as you knead, gluten develops and produces an elastic dough. For shortcrust you want the opposite: low gluten, "soft," or pastry flour. The flour package provides information about the USDA recommended daily allowance percentage of protein (gluten) — bread flour is about 20 percent, most all-purpose flour is 15 percent, and there are a few brands (White Lily is one) that are only 10 percent protein. For crisper pastry use one of the low-protein flours.

+ *The proportion of fat to flour.* The higher the proportion of fat, the shorter the pastry will be. "Short" means crumbly and crisp. I recommend butter for its better flavor. If you are dissatisfied with the shortness of your pastry, try replacing a tablespoon or two of the butter with vegetable shortening. The weight of fat should be at least half the weight of the flour for shortcrust pastry. A quarter-pound of butter is one stick or eight tablespoons; a half pound of flour is about two cups.

+ *The amount of liquid.* Be cautious — use just enough liquid to hold the dough together. Different flours absorb different amounts, so start out with a little less than the recipe calls for. You can always sprinkle on a little more water if the dough is too dry, but you can't remove any when you've added too much. Water is the most common liquid called for in pastry-making but it is sometimes combined with egg yolks or lemon juice.

+ *Handling the dough.* A light touch gives the best results. If you over-handle the dough the gluten will develop and you'll end up with tough pastry. Good shortcrust dough is a little difficult to handle but the resulting texture is worth the effort.

You can make dough with a mixer or food processor but I recommend making it by hand until you know what good shortcrust is like. It is a very pleasant experience — you can feel the butter being surrounded by the flour, rather than being mixed into it, and you are less likely to overwork the dough.

If you do use a processor or mixer, pay close attention and stop as soon as the dough barely holds together. If there are large bits of butter visible, push the dough out a couple of times with the heel of your hand to incorporate them rather than continue mixing.

When the dough is made, wrap it up and let it rest in the refrigerator for 30 minutes to an hour (longer is fine but the dough may be too stiff to roll and need to sit out at room temperature). In very hot weather you may need to keep the dough you are not using in the refrigerator.

• *Rolling out the dough.* Lightly flour the rolling surface (the countertop, a large board or marble slab) and your rolling pin. Roll the pastry out, turning it between rolls and lightly dusting with flour if the dough starts to stick. When the pastry is thin and large enough to fill your baking tin, either drape it over the rolling pin and unroll into the pan or fold it loosely into quarters and unfold in the pan. This minimizes stretching (stretched dough shrinks when cooked). Make sure the dough fits snugly into the pan by pushing the dough down the sides rather than stretching it up.

• *Baking "blind."* This means baking or partially baking the unfilled crust to avoid sogginess. Prick the surface of the dough a few times with a fork, lay in a piece of aluminum foil and fill with dried beans (which you then save to reuse for next time as they will not be edible after baking). Bake in a 425°F oven for 15 minutes. At this point you can remove the foil and beans and continue with your recipe or turn down the oven to 350°F and bake the empty crust for 20 to 30 minutes until it is dry to the touch.

Shortcrust Pastry

2 cups flour
pinch of salt
8 tablespoons (1 stick) unsalted butter
Optional: replace 1 to 2 tablespoons butter
   with shortening
4 to 6 tablespoons cold water
Optional: 1 egg yolk, lightly beaten (reduce
   the amount of water to compensate)
For sweet pastry: 2 tablespoons sugar

Mix the flour and salt. When making sweet pastry, mix the sugar with the flour and salt. Cut the butter and shortening into 6 to 8 pieces and add to the flour. Start incorporating the butter into the flour with a pastry cutter or two knives held parallel. Use your fingertips as the butter pieces get smaller. When the mixture starts to look like large raw oatmeal flakes, add most of the liquid. Mix lightly; add a little more liquid if the pastry is not going to come together. Form into a ball, wrap and refrigerate for 30 minutes to an hour.

If you use a food processor, flick it on and off a couple of times to combine the dry ingredients. Add the butter, cut into pieces, and pulse 5 to 10 times to achieve the flaky oatmeal-like state. Add the liquid while flicking the machine off and on. Continue to pulse (up to 20 times) until the dough just barely comes together. Wrap and refrigerate.

This will make a top and bottom crust for an average-sized pie.

Sweet & Savory Pies

The Independent
October 5, 1989

As I PROMISED, here are two recipes that make use of the shortcrust pastry instructions from my last column.

The savory fish pie is English. Its filling can be made a day in advance and refrigerated until you're ready to cover it with pastry and bake it. Use a firm, white fish with a good texture like cod or haddock, or ask your fish dealer to recommend one. You can vary the recipe by adding a teaspoon or two of curry powder with the flour when you make the white sauce or using shrimp or scallops instead of mushrooms.

When you choose fruit to fill the tart remember that some varieties cook better than others. Granny Smith apples have a good texture and wonderful flavor when cooked; Stayman and Winesap are two other varieties to look for. With pears, select firm, not-quite-ripe ones; and with cherries, less sweet ones make for better baked flavor.

Savory Fish Pie

**2 pounds fresh fish fillets, or a combination
   of fresh and smoked fish fillets**
1½ cups milk
1 bay leaf
4 peppercorns
3 to 4 parsley stalks
salt
2 tablespoons butter
3 tablespoons flour
**2 ounces small, whole mushrooms,
   cleaned and trimmed**
¼ to ½ cup finely chopped parsley
shortcrust pastry for a single crust pie
   (see page 157)

**1 egg yolk beaten with a teaspoon of water,
   or milk for glazing**

Put the fish, milk, bay leaf, peppercorns, parsley stalks and a pinch of salt into a sauce pan. The milk should just cover the fish; add a little more if necessary. Bring to a gentle simmer, cover loosely and poach until the fish is opaque and just barely done (15 to 20 minutes, depending upon the thickness of the fish). Remove the fish from the liquid, save the milk but discard the bay leaf, peppercorns and parsley stalks. Remove skin and bones from the fish.

Make a medium-thick white sauce: Melt the butter over low heat and stir in the flour; stir and cook a few minutes regulating the heat so the mixture doesn't take on any color. Stirring with a wire whisk, pour in one and a half cups of the warm poaching liquid, turn up the heat and bring to a boil. If the mixture becomes lumpy, whisk vigorously, or briefly blend the sauce in a blender or food processor. Simmer for five minutes and check seasoning. If the sauce needs sharpening, add a teaspoon of capers or white wine vinegar. Stir in the parsley and gently mix the sauce with the fish and mushrooms. Place in a pie pan. (A ceramic pan is fine, as this pie has no bottom crust to get soggy.)

Roll out the pastry for a lid. Moisten the rim of the pan and cover the pie with the pastry, pressing down the edge for a good seal. Trim away the excess, crimp or decorate the edge and make a couple of slashes in the top for steam to escape. If you're feeling fancy or have a young assistant, make fish shapes from pastry scraps. Moisten their undersides and place them on the pie. Brush the crust with egg yolk-water mixture or milk for a glazed finish.

Bake at 425°F for 10 minutes. Turn the oven down to 375°F and continue baking 20 to 30 minutes until the crust is done. Serve hot or warm.

Open-Faced Fruit Tart

sweet shortcrust pastry dough *(see page 157)*
fruit
sugar
lemon juice
jam or jelly
brandy

The "singing chef," who presided at one of my favorite London restaurants of the same name, usually offered a freshly made fruit tart after the meal, featuring whatever fruit was in season with double cream on the side (those who hate English cooking must have missed out on the dairy products). Fillings included apples, pears, peaches, plums, apricots, cherries, currants (red and black) and less frequently, berries. The fruits appeared in various combinations — apple and plum, and apples over a homemade sweet apple sauce are two I especially liked — and the finished tart was usually glazed with jelly or thick fruit syrup.

To produce your own, you will need a metal tart tin (not ceramic — the crust won't get as crisp) with a removable outer rim. The rim enables you to put the finished tart on a large plate to present it elegantly.

Roll the pastry out and fill the tart tin. Trim away the excess by rolling the rolling pin over the edges. Cover with aluminum foil, fill with beans and bake "blind" for 15 minutes at 425°F.

While the pastry bakes, peel and seed the fruit and cut it into attractive pieces — apples into thin slices; plums into halves; peaches and apricots into halves, quarters or thick slices. Toss the pieces with a tablespoon or two of sugar and a little lemon juice. Remove the foil and beans from the pastry, and arrange the fruit on the crust in a pleasing pattern. Remember that fruit shrinks when it cooks, so be generous with the filling. Bake at

375°F for 45 to 60 minutes, until the fruit is tender. If the edges of the pastry threaten to burn before the tart is done, cover them with a strip of foil and continue baking.

Remove the tart from the oven and let it cool while you prepare a glaze from a 1/4 to 1/2-cup of jelly simmered briskly with a couple of tablespoons of brandy. Select a jelly or jam to complement the fruit filling — apricot with apples, red currant or raspberry with pears, for example. To achieve a smooth glaze, sieve the jelly or jam if it contains seeds or pieces of fruit.

You can use apple peelings to make a thick syrup (do this only if the apples are pesticide-free). Boil them with sugar and water while the tart bakes. Drain well, pushing down to extract as much liquid as possible. Taste and add lemon juice, brandy, a very tiny pinch of salt, or vanilla or almond extract to adjust the flavor. Reduce over a high heat, stirring until you have a thick syrup.

Spoon the glaze over the fruit. The tart is best warm or at room temperature on the day it is made, although no one has ever complained about leftover tart whether warm or cold.

The quantities of ingredients depend on the size of your tart tin. A 7 1/2-inch tart tin will need pastry made with 3/4 of a cup of flour, 3 to 4 tablespoons of butter and a couple of tablespoons of water; it will hold a filling made with two large apples, two to three peaches, a few more apricots or even more plums. A 10-inch tart tin will need pastry for a single-crust pie. You'll soon learn the amounts of various fillings for the size of tin you have.

Shortcrust By Any Other Name

The Independent
October 19, 1989

I MUST APOLOGIZE FOR any confusion I caused in my previous pastry articles by using the term "shortcrust." It wasn't until a couple of friends questioned me that I realized the term was probably more English than American. Living in London when I started cooking daily, I successfully kept "chips," "french fries," "crisps" and "potato chips" separate in the bilingual compartments of my mind. Some Anglicisms, though, seem to have stuck with me. Shortcrust dough means pie dough.

This week I risk confusing other categories by making shortcrust with yeast. This produces a yeasty-flavored pie dough that seems less rich than traditional shortcrust and is wonderful with savory fillings. (It's not a bread dough suitable for pizza.)

If you are nervous when you think about using yeast, relax. The only thing you need to remember is that too much heat kills yeast, and dead yeast won't raise anything. Otherwise, yeast is very accommodating. Sugar and warmer temperatures will speed it up; salt and cooler temperatures will slow it down. You can learn to use these characteristics to plan the time of baking to suit your convenience.

Yeast-Raised Shortcrust

1¼ cup bread flour
¼ ounce cake yeast or 1½ teaspoon dry yeast
2 tablespoons warm water
1 egg
1 teaspoon salt
3 tablespoons cream

In a small bowl or cup, cream the yeast with the warm water. If you are using dry yeast, sprinkle it onto the warm water, let it sit a couple of minutes, then stir to a creamy liquid.

Put the flour into a 1½-quart bowl or larger and stir in the salt. Add the egg and yeast, and mix. Add the cream or butter and, using your hands, mix the dough. Form into a ball, sprinkle with flour and let the dough double in bulk in a warm spot (1½ to 2 hours, depending on the temperature of the ingredients and the spot you choose).

When the dough has doubled, punch it down, work it briefly and form into another ball. At this point you can fill your pie pan with the dough and proceed with your recipe, put the dough in a cool spot and wait a bit to cook your tart, or refrigerate the dough and use it the next day. I imagine, if you really want to plan ahead, you could even freeze it and let it thaw all day in the refrigerator to use in the evening. Place the dough in the center of a buttered and floured 8 x 11-inch pie pan or tart tin. Use your knuckles to press the dough out to the sides of the tin. Let it sit in a warm spot — the top of the stove while the oven heats to 425°F is ideal — while you prepare a filling; the dough will rise a bit, then you can easily work it up the sides of the pan. Try something fancy with the edges if you're inclined.

Fill the pastry and bake your tart, usually 15 minutes at 425°F, then 10 to 15 minutes at 375°F. If the filling or edges of the crust begin to get too brown before one or the other is completely cooked, cover with aluminum foil.

This recipe is adapted from Elizabeth David's *English Bread and Yeast Cookery,* a delight to read as well as a source of some interesting recipes.

Mushroom Tart

> **8 ounces mushrooms, cleaned and sliced**
> **4 shiitake mushrooms, cleaned and sliced,**
>   **or 4 dried shiitake or porcini mushrooms,**
>   **softened and sliced**
> **I small onion, chopped**
> **2 cloves garlic, finely chopped**
> **3 tablespoons butter**
> **salt and pepper**
> **a tiny pinch of nutmeg**
> **2 eggs**
> **I cup cream, half-and-half, or milk**
> **I heaped tablespoon chopped parsley**

Wipe, don't wash, the mushrooms to clean them. If you are using dried mushrooms, place them in a small bowl, cover with boiling water and let them sit 20 to 30 minutes to soften. Drain well and slice very thinly.

Cook the mushrooms, onions and garlic in the butter over a medium high heat, stirring frequently, until the juices have almost completely evaporated (about 10 minutes). Season with salt, pepper and nutmeg. Be cautious with nutmeg, it's possible to overpower other flavors with just a little too much. Spread this mixture on the pastry dough.

Beat the eggs, cream and parsley together and pour over the mushroom mixture. If you place your pie pan or tart tin on a larger baking sheet you won't have to worry about any overflow triggering your smoke alarm when it inevitably blackens on the bottom of the oven. Bake at 425°F for 15 minutes. Turn the oven down to 375°F and

bake for another 15 minutes. The filling will jiggle slightly but not be liquid when the tart is done.

This is absolutely delicious and will serve six as an appetizer or four for a light meal. Using the strongly flavored dried or fresh mushrooms greatly enhances the flavor of the more common white mushrooms.

Roquefort Quiche

> **4 ounces Roquefort cheese**
> **3 tablespoons cream**
> **2 eggs**
> **4 tablespoons milk**
> **pepper**
> **nutmeg**

Mash the cheese with the three tablespoons of cream. Use a fork and leave it a little lumpy.

Beat the eggs and milk together. Combine the two mixtures and season with pepper and nutmeg. Roquefort is usually fairly salty so you may not need any salt; taste it to see. Pour this mixture into your pastry-lined pie tin.

Bake for 15 minutes at 425°F, then for 10 minutes at 375°F.

This makes a thinly filled quiche but one so rich it will serve four to six.

The recipe is also adapted from *English Bread and Yeast Cookery.* Any strong-flavored cheese that maintains good texture when cooked can be substituted — sharp cheddar or some Danish blues; Julia Child suggests Camembert. Experiment, but try the Roquefort first; it's a very interesting flavor.

True Hominy

The Independent
November 2, 1989

A WEEK OFF, some interesting new cookbooks, and I discover a new ingredient — hominy! Don't laugh; I mean new to me. I've always liked grits, which is hominy dried and ground, but whole kernel hominy, I am beginning to *love*.

The flavor is much like masa, the primary ingredient of corn tortillas. This is not surprising since masa and hominy come from the same corn. The first step in preparing both involves soaking mature (dried) corn in water and lye until the hulls loosen and can be removed. The corn, or hominy, is then rinsed thoroughly, covered with fresh water and simmered until it is soft and tender.

This technique was in use in the Americas long before Columbus arrived and, according to Harold McGee's *On Food and Cooking,* hominy helped native Americans avoid pellagra, a disease to which people who rely on corn as a primary food are highly susceptible. Treating the corn makes the available proteins more balanced and the niacin more usable for human nutrition.

Hominy is a principle ingredient of the Pueblo Indian-inspired Southwestern American stew known as posole. The version in Ruth Adams Bronz' *Miss Ruby's American Cooking* is terrific. The book is a collection of recipes served at Miss Ruby's Cafe in New York City and reads like a compilation of the best recipes from each of many church or community cookbooks from around the country. After trying several recipes, I'd accept an invitation to the cafe in a minute.

Miss Ruby's Posole is a thick stew, rich and well-seasoned. Other versions are thinner, more like a soup, and served with a selection of garnishes. I offer you a modified version of Miss Ruby's

The next cookbook I explored is the newly revised and enlarged Bill Neal's *Southern Cooking.* He has added 25 new recipes, many of which are featured and often requested at Crook's Corner in Chapel Hill. The mushroom and hominy recipe here is in both the old and new editions of the book, but if you've always wanted Bill Neal's recipe for shrimp and grits or fried bean cakes, investigate the new edition.

If you're inclined to start from scratch with dried corn or hominy, consult Diana Kennedy's *Art of Mexican Cooking: Traditional Mexican Cooking for Aficionados.* Now, I'd like another week off to try many of the recipes in that cookbook.

Pork with Green Chiles & Posole

1½ pounds pork shoulder, trimmed and cut into 1-inch pieces
2 tablespoons cooking oil
1 small onion, chopped
2 garlic cloves, finely chopped
pinch dried oregano
½ teaspoon ground cumin
1 can chopped green chiles
1 can chopped fresh tomatillos
2 whole pickled jalapeño peppers, chopped
salt and pepper to taste
1 can white hominy, or cooked dried hominy, rinsed
2 cups chicken stock
12 corn tortillas

Sauté the pork in the cooking oil over a medium high heat. Remove it and sauté the onion and garlic until the onion is translucent. Stir in the oregano, cumin, pork, chiles, tomatillos, jalapeños, salt, pepper and hominy. Add the chicken stock and bring to a simmer. Cover loosely and simmer for 1½ to 2 hours or until the pork is very tender and beginning to shred. Add more stock if the dish threatens to dry out. Warm the tortillas. The recipe serves three to four.

The green chiles are only mildly hot; jalapeño peppers are very hot; both are widely available. Tomatillos look like green tomatoes but are very different in flavor; do not substitute. They can be found fresh or canned in many local stores.

The cookbook's author recommends serving this dish with refried beans and Spanish rice.

Bill Neal's Hominy with Mushrooms

    6 slices bacon
    2 cups mushrooms, cleaned and sliced
    ¾ cup scallions, chopped
    I clove garlic, minced
    20-ounce can hominy, drained
    2 tablespoons chopped pimiento
    ½ teaspoon salt
    freshly ground black pepper
    2 tablespoons chopped fresh parsley

Cut each piece of bacon lengthwise, then into squares. Place in a cold skillet or sauté pan and render over low to medium heat until the bacon browns. Remove it before it becomes crisp. Increase heat and add the sliced mushrooms, sautéing well until liquid evaporates. Add the scallions and minced garlic, stirring well until the scallions wilt. Increase heat to high and add the hominy. Continue stirring and add the pimiento, salt, bacon and pepper. Remove from heat, stir in the fresh parsley and serve immediately.

Serves four. While this dish is good at any meal, I like it best with biscuits and scrambled eggs for breakfast.

[*Reprinted by permission from University of North Carolina Press. — ed.*]

Tea Cakes for Two

The Independent
November 23, 1989

WHILE WE AMERICANS seldom "take tea" as the English do in the afternoon or have time for "coffee" as we once did in the mornings, we can still find occasions for serving many of the baked goods that used to appear at such times.

The upcoming holiday season promises a variety of suitable gatherings with houseguests, friends or family at your place or theirs. If you do a little timely baking and freezing right now you can have some treats on hand to serve for breakfast or with tea later in the day. The following tea breads and cakes also make good presents for those who've shown you hospitality.

These recipes contain little or no sugar, but some sweetness is provided in two of them by dried fruit or candied citrus peel. Look for good quality candied peel — not slimy or full of additives (how do they make those cherries look like that?).

Saffron was all the rage in the British Isles during the Middle Ages, and the saffron bread comes from Cornwall where the saffron crocus was once grown. It is an example of a yeast-raised fruit bread and, in addition to being delicious, keeps very well.

Saffron Bread

    pinch saffron
    2 tablespoons water
    ½ ounce fresh yeast or I scant teaspoon
        dried yeast
    4 cups bread flour
    ⅔ cup sugar

¼ teaspoon nutmeg
¼ teaspoon cinnamon
pinch salt
6 ounces (1½ sticks) butter or combination
    of butter and shortening
5 fluid ounces milk
1 cup dried mixed fruit (currants, raisins,
    chopped dried apples) and chopped
    candied citrus peel

Infuse the saffron in two tablespoons of water by bringing the water slowly to a simmer, turning off the heat and letting it sit.

Dissolve the yeast in ¼ cup warm water.

Mix the flour, sugar and spices. Cut in the butter or butter and shortening combination.

Add the milk to the saffron and water infusion. Heat until warm.

Add the yeast and milk mixtures to the flour. Mix to a soft dough — the bread hook on an electric mixer is perfect. If you don't have a bread hook, knead until smooth and elastic, 5 to 10 minutes. Place the dough back in the bowl, cover and let it sit in a warm place until doubled in bulk, 2 to 3 hours.

Punch the dough down; knead in the fruit and peel. Place the dough in a large, well-greased loaf pan and let it rise for 30 minutes. Bake at 425°F for 40 minutes. When the bread is done it will sound hollow when you thump the bottom of the loaf. Saffron bread is good warm, cold or toasted. This recipe and the next are adapted from Jane Grigson's *English Food*.

Cider Cake

2 cups flour
½ teaspoon grated nutmeg
1 teaspoon baking powder
pinch salt
5 ounces (1¼ sticks) butter
¾ cup sugar
2 eggs
2 tablespoons brandy or Calvados or bourbon
½ cup sweet (not hard or alcoholic) cider

Preheat the oven to 350°F. Sift the flour and measure. Resift with the nutmeg and baking powder.

Cream the butter and sugar until fluffy; add the eggs and beat well.

Put the brandy into a measuring cup. Add cider to make 5 fluid ounces.

Add the flour and cider mixtures alternately to the butter, sugar and eggs until everything is well mixed. Pour into a well-greased pan (about 7 x 9 x 2 inches) and bake at 350°F for 45 minutes. Cool for about 5 minutes, then remove from the pan and cool on a rack. Serve with butter for breakfast or tea.

Teacakes

½ ounce fresh yeast or 3 tablespoons
    dried yeast
3¼ cups bread flour
1 teaspoon dried orange peel or
    ¼ teaspoon nutmeg
1 teaspoon salt
3 tablespoons butter, softened
¼ cup currants or sultanas (golden raisins)
1 egg, beaten
⅓ cup warm milk
½ cup warm water

Cream the yeast with 2 tablespoons of warm water.

Combine the flour, orange peel or nutmeg and salt. Cut in the butter. Add the currants or sultanas. Add the yeast, beaten egg, warm milk and water and mix to form a soft, pliable dough. You may need to add a little more water.

Knead for 5 to 10 minutes, until the dough is smooth. Return to the bowl, cover and let it rise for 2 to 3 hours, until doubled in bulk.

Dust your hands with flour and punch down the dough. Knead briefly and shape into 8 round, flattened rolls. Place them on a greased baking sheet. Cover with a tea towel and let them rise on top of the stove for 20 to 30 minutes while the oven heats to 350°F. Bake for 30 to 35 minutes until the rolls are lightly browned and sound hollow when tapped. Serve warm with butter. To reheat, slice and toast on the cut side only, if possible. Adapted from Caroline Conran's *English Country Cooking At Its Best*.

The Party Faithful

The Independent
December 7, 1989

SOME PEOPLE HAVE JUST WHAT IT TAKES to throw a really good party. They've got the right space (just a little crowded), the right guest list (most of the people you'd hoped to see, and some interesting strangers thrown in) and terrific food and drink.

If you've got holiday party plans — modest or elaborate — here is a recipe that has stood the test of time, appearing — then disappearing — at many great gatherings.

Holly McDonough's Burgundy Mushrooms

4 pounds mushrooms (all sizes)
1 pound butter
1 quart burgundy
1½ tablespoons Worcestershire sauce
1 teaspoon dill
1 teaspoon pepper
1 teaspoon garlic
1 cup boiling water
4 beef bouillon cubes
4 chicken bouillon cubes

Clean the mushrooms. Don't wash them, but wipe with a paper towel; or, if your relatives give the kind of gifts mine do, use a mushroom brush. Put everything into a large pot and bring to a boil. Simmer, covered, for 5 to 6 hours then uncover and simmer for three hours.

Provide plenty of toothpicks and serve hot. Your kitchen will smell great for the 8 or 9 hours it takes to cook. This dish can be made in advance, refrigerated and reheated at party time.

In the Soup

The Independent
January 11, 1990

A S THE TEMPERATURE DROPS, soup production rises. But let me warn you, when you start making soup from scratch, you'll get spoiled. You'll no longer want to eat packaged soups from the supermarkets, no matter what the labels promise, because the ones you make at home are so much better. The major difference is what you *don't* put into the pot — MSG or too much salt, for example.

Luckily, it's not hard to prepare soup for a good hot meal. And while you're at it, make that several hot meals; it's not much more work to make a bigger pot and freeze leftovers in useable portions. While I haven't tried many microwave soup recipes because I like to savor the scent of slowly simmering soup, the microwave oven is useful for thawing and reheating on the spur of the moment.

There are a few simple things to know that will help you prepare soups. Use water if you don't have good stock, or if you must have stock but don't have time to make it, use a low-salt canned broth or stock. Taste your soup carefully for salt and pepper; too little is as disappointing as too much.

Simmer, don't boil; and don't overcook, which will cause the soup to lose its flavor and nutrients. Use a large enough pot so that you can stir things around easily and add ingredients without worrying about the soup boiling over

These two recipes are my current favorites. Each is enriched and thickened in an unusual way — the pea soup with a white sauce, and the cheese soup with cream cheese. I recommend either soup with good bread for a cozy meal on a cold wet day.

Split Pea Soup

4 strips thickly sliced bacon, diced
1 medium onion, diced
1 pound green split peas
3 quarts water
1 ham hock or ham bone
1 bay leaf
freshly ground black pepper
¼ pound baked ham, diced

WHITE SAUCE:
3 tablespoons butter
2 tablespoons flour
1½ to 2 cups milk

Sauté the bacon until it begins to render its fat. Add the diced onion and cook, stirring frequently, until the onion softens and starts to look transparent. Add 3 quarts of water, the split peas, the ham hock or bone, bay leaf and pepper. Cover loosely and simmer until the split peas are very tender, which will take 1½ to 2 hours. Remove the bay leaf and any bones, and roughly puree everything else in a blender, food processor or food mill.

Now you'll make the white sauce. If the soup seems thin, use the smaller amount of milk in the sauce; if your soup seems thick, use more milk. Melt the butter in a small, sturdy saucepan over low heat. Sprinkle in the flour and cook for 3 minutes stirring constantly with a wire whisk. Then turn up the heat and add the milk. If you are wary of lumps, heat the milk just about to a boil, add to the butter and flour mixture (culinarily known as a roux) all at once, and bring up to a boil while stirring. Turn down to a simmer, salt and pepper to taste and cook for 2 minutes. If you are even more wary of cleaning up spilt milk that has boiled over when you weren't paying attention, add the milk in several lots, starting small — about ¼ cup. Let it come to a boil and whisk madly until the two mixtures amalgamate. Add the rest of the milk in increasing doses, following the same procedure each time. When all the milk has been added, turn the heat down, salt and pepper to taste and simmer for 2 minutes.

Stir the white sauce into the soup, add the ham pieces and simmer for 15 minutes, stirring occasionally. Serve very hot. This soup freezes well and is a good way to get one more good meal out of a ham bone.

The recipe came into my kitchen as Diner Split Pea Soup from one of Jane and Michael Stern's newspaper columns.

Creamy Potato-Cheese Soup

3 to 4 tablespoons butter
2 cups chopped onions
1 large garlic clove, minced or pressed
2 large potatoes, peeled and coarsely chopped
1 large carrot, coarsely chopped
3 cups vegetable stock or water
1 teaspoon dried dill or 2 tablespoons fresh dill
4 ounces cream cheese
1½ cups milk
1 cup grated smoked cheddar cheese (3 ounces)
salt and black pepper to taste
chopped fresh parsley

In a large soup pot, sauté the onions and garlic in the butter until the onions are translucent. Add the potatoes and carrots and sauté 5 to 10 minutes longer. Add the stock or water and dill, and simmer until all the vegetables are tender.

Puree the vegetables with the cream cheese and milk in a blender or food processor. Return the soup to the soup pot. Season with salt and pepper. Stir in the cheddar cheese and reheat gently.

Serve each cup or bowl garnished with chopped fresh parsley. Serves four to six.

In the Soup

This is adapted from *New Recipes From Moose-wood Restaurant,* a fine collection of very satisfying dishes from the Moosewood Collective. The first time I made this soup, I bought smoked cheddar by mistake — it was so good I continue to use it by choice. The soup freezes well. When reheating don't let it boil; simmer briefly, stirring often.

Lasagne from the Larder

The Independent
February 1, 1990

EVERY NOW AND AGAIN YOU FIND yourself with a pleasant problem: how to turn an afternoon with friends into dinner for four to six hungry people without a trip to the supermarket. The solution: A spur-of-the-minute dish that can be assembled from ingredients on hand in your pantry and refrigerator. One of my favorites is some variation of lasagne.

The necessities include the appropriate pasta, some tomato sauce (homemade or good store-bought), parmesan cheese, ingredients for white sauce (butter, flour, milk) and, for the recipe below, frozen spinach and a few dried mushrooms.

You can vary things according to what you've got on hand. Substitute a half-pound of ground meat browned and simmered in the tomato sauce for the spinach, or make Eggplant Parmesan by using fried or baked eggplant slices instead of pasta. If you've got some leftover lamb as well as eggplant in the refrigerator, go further afield by making Moussaka. The permutations are endless — I've got a Moussaka recipe in what seems otherwise to be a pretty authentic Greek cookbook that calls for veal and artichoke hearts.

This recipe takes 30 to 45 minutes to assemble; you can cut that time down if you have an assistant or two. Take the 45 to 60 minutes the dish is in the oven to clean up a bit, set the table, make a salad, open the wine, relax and continue to chat with your guests.

Spinach Lasagne

6 to 9 lasagne noodles
1 package frozen spinach or 1 pound fresh
2 cups béchamel (white) sauce
1 quart tomato sauce
4 ounces parmesan cheese, grated (1 cup)
Optional: 4 to 6 dried mushrooms

If you include dried mushrooms, soak them in very hot water for 15 to 30 minutes while you prepare other segments of the lasagne. Drain well and chop very finely.

Cook the lasagne noodles in lots of rapidly boiling water, stirring often. They will be just done (al dente) in 10 to 16 minutes. Drain and rinse with cold water to keep them from sticking together before you assemble the dish.

I've been meaning to try the uncooked pasta method of making lasagne, but haven't worked up the nerve after a friend's strange experience with it. (Is one to use uncooked *fresh* — and therefore soft — pasta, or uncooked *dried* pasta, I wonder?)

Cook the spinach according to the package directions and drain well. You can use a pound of fresh spinach, cooking it by your favorite method, and draining well.

Make the white sauce. My January 11th article about soups *(see page 166)* offered a couple of stovetop methods, and below is a microwave version that's not lumpy and frees you to prepare other ingredients while it's cooking.

Assess the flavoring of the various components of the dish. The tomato sauce might need a little basil; if it is very salty hold back on salt in the other elements. Assemble the lasagne. Start with a thin coating of tomato sauce on the bottom of an 8 x 8 x 2-inch pan (other shapes, as long as they are two inches or more deep and 65 to 75 square inches in area, are fine). Put down a layer of noodles; cover with a third of the tomato sauce, half of the spinach, half of the béchamel sauce and a third of the grated parmesan cheese. The second layer is the same, except sprinkle the optional finely chopped mushrooms over the spinach layer. The last layer should be noodles, tomato sauce and parmesan cheese.

Bake at 375°F for 45 minutes to an hour, until it is quite hot, bubbling and starting to brown on top. Let the lasagne settle for 10 minutes before cutting.

This will serve four to six depending on how hungry they are and how much salad you serve with it. A robust red wine is also a good accompaniment.

Microwave Béchamel

(See also traditional Béchamel Sauce, page 124.)

For two cups:
4 tablespoons unsalted butter
4 tablespoons flour
2 cups milk
1 teaspoon salt
pepper

Use a 4-cup measuring cup or deep bowl that can be used in a microwave oven to heat the butter for 1½ minutes (if at room temperature) to 2½ minutes (if very cold). Cover loosely with a paper towel while heating.

Uncover and whisk in the flour. Cook uncovered for 2 minutes.

Whisk in the milk; cook for 3 minutes. Whisk and cook for 2 more minutes.

Remove from the oven and whisk thoroughly. Season to taste.

Lasagne from the Larder

All cooking levels are HIGH or 100 percent for a high wattage (650 to 700-watt) oven. Omit the salt if using regular salted butter.

What the Doctor Ordered

The Independent
February 22, 1990

UNDER THE WEATHER? Tastebuds in a fog? Some people don't want to eat anything when they've got a cold or the flu. Me, I get extremely nervous about my health when I'm not interested in eating. I always believe that there's something I can take internally to make me feel better. Usually, I'm right. Soup — chicken or otherwise — will open a stuffed-up head and soothe a sore throat as it provides nourishment. Plain pasta or mashed potatoes usually sit well on a stomach that has been feeling queasy. Hot peppers generally help avert disaster when something nasty is coming on.

A longing for that first full-flavored meat is a sure sign that my recovery has begun — the day when I'm ready for something real, something with texture and flavor. It's at that point that I need to feel like I've rejoined the land of the living.

The following recipe for Vinegar-Splashed Chicken is a good choice for "recovery day": It's not so complicated that it challenges a recovering digestion but is an interesting and full-flavored dish. The dark red color looks lovely with rice and simple steamed or microwaved broccoli.

Instructions to "serve with plain, boiled rice" caused me problems in my early cooking days. But what I have learned from experience has reduced my terror of plain, boiled rice. I'm now careful to:

♦ Buy good quality rice. Although brown rice is more nutritious, there are times when only white will do. Asian markets often stock high quality white rice.

- Wash the rice well to remove the floury coating that becomes gummy when cooking.

- Use a little less than twice the volume of water as rice. If the rice is too dry near the end of the cooking time, add a little water. (It is much harder to get rid of unwanted moisture.)

- Bring the water to a boil, add the rice, stir once and bring back to a boil. Then turn the heat very low, cover the pan tightly, and simmer gently.

- Do not lift the lid or stir the rice while it's cooking. Check the rice after about 15 minutes of simmering. When it's done, it can be kept warm tightly covered off the heat: small quantities for 10 to 15 minutes; large quantities for up to 30 minutes. Gently fluff up the rice with a fork just before serving.

Vinegar-Splashed Chicken

1½ **pounds boneless chicken**

MARINADE:
½ **teaspoon Szechuan peppercorns**
3 **tablespoons soy sauce**
1 **tablespoon dry sherry, or white wine**
1 **teaspoon sugar**
1 **tablespoon minced, peeled ginger**
2 **large cloves garlic, minced**
2 **green onions, finely chopped**
1 **teaspoon sesame oil**
1 **tablespoon Chenkong or red wine vinegar**
3 **tablespoons oil**

Cut the chicken into 1-inch squares. Toast the Szechuan peppercorns in a medium-hot skillet, rolling them around to keep from burning. When they start to smell strong, remove from the heat and crush. Mix the peppercorns, soy sauce, sherry or white wine and sugar together for the marinade. Add the chicken and toss to coat evenly. Let it marinate for 15 to 30 minutes.

Prepare the other ingredients. Heat a wok or heavy skillet over high heat. Add the oil and swirl. Scatter in the ginger, garlic and green onions. Stir for a few seconds and add the chicken with the marinade. Stir vigorously for about 2 minutes or until the chicken just starts to stiffen. Turn the heat to low, cover the pan and simmer for 3 minutes. Uncover, turn the heat back up to high and stir for about 2 minutes or until the sauce starts to thicken into a glaze. Sprinkle in the sesame oil and stir; splash in the vinegar and stir briskly in a folding motion. Serve hot.

This will serve three to four as a main course, more with other dishes. I adapted this recipe from my favorite Chinese cookbook, *The Key to Chinese Cooking* by Irene Kuo. This book taught me the techniques that turned my decent Chinese cooking into good Chinese cooking. Kuo even proposes a strategy for stir-frying on an electric stove (it calls for two burners, one on high and one on low, thus eliminating the wait for the burner to heat up or cool off).

There is no substitute for Szechuan peppercorns, and they can be found in Asian markets or Chinese sections of fancier food stores. Chenkong vinegar has a distinctive flavor and is worth getting if you see it. Regular red wine vinegar has a less interesting flavor but makes a delicious dish.

What the Doctor Ordered

Asparagus:
The Sprigs of Spring

The Independent
March 15, 1990

FOR SOME, SPRING IS A HILLSIDE of daffodils dancing in the sun; for others it is the appearance of favorite seasonal food items — asparagus for one.

Asparagus has been savored for thousands of years and, like leeks and onions, is a member of the lily family. Leeks, in fact, have been known as "poor man's asparagus" (not by anyone checking the price of leeks in my local stores) and are good sauced and served, hot and cold, in many of the same ways as asparagus.

I saw my first decent asparagus this spring the day after looking up one recipe and reading many others in *Cooking With Pomiane* by Edouard de Pomiane. It was fate, I decided as I purchased the ingredients for his Asparagus and Potato Salad.

Edouard de Pomiane can be thought of as the Julia Child of his day (the first half of this century). He was an early multi-media person who greatly influenced French cooks in print, on radio, and in the lecture hall. He saw himself as a scientist and invented "gastrotechnology" — the scientific explanation of accepted principles of cookery — and freed countless cooks with the ideas he advanced in his sensible, charming and witty style.

Anyhow, there before me were some good-looking asparagus — tightly budded, undamaged spears with smooth tender skin, not withered or woody, and priced somewhat lower than a king's

ransom. I picked out about ⅓ to ½ pound per person of evenly sized spears (so they would cook in the same amount of time).

When I got home I stored the spears in the vegetable crisper of my refrigerator, wrapped loosely in a plastic bag in order to preserve moisture. Because I would shortly be cooking them I did not follow the advice offered by Marian Morash in *The Victory Garden Cookbook,* which was to trim the stem ends and store the asparagus upright in an inch of water in the refrigerator. I may try this if I am purchasing asparagus that won't be used the same day. As time passes after harvest, asparagus loses sugar and becomes woody, but it should keep well for a couple of days in the refrigerator.

At dinner time, I prepared the asparagus by snapping off the tough ends (the asparagus knows where to break, the cook just provides the impetus). I saved the tough ends in the freezer to make soup (with the asparagus cooking liquid) someday soon. *Mastering The Art of French Cooking* by Child, Bertholle and Beck recommends a tapered peeling of the tough outer parts of the stem in order to maximize usable asparagus. I use this technique when soup is not planned.

Though several of my respected cookbooks unequivocally state that simmering is the best method of cooking, I have never been disappointed by steaming asparagus. The main trick is to avoid overcooking it. Pay attention and start testing early on. You will learn to recognize a change in smell as the asparagus becomes done. I like to maintain a slight crispness — cooked through but not flabby. Between 4 and 12 minutes is usually just about right depending on the type and thickness of asparagus.

Jane Birchfield in *Great Aunt Jane's Cook and Garden Book* brings the trimmed asparagus to a boil, turns off the heat, and lets it sit until "tender but not the least bit limp." Once it's cooked, drain the asparagus well. This sounds like a good idea for a cook with a lot going on at once in the kitchen.

You can serve asparagus simply with melted butter and salt and pepper, or with butter and a dusting of finely grated parmesan cheese or a squeeze of lemon. Its flavor is especially good with many members of the hollandaise sauce family — hollandaise, mousseline (hollandaise with whipped cream) or maltaise (hollandaise flavored with orange). If you are nervous about saturated fat, you'll be glad to know that asparagus is good either hot or cold with olive oil and lemon juice. It's delicious cold with a simple vinaigrette (olive oil, wine vinegar, pinch of dry mustard and freshly ground pepper) or homemade mayonnaise with lots of lemon. I've not had time to try whipped cream seasoned with grated horseradish, lemon juice and salt, but that's on the list for later this spring.

If the asparagus is coming into season, can those further signs of spring — fresh peas and strawberries — be far behind?

Asparagus & Potato Salad

 I pound asparagus
 I pound new or boiling potatoes
 ½ cup mayonnaise
 3 to 4 tablespoons cream
 lemon juice
 salt
 I teaspoon grated lemon zest

Trim and rinse the asparagus and cut into 1½ to 2-inch lengths. Steam until just tender. Rinse with cold water to stop the cooking and drain well.

Scrub the potatoes and simmer until tender. Cool and peel them (not absolutely necessary but it produces a more refined dish). Cut them into three ¼-inch cubes.

Combine the mayonnaise and cream and season to taste with the salt and lemon juice. The mayonnaise you use will determine the exact amounts; some are very salty and lemony. Lemon zest is the yellow part of the peel — avoid using any of the bitter white pith. You can grate it finely or cut off a piece and slice it into impossibly thin julienne strips. Gently mix the dressing with the potatoes and asparagus. Chill for a couple of hours before serving.

This will serve four to six people, and leftovers remain very good for up to three days. My contribution to de Pomiane's recipe is the lemon zest; a little freshly grated parmesan cheese is fine as well.

Asparagus à la Flammande

 I pound asparagus
 I hard-boiled egg yolk
 7 tablespoons melted butter
 squeeze of lemon juice
 salt

Trim, rinse and cook the asparagus until just done. Drain carefully.

Crush the egg yolk thoroughly and gradually work in the hot melted butter. Season to taste with salt and lemon juice. Pour the sauce over the asparagus and serve.

Hot, Quick & Saucy

The Independent
April 23, 1990

YOU'RE TIRED AND CRANKY after a less-than-the-best day at work, but you still want something unusual for dinner for the two of you. Your spirits lift when you remember that container of pasta stuffed with fancy filling stashed in the freezer.

All you need to do is boil some water, put in the pasta and check for doneness from time to time (6 to 12 minutes is usually about right). When the pasta's *al dente,* you drain it, sauce it and serve with a big fresh salad, some bread and some compatible wine. Simply elegant.

Store-bought filled pastas (ravioli, tortellini and so on) usually contain cheese combined with a couple of other ingredients: spinach, nuts, pesto and mushrooms are some common ones. Read the ingredient list so you can select pasta with the most "real" ingredients, e.g., parmesan or Gruyère cheese rather than just "cheese" or "processed cheese." Look for garlic or onion rather than garlic power or onion powder or flakes.

The better pastas can be pricey, but real ingredients are worth going to some expense. Don't, however, assume that the most expensive is the best; you still need to read the ingredient list. Two brands I've liked are Contadina and Putney Pasta; both are available locally.

Saucing your selection requires a little thought. To avoid overwhelming the filling flavors, aim for simplicity and compatibility. Keep in mind that in food, as in life, opposites attract, so be open to contrasts.

I love the heady, earthy flavor of pesto with just about anything, and think it goes especially well with cheese, nut or mushroom fillings. Cream-based sauces are good with spinach or mushroom fillings. Mushroom sauce complements meat or cheese fillings. Try anything you fancy, including combinations you've liked in other dishes.

Start out with just a few ingredients to lessen your chances of disaster, but don't be afraid to fail. A shot of leftover pesto or a teaspoon of anchovy, tomato or olive paste has livened up many a sauce at the last minute.

If there's a pool of sauce left at the bottom of the serving dish, you've used too much for the amount of pasta. Aim for a thorough but light coating. A generous half-cup of most sauces will adequately cover the typical 9- to 10-ounce package of pasta and serve two.

Don't automatically sprinkle grated parmesan or Romano cheese on the finished product. Taste first, and try a little sauce with cheese before you make up your mind.

Here's a list of seven simple pastabilities followed by a couple of recipes that are slightly more complicated.

Pastabilities

1. Chop some garlic and fry it in olive oil until it turns golden. Hot dried red peppers are a typical addition to this sauce; put some in with the garlic. Before mixing with the pasta, you might want to strain out the garlic and pepper. Finish with a generous handful of finely chopped fresh parsley.

2. Toss cooked pasta with butter, grated cheese and lots of freshly ground black pepper.

3. Warm thin strips of good ham in butter, mix with pasta and sprinkle generously with parmesan.

4. Cook fresh peas, chopped ham and sliced mushrooms in butter or olive oil. Serve with parmesan.

5. Peel and chop some absolutely ripe fresh tomatoes when they're in season. Mix with finely chopped garlic, fresh basil and olive oil. Let the sauce sit while you prepare the rest of the meal.

6. Chop or slice mushrooms and sauté in butter or olive oil. Add some thick cream and stir everything around over high heat until the sauce comes together. Fresh thyme is a good addition, as is a shot of lemon juice. This sauce is fabulous.

7. Simmer some cream with garlic while everything else cooks. Just before serving, remove the garlic and stir in grated parmesan. Serve with additional parmesan.

Veronese Mushroom Sauce

1 tablespoon butter
2 tablespoons olive oil
1 small onion, finely chopped
handful of finely chopped parsley
1 small clove of garlic, finely chopped
2 teaspoons flour
1/2 pound of mushrooms, cleaned and sliced
squeeze of fresh lemon juice
salt and pepper
additional tablespoon of butter (optional)

Lightly fry the onion, parsley and garlic in the butter and olive oil. Sprinkle in the flour and stir it around. Add the mushrooms, season with the lemon juice, salt and pepper and simmer until the mushrooms are just cooked. Stir frequently. You will achieve a "slightly thickened mushroom stew" rather than a sauce.

This and the following recipe are adaptations from Elizabeth David's fascinating *Italian Food* first published in 1954, revised in 1964 and updated in 1987. Serious students of Italian cooking will want to see this beautiful (though expensive) book. It is an excellent reference and a source of delicious recipes.

Ricotta Sauce

1/2 cup ricotta cheese
3 tablespoons grated parmesan cheese
1 tablespoon butter
3 to 4 tablespoons cream
nutmeg
salt and pepper

Blend the cheeses and butter together. Add enough cream to make the sauce pourable and season to taste with a scrap of nutmeg and salt and pepper. Mix the sauce and cooked pasta in a heated serving dish and serve on hot plates with extra parmesan.

Do take the time to heat the plates; it makes a real difference to the finished dish.

Hot, Quick & Saucy

American Cooks Cook American

The Independent
May 3, 1990

I ENTHUSIASTICALLY RECOMMEND the first two cookbooks in the "Knopf Cooks American" series: Bill Neal's *Biscuits, Spoon Bread and Sweet Potato Pie* and Bruce Aidells and Dennis Kelly's *Hot Links and Country Flavors.* They are both handsome, sturdy, hardback books, but, practically, not so big nor so beautiful that you'll be afraid to spread them open on the kitchen counter while you cook. And the recipes are classics — so good you will be cooking them for years to come.

Biscuits, Spoon Bread and Sweet Potato Pie is Bill Neal's second cookbook and his second Southern cookbook, and in it he focuses on the breads and sweets of Southern cooks. It is full of great recipes. The Strawberry Shortcake and Frozen Strawberries recipes below were two I had to try as soon as I spotted some good, relatively inexpensive strawberries for sale.

Biscuits is a low- to medium-tech book; you'll be using your hands and spoons more than food processors and fancy gadgets. Neal assumes that you know how to do things such as whip cream, and therefore he focuses on the details that make all the difference to a recipe. For example, he directs you to slice the strawberries and let them sit with the sugar outside the refrigerator for half an hour to maximize the berry flavor before assembling the shortcake.

This elegantly written cookbook contains lots of interesting historical information and would be a great present for people who've just moved to the area, or are moving away from the South, or never paid attention when their mothers offered to show them how to bake perfect cornbread or black-bottom pie.

Hot Links and Country Flavors is about sausage — making it from scratch as well as using it (homemade or store-bought) in hearty, satisfying recipes. The book contains clear instructions and basic information on ingredients, equipment and techniques for the home kitchen. There is mail order information if you can't locate what you need locally (sausage casings, for example). If you aren't tempted to make your own, there are plenty of recommendations about what to look for in good store-bought sausage.

The chapters focus on different regions of America, and the last covers New American Cuisine (you know, wild boar, sun-dried tomato and goat cheese recipes). The recipes I've tried and adapted below (Tortilla and Chorizo Pie and Smoked Sausage and Black Bean Salad) are from the Southwest chapter; I'll be trying some of the Pennsylvania Dutch and Basque recipes soon. Once again, I wanted to cook nearly everything in the book.

Frozen Strawberries

> I pound ripe strawberries
> ¾ to I cup sugar, to taste
> ½ to ¾ cup water, to taste
> juice of I lemon
> good dry red wine such as cabernet sauvignon

Cap and slice the berries. There should be about three cups. Toss with the sugar and mash well with a pestle or potato masher to break the cellulose structure down for easy sugar absorption. Avoid a puree: the sense of whole fruit should remain. Add a little water and lemon juice. Taste;

it should be quite sweet. Set it aside for one hour to macerate, then pour into a shallow pan and freeze. Stir it up every hour for six hours until firmly set; do not try to incorporate air or try to make it fluffy. Serve with a tablespoon (or more) of the dry red wine over each serving. Makes eight servings.

Bill Neal's
Strawberry Shortcake

FOR THE SHORTCAKE:
3 cups all-purpose flour
3 tablespoons sugar
4 teaspoons baking powder
¾ teaspoon salt
¾ cup butter
I egg
½ cup heavy cream

TO ASSEMBLE:
unsalted butter
4 cups sliced strawberries
sugar, to taste
I cup heavy cream, lightly whipped with
    about 1 ½ tablespoons sugar

Slice and add sugar to the berries and let them stand at room temperature for about 30 minutes before assembling.

Sift flour, sugar, baking powder and salt together. Work the butter through with the fingertips. Beat the egg, milk and cream together and stir into the dough. Turn out on a lightly floured surface and give the dough a very light kneading, 8-10 quick strokes. Divide into 2 portions. Shape into 8-inch rounds about ⅔-inch thick. Transfer gently to the lightly buttered baking sheet. Prick about 8 times with a fork. Bake about 18 minutes in an oven preheated to 450°F until light brown.

Split each biscuit and spread each layer with unsalted butter. Assemble the shortcake by gener-

ously spreading strawberries over each split layer as you stack them. Top with the last layer of biscuit. Pour over the whipped cream and serve. Makes eight to 10 servings.

[Reprinted by permission from University of North Carolina Press. – ed.]

Tortilla & Chorizo Pie

2 tablespoons olive oil
3 or 4 fresh Anaheim or other mild green chiles
6 to 8 tomatillos, husks removed and parboiled
    five minutes, or a 16-ounce can
2 medium onions
4 cloves garlic
I bunch fresh cilantro
I or more cups chicken stock
salt and pepper to taste
1½ pounds chorizo or other fresh Southwest
    sausage, in bulk or removed from casings
2 cups finely chopped onions
16 corn tortillas cut into sixths
oil for deep frying
6 cups shredded jack cheese

GARNISHES:
avocado slices
fresh cilantro sprigs

To make the sauce, coarsely puree the olive oil, chiles, tomatillos, onions, garlic and cilantro in a food processor. Combine with the chicken stock in a sauce pan and simmer for five minutes. Taste for salt and pepper, and reserve.

Fry the chorizo over medium-high heat, breaking up the meat with a fork, for about 5 minutes. Pour off all but about 2 tablespoons of the fat, add the finely chopped onions and cook another 5 minutes, until the onions are soft.

Meanwhile deep-fry the tortilla wedges in batches for 1 to 2 minutes, until they are crisp but not brown. Drain well on paper towels.

To assemble the chilequiles, oil a 3- to 4-quart casserole. Make layers of tortilla chips, chorizo, jack cheese and sauce. Repeat until all the ingredients are used. Press down with a plate, making sure all the solids are covered with liquid. If not, add more stock. Cover with foil and refrigerate overnight so the tortillas absorb the liquid. The next day, remove the plate and sprinkle the top with more shredded jack cheese. Bake, covered, in a preheated 350°F oven for 45 minutes. Garnish with avocado slices and cilantro sprigs. Makes 5 to 6 servings.

Smoked Sausage & Black Bean Salad

1 pound smoked sausage, diced
1½ cups vinaigrette
4 cups cooked black beans
1 red onion, finely chopped
1 red bell pepper, diced
1 jalapeño or other hot green chile, finely chopped
1 teaspoon minced garlic
2 cups chopped fresh cilantro or flat-leaf Italian parsley

In a heavy skillet, fry the sausage over medium-high heat until the fat is rendered, about 5 to 10 minutes. Discard the fat. Add the vinaigrette to the beans while they are still hot. Cool, then mix in the sausage and the remaining ingredients. Makes four to six servings.

Zucchini Home Improvements

The Independent
June 27, 1990

THE SINGLE BEST TIP I CAN OFFER to improve the flavor and texture of any zucchini dish you may be contemplating is this: Think small — four inches or less. If you're growing your own, pick often and toss any huge ones onto the compost heap or into the chicken coop.

I know, we've all had marvelously clever recipes that disguise or cope with the watery, coarse texture of a large specimen, but why bother? The delicate, creamy taste and texture of young, firm zucchini are not only better than those of larger zucchini, but also other summer squash.

And you should be contemplating zucchini dishes right about now. Though it is available year 'round, it is most abundant from late spring through summer. This means the cheapest, best zucchini are appearing in food stores and at farmer's markets.

In addition to diminutive size, look for perfect, whole, unblemished, firm zucchini; they should seem heavy for their size. Color varies according to the variety, ranging from pale yellowish to very dark green, with many striped variations. Examine the blossom end (opposite where the stem has been cut) for any signs of rot. Plan to use them within two or three days and wash them off just before proceeding with the recipe.

Some recipes direct you to sprinkle cut zucchini with salt and let them sit to draw out some water or reduce bitterness. If you choose small, underripe squash, you should not have a problem with bitterness. You may want to draw out some water, however, depending on the recipe.

Zucchini has a real affinity for fresh herbs — try tarragon, chervil, basil, parsley, chives. Or try a hint of rosemary, alone or in combination, with hot zucchini, simply and slowly cooked in butter; or with lightly poached zucchini, cooled and tossed with olive oil and lemon juice.

Three of the following recipes originated somewhere near the Mediterranean where many of the best uses of zucchini occur, even though squash was originally a New World foodstuff.

Zucchini Stuffed with Corn & Cheese

4 small zucchini
1 cup corn kernels
⅔ cup ricotta cheese
1 to 2 tablespoons chives, finely chopped
salt and freshly ground black pepper
¾ cup grated sharp cheddar cheese

Blanch the squash in boiling salted water for five minutes. Cool slightly (dousing in cold water will speed the process). Halve and scoop out the seeds, forming cavities.

Coarsely puree the corn and ricotta cheese in a food processor or food mill. Add the chives and season with salt and pepper. Fill the squash halves with the mixture, mounding slightly. Cover with grated cheese. Place in a buttered casserole and bake, covered, in a preheated 350°F oven for 15 minutes. Uncover and bake 20 minutes or longer, until the squash is tender and the topping is browned.

Serves four. This is adapted from *The Victory Garden Cookbook* by Marian Morash, a valuable resource for the cook, as well as the cooking gardener, because it is full of useful information about selecting and using various vegetables at their best whether you are making your choices in the garden or in the supermarket.

Sweet-Sour Zucchini, Sicilian Style

2 pounds zucchini
1 large clove garlic, crushed
2 tablespoons olive oil
2 tablespoons wine vinegar
2 tablespoons water
2 tablespoons pine nuts
2 tablespoons sultanas (golden raisins)
4 anchovy fillets, chopped small
salt, pepper

Cut the zucchini into strips about 2 to 3 inches long. Salt them. Let them sit for at least half an hour. Drain and pat dry.

Cook the garlic slowly in the oil and, after a couple of minutes, add the zucchini strips. Keep them moving until they are coated in oil and just beginning to color. Pour in vinegar and water, cover and simmer for 10 minutes. Remove the cover, add the nuts, sultanas and anchovies and cook more rapidly until the liquid is reduced to about two tablespoons Keep stirring, so that the zucchini are bathed in the flavors of the sauce. Correct the seasonings and serve with bread.

Serves six. Adapted from Jane Grigson's *Vegetable Book,* a delightful mixture of delicious scholarship and wonderful recipes.

Tunisian Zucchini Salad

1½ pounds zucchini
2 cloves garlic, very finely chopped
4 tablespoons olive oil
2 tablespoons lemon juice
2 teaspoons caraway seeds, crushed
pinch of cayenne pepper
salt and freshly ground black pepper

Boil the zucchini in a little salted water until just tender. Drain, allow to cool, and then cut into ½-inch rounds. Combine the other ingredients and pour them over the zucchini. Toss well and serve.

Serves four. Adapted from *Recipes For An Arabian Night* by David Scott.

Afghan Zucchini with Yogurt

    2 cups yogurt
    1½ pounds zucchini
    ¼ cup vegetable oil
    1 large onion, chopped
    2 medium tomatoes, sliced or chopped
    salt
    red pepper

Drain the yogurt in a coffee filter, paper towel or fine sieve for an hour to thicken it.

Cut the zucchini into 1-inch pieces. Fry the chopped onion in the vegetable oil over a medium heat until it is very soft and beginning to turn golden. Then add the zucchini; fry it for a couple of minutes before adding the tomatoes, salt and pepper. Cover and cook over a low heat for 10 to 15 minutes. Uncover, turn up the heat a bit and evaporate most of the liquid, stirring frequently.

Put half the yogurt on a warmed dish and arrange the zucchini mixture on it. Top with the remaining yogurt. Pour any cooking juices over the top layer and serve immediately. Serves four.

Adapted from *Noshe Djan: Afghan Food & Cookery* by Helen Saberi — a sterling example of a cookbook written by someone who married into a very different culture, learned about the cooking and couldn't resist sharing.

Kernels of Truth

The Independent
July 18, 1990

IT IS TRUE — the best corn on the cob is corn that's picked, shucked as you run to the kitchen where the water is coming to a boil, cooked until just done and served immediately. This haste pays off because the sugars in the corn start to turn into starch as soon as the ears are separated from the plant, gradually making the corn less sweet and less juicy.

As this scenario is possible only with home-grown, look for locally grown corn that was rushed to market, stored in refrigeration. Buy it soon thereafter and eat it the same day.

Shop where you can peel back the husk and look for tightly packed, juicy kernels with milky, not watery, juices. The husks should be green, not dry, and the silk should be golden, not dark brown. There should be no hint of decay. I'm not bothered by the worm or two, as long as they haven't eaten much, and I can avoid eating them. I hope their presence signals a lack of chemical pesticides.

I won't suggest particular varieties; to my mind freshness is much more important than whether the corn is white or yellow, and I like the flavor of both. Store the corn in your refrigerator and remove the husk and silk just before cooking. I usually rinse under running water because that makes it a bit easier to get out the stubborn strands of silk stuck between the rows.

You can boil corn in unsalted water for 3 to 10 minutes; the timing depends on freshness and variety. If you steam it, don't pile up more than a couple of layers or the bottom ears will be overdone while the top are not quite done. Steaming will take somewhere between 4 and 12 minutes.

The microwave treats corn on the cob very well. You can either clean the corn, wrap it loosely in waxed paper and arrange it on the bottom of your oven, or cook the whole ear — husks, silk and all. The second method means you have to deal with hot husks and silk, but they come away fairly easily when the corn is cooked. You might want to peel the husks back gently to inspect for worms before proceeding.

Cook on high or full power and start testing one ear after 2 minutes, four ears after 5 minutes. If you are not using a turntable, stop and rearrange the ears at halftime. The corn will continue to cook when you remove it from the microwave so try to stop just before it is done. A little practice will make perfect.

If you want to use your outdoor grill, soak the unhusked corn for at least half an hour in cold water and cook it over hot coals for 20 to 30 minutes, turning it every 5. Here again, some people peel back the husks to remove the silk before cooking.

Once the corn is cooked you can serve it with a little salt and plain or fancy butter (mixed with herbs or pureed peppers, for example). I've never tried leftover pesto, but that sounds all right, too.

When a recipe calls for the kernels to be cut from the cob, use a sharp knife and do the cutting over a bowl to catch any liquids. Don't cut into the cob. One ear of corn will yield approximately a half-cup of kernels.

Corn is a New World foodstuff; it was probably domesticated 5,000 years ago in either Mexico or Peru. Although the early European explorers took it back to the Old World, only the Italians did much with it, mostly in the form of polenta (cornmeal). The rest of the continent, until very recently, fed it to their livestock. This means you want to look to American — North, Central and South — cookbooks for inspiration.

Sausage Creole with Corn Pancakes

2 pounds hot Italian sausage
olive oil, if necessary
½ cup finely chopped onion
¼ cup finely chopped celery
½ cup finely chopped green pepper
2 to 4 finely chopped green onions
¼ cup minced fresh parsley
2 bay leaves
2 whole cloves
very small pinch of nutmeg
salt and pepper
pinch cayenne pepper
2 teaspoons finely chopped fresh basil, or
** ½ teaspoon dried**
¼ teaspoon thyme
6 tomatoes, peeled, seeded and chopped, or
** 1 large can Italian tomatoes**
8 to 12 corn pancakes (recipe follows)

Cut the sausage into 1-inch lengths and brown lightly in a hot skillet. Drain away the fat and remove the sausage from the skillet.

Add a little olive oil, if needed, and sauté the onions and celery until they soften and the onion looks transparent. Add the green pepper and green onion and sauté for a few minutes more. Add the parsley, bay leaves, cloves, nutmeg, salt, pepper, cayenne pepper, basil and thyme and stir around briefly before adding the tomatoes. Bring to a rapid boil, stir and break up the tomatoes a bit before turning down to a simmer and adding the sausage. It should be done in about 20 minutes but taste and adjust the seasonings after 10. Add a little

Tabasco sauce if you'd like it hotter or a squeeze of lemon juice if it needs to be more tart.

To serve four: Line up slightly overlapping corn pancakes on one half of a plate. Serve the sausage on the side but spoon sauce over the pancakes.

Venezuelan Corn Pancakes

1½ cups corn kernels (3 ears)
½ cup sour cream
1 egg
3 tablespoons flour
¼ teaspoon salt
pinch of freshly ground pepper
2 tablespoons melted butter

Blend or process all the ingredients until fairly smooth.

Using a scant quarter cup of batter, make the pancakes, 3 to 4 at a time on a medium hot, well-greased griddle.

This will make from 8 to 12 pancakes, depending on how scant the quarter cup of batter is. Adapted from *The Book of Latin American Cooking* by Elisabeth Lambert Ortiz, which contains many other interesting recipes using corn, including a simple pureed corn sauce served with cauliflower.

Bill Neal's Shrimp & Corn Pie

8 cooked biscuits
2 tablespoons melted butter
1 pound large shrimp, peeled and deveined
2 tablespoons dry sherry
2 tablespoons butter
1½ cups sliced small mushrooms
½ cup chopped scallions
½ cup chopped red or green bell pepper
1 cup cut fresh corn kernels (2 ears)
¼ teaspoon pepper

¼ teaspoon grated cayenne pepper
pinch grated nutmeg
½ teaspoon salt
3 eggs
1 cup milk

Preheat broiler. Split the biscuits and line the bottom of a baking dish with them. Brush the split halves with the melted butter and toast under the broiler until golden and crisp.

Toss the shrimp with the sherry.

Melt 2 tablespoons of butter in a skillet and sauté the mushrooms over a medium heat. Stir in the scallions and bell pepper and cook until just wilted. Remove from heat and pour the vegetables into a mixing bowl with the corn, pepper, cayenne, nutmeg and salt.

Beat the eggs with the milk and pour over the vegetables. Arrange the shrimp on the biscuits. Pour the vegetable mixture over the shrimp and biscuits. Bake in a 325°F oven for 50 minutes or until the custard is set. Do not brown or let puff.

I've never had anything quite like this absolutely delicious recipe from Bill Neal's *Southern Cooking.* The different flavors and textures are all there together but none overwhelms the others. Serves four.

[*Reprinted by permission from University of North Carolina Press. – ed.*]

Hot Off the Presses

The Independent
September 19, 1990

Last Sunday was a milestone of sorts in my family. My mother joined the rest of us when she plugged in her first microwave oven. I was a little surprised that it took her so long. After all, this is a woman who had a food processor even before James Beard proclaimed them to be serious kitchen appliances.

Not that I'm accusing anyone without a microwave of being a Luddite. Some of my best friends don't microwave. But I bet their children will, in a future with a microwave in every kitchen rather than a chicken in every pot. I do wonder what will be cooked in them, and I hope it will be more interesting than 95 percent of the recipes in the instruction book that accompanied my microwave oven. Even discounting the weird color balance of the photograph, I had no interest in cooking chicken with mayonnaise, dried onion soup mix, bottled Russian dressing and apricot-pineapple preserves no matter how much time I could save.

Someday there won't be a need for separate microwave cookbooks; the relevant information will be incorporated into the standard books. But for now, there are some good, basic microwave cookbooks that will help you learn how to use the oven while you cook worthwhile recipes. Barbara Kafka's *Microwave Gourmet* has become a classic. Another more recent volume is Jean Anderson and Elaine Hanna's *Micro Ways*.

Anderson and Hanna's book is up-to-date and relaxed. Being current is important because the use of the microwave is evolving rapidly, and what's accepted wisdom one day is often debunked the next. Their relaxed approach is nice; unlike some cookbooks that lock you into rigid proportions and ingredient lists, *Micro Ways* teaches you the variables that will help you master microwave cooking in order to cook what you really want to cook. For example, container size and shape can be crucial to a recipe's success, and this book offers useful advice about which container variables are important when you change the number of servings or adapt one of your favorite non-microwave recipes.

Currently, my particular interest in microwave cooking is ethnic-food cookbooks. The two I'm currently trying out are *Moghul Microwave: Cooking Indian Food the Modern Way* by Julie Sahni and *Mexican Microwave Cookery* by Carol Medina Maze.

Sahni's book is exciting. She believes that a cook should be familiar with various cooking techniques and choose the best one for a particular recipe. In that vein, she treats the microwave as just another kitchen tool that happens to do certain things very well and has avoided writing the sort of cookbook. where every recipe, no matter how contrived, uses the featured appliance.

Sahni finds the microwave good for producing dishes where "trapped moist heat is used to create succulent food with complex flavors which makes it suitable for Moghul cooking — classic rather than regional Indian food." She's aimed for recipes where flavor, appearance and healthfulness are improved or significant time is saved. And she has succeeded admirably — every recipe I've tried from *Moghul Microwave* has been superb.

Mexican Microwave Cookery is not as good as Sahni's book. It contains a number of instances where there seems to be no advantage to using a microwave. (And I am always suspicious of even a few recipes calling for a can of cream-of-anything soup.) Nevertheless the book has been useful for learning microwave techniques to apply to the Mexican food I like to cook, and many of the recipes are quite good.

Fragrant Beef with Peas (Keema Matar)

I teaspoon ground cumin
2 teaspoons ground coriander
½ teaspoon turmeric
I teaspoon cayenne pepper
3 tablespoons light vegetable oil
¾ cup finely chopped onion
I teaspoon finely chopped garlic
I tablespoon grated or crushed fresh ginger
I pound lean ground beef
2 tablespoons tomato paste
⅓ cup plain yogurt, coconut milk or water
¾ cup green peas (fresh or frozen)
2 tablespoons heavy cream, half-and-half or milk
I teaspoon garam masala or ground roasted
   cumin seeds
kosher salt to taste
4 tablespoons chopped fresh coriander (cilantro)

Combine cumin, coriander, turmeric and cayenne in a small bowl and reserve.

Place oil, onion, garlic and ginger in a 10-inch microwave-safe skillet. Cook, uncovered, at 100-percent power in a 650- to 700-watt carousel oven for 8 minutes (or until onions are lightly colored). Stir in the spice mixture and continue cooking, uncovered, for an additional minute. Remove from oven.

Add beef, tomato paste and yogurt and mix thoroughly. Cook, covered, at 100-percent power for 8 minutes (or until beef is fully cooked), stirring once. Uncover, add peas and cream, and replace cover. Cook, covered, for 2 more minutes (or

until sauce comes to a boil). Remove from oven. Uncover, stir in garam masala, salt to taste, add 2 tablespoons coriander and replace cover. Let the dish stand for 5 minutes, then uncover and serve sprinkled with the remaining coriander.

Serves four. Sahni offers menu suggestions as well as information about making this dish ahead of time. Don't worry about ingredients that are not on your usual shopping lists (garam masala, a spice mixture, for example). She defines and explains how to use or prepare them clearly and most are readily available in supermarkets or specialty stores in the Triangle.

Fish in Red Sauce (Pescado en Salsa Roja)

3 tablespoons vegetable oil
1½ pounds rockfish or red snapper fillets
6-ounce can tomato paste
I cup water
¼ cup chopped onion
3 garlic cloves, chopped
2 tablespoons red chile powder
½ teaspoon dried leaf oregano
½ teaspoon ground cumin
I teaspoon salt
I lime or lemon, cut in wedges

Pour 2 tablespoons oil into a 12 x 8-inch casserole. Place fish fillets in dish, turning to coat both sides with oil. Cover with waxed paper, microwave on 100 percent for 4 minutes turning fish after 2 minutes. Set fish aside.

To make Salsa Roja, place remaining tablespoon oil, tomato paste, water, onion, garlic, chile powder, oregano, cumin and salt in a blender or food processor. Process until pureed. Pour mixture into a 1-quart bowl. Cover with waxed paper microwave on 70 percent for 10 minutes, stirring every 3 minutes.

Pour cooked salsa over cooked fish. Cover

with waxed paper; microwave on 70 percent for 2 minutes. Serve immediately with lime or lemon wedges.

Serves four to six. Red chile powder is ground dried red chiles, not a commercial chili powder mixture which usually contains garlic, cumin, oregano and other spices.

Summer Seasons

The Independent
September 5, 1990

THE CURRENT TORRID WEATHER not withstanding, summer is on the way out. The day when a decent fresh tomato will not be seen at any store in town is all too rapidly approaching. Now's the time to take advantage of the later summer's bounty — to squeeze a few more moments of enjoyment from fresh fruits and vegetables that either won't be around, or won't be worth buying in a month or so.

Before their harvest fades, take a few minutes to preserve some fresh herbs. Barbara Kafka recommends drying fresh herbs in a microwave oven (from *The Microwave Gourmet*), a method that I tried successfully. Here's how to do it: Wash one to two cups of herbs. Dry them by gently blotting or giving a whirl in a salad spinner. Separate the leaves from the stems and scatter on a paper towel. Leave uncovered and microwave on high, stopping every minute to toss them about and check for dryness. Kafka suggests four minutes for two cups of herbs; I have found it varies by herb and amount. One and a half cups of oregano took three minutes, for instance.

I've tried other herb-drying methods over the years but this is the best yet for basil, tarragon and oregano. I plan to try other herbs soon.

Gazpacho and corn chowder will make use of late summer produce — corn and tomatoes. Here are my favorite recipes for each. The gazpacho, the only version I ever make, calls for fresh, ripe, raw tomatoes, thus avoiding the cooked tomato taste of canned tomatoes or tomato juice. I use a two-step process — blending or processing part of the ingredients to a puree and then stirring in coarsely chopped ingredients and garnishes.

While the corn chowder can be made with good quality frozen corn, and sweet green and red peppers are available year 'round, the soup is at its best with fresh and seasonal ingredients. Some versions call for chicken stock, but it's not necessary. Fresh black pepper is, however; you want a little bite to it, so if you grind your own (the easiest way to get really fresh pepper), grind it a little more coarsely for this soup.

Gazpacho II

    4 medium tomatoes, peeled and seeded
    1 cucumber, peeled and seeded
      (if you're feeling refined)
    1 to 2 cloves garlic
    2 sweet peppers, green or red
    3 tablespoons olive oil
    ¼ cup red wine vinegar
    1 medium onion
    salt and freshly ground black pepper
    a small pinch of cayenne pepper or
      a large pinch of paprika
    Optional: ½ cup bread crumbs
    A selection of chopped optional extras:
      pitted black olives; hard boiled eggs;
      green onions; croutons

Puree three of the tomatoes, half of the cucumber (if the skin is waxed, peel it away, whether you're feeling refined or not), all the garlic, one sweet pepper, the olive oil, vinegar, onion, salt and pepper and cayenne pepper or paprika in a blender or food processor. Chop the remaining tomato, cucumber and peppers and stir into the puree. Add the bread crumbs if you are using them and chill. I add the bread crumbs about only one third of the time I make gazpacho. The bread should be a white bread with a dense, elastic crumb.

Just before serving, add chopped ice or ice water to thin the soup to your liking, check the seasonings (if it seems to lack that certain indefinable something, try a little more vinegar) and stir in your choice of optional extras.

Serves four and is sure to start some arguments about authenticity. Leftovers are good for several days.

Corn Chowder

    3 to 5 slices bacon, chopped
    1 onion, chopped
    4 potatoes, cubed
    1 sweet green or red pepper, chopped
    2 cups water
    1 cup milk
    2 cups corn kernels (from 4 ears)
    salt and freshly ground black pepper
    paprika

Fry the bacon until crisp. Stir in the onion and cook until it softens. Add the potatoes and sweet peppers. Cook and stir for a minute, until they absorb some of the fat. Add the water, and briskly simmer for 10 minutes, until the potatoes are just starting to get tender. Add the milk and corn, season to taste with salt and pepper and simmer for 10 more minutes, or until the corn has cooked through. Sprinkle with paprika and serve.

Serves four. The recipe started life in *The American Heritage Cookbook,* a delightful combination of scholarship and good cooking.

To Sir (Isaac Newton) with Love

The Independent
October 10, 1990

I F YOU'VE BEEN PAYING ATTENTION to tempera-ture alone, you might have missed the fact that fall is here. But if you've been watching the quality of light as the sun sinks ever earlier into the west, or the varieties of apples in the stores, you know that the seasons have changed. Accordingly, your cookbook reading, like mine, may be turning to ways to exploit those varieties.

Apples are available most of the year, either from cold storage or imported from the southern hemisphere, but the best selection of high quality apples is coming in right now. They may seem a little funky if you're looking at organic fruit. Don't worry if what you see is less than some platonic ideal: A good apple can be small, oddly shaped or unevenly colored. Avoid bruised or mushy-feeling fruit; look for firm, fresh-smelling apples. (A bruise or two in otherwise good fruit might be all right if you're planning to use it right away and can negotiate a price reduction.)

Try lots of varieties to find those you like. I've eaten so many mushy, tasteless Red and Golden Delicious over the years that I usually go for something else, like Pippins or Macintoshes or whatever smells best. If you're in doubt, I settle for the ubiquitous Granny Smiths — they keep well and are reliably tart and crisp.

Store your apples in the refrigerator if they are going to be around for more than a couple of days. And do look them over every so often — one rotten apple *will* spoil the bunch.

Don't confine yourself to apple pie, apple crisp or some other sweet dish. Here are some savory apple recipes for you to try, including one of my favorite uses of the microwave oven: fresh, fast applesauce.

Microwave Applesauce

Per person:
1 large or two small apples
1 scant tablespoon water or cider
1 teaspoon to 1 tablespoon brown sugar
1 teaspoon butter
a scant pinch of salt
**a hint of nutmeg or cinnamon or Chinese
    five-spice powder**

Peel, core and roughly chop the apples. Place them in a microwave-safe container with water or cider. Cover and cook on high until very tender, stirring a couple of times. Two apples take about three minutes to get tender; 12 smallish ones, nine minutes. You want the apples to get mushy, so timing is not crucial.

Remove from the oven and mash the apples while stirring in the brown sugar, butter, salt and spices. Take account of what you'll be serving the applesauce with and adjust the sweetness and seasonings accordingly.

Any leftovers are good hot, warm or cold for breakfast, lunch or dinner. Make sure the spices are fresh — either grind your own or buy small quantities of ground spices and replace them frequently.

Chicken with Apples & Hard Cider

2 tablespoons butter
**2 tart cooking apples, peeled, cored
    and thinly sliced**
1 chicken, disjointed
salt and pepper

rosemary
thyme
I cup hard cider
$\frac{1}{2}$ cup heavy cream

In a large skillet, sauté the apples in a tablespoon of the butter over medium heat. Remove with a slotted spoon and set aside.

Pick over the chicken for stray pin-feathers and the like, rinse and dry it well. I like to cut each breast half into half again (using good kitchen shears or a heavy cleaver). Add the remaining butter to the skillet and brown the chicken over medium-high heat. Sprinkle with salt, pepper and a good pinch of rosemary and thyme toward the end of the browning. Add the cider and bring to a boil. Turn down the heat, cover the pan and simmer until the chicken is done, 25 to 40 minutes.

Remove the chicken to a hot serving platter and keep warm. Bring the liquid in the pan to a boil and reduce by about half, stirring all the while. Be sure to stir up any of the delicious sticky bits on the bottom of the pan. Add the apples and the cream, bring them to boil once again, stirring until the sauce comes together. Correct the seasoning, pour the sauce over the chicken and serve.

This serves four. Crisp sautéed potatoes and a green salad are admirable accompaniments. Over the years I have created many an excellent dish that ultimately can be traced to the basic sautéed chicken recipe found in *Mastering the Art of French Cooking* by Child, Bertholle and Beck. This variation occurred one evening when all the necessary ingredients were on hand. It was so good, I immediately wrote down what I had done. If you have no hard cider, use a tart sweet cider (hard cider is alcoholic, sweet is non-alcoholic). To reduce the amount of fat, substitute yogurt for the cream but add it at the last minute and heat it through without boiling.

Grandma Margaret Flemming's Pork Chops & Rice

4 to 6 pork chops
2 tablespoons butter
salt and pepper
thyme
rosemary
I cup rice
water
I onion, sliced into 4 to 6 slices
I apple, peeled, cored and sliced
** into 4 to 6 slices**

Using a large iron skillet with a cover, brown the pork chops in the butter. Sprinkle with salt, pepper, thyme and rosemary and remove from the skillet.

Lightly fry the rice in the drippings, stirring frequently. When the rice looks "milky," turn off the heat, sprinkle with salt and pepper and barely cover the rice with water. Let the pan sit, covered, for 5 minutes while you preheat the oven to 350°F and prepare the onion and apple.

Arrange the chops on the rice and place an onion slice and an apple slice on each. Add a little more water but not enough to cover the chops. Cover the pan and bake for an hour. Check after 30 to 40 minutes to see if it is drying out too rapidly and add a little more water if necessary.

Serves four. If you want to serve six, get thick pork chops and use 1½ cups of rice. When I was a kid, my siblings and I would hope for the serving with the most crusty bits of rice from the bottom of the pan. I specify an iron skillet to maximize this pleasure, though any ovenproof casserole of the right size can be used. Brown rice also works well; just cook the dish a little longer and check the liquid level twice.

A Red Hot Christmas

The Independent
November 21, 1990

A S BEFITS A TEXAS BIRTH, my first food memory is the night on the river in San Antonio when fresh, hot tortillas entered my consciousness. I was somewhere around 3 years old, and I wanted to sit at that table and eat them forever.

Though I have many years of experience with Mexican food, I'm not a snob about it. If it's done well, I love it: "authentic," Tex-Mex, New Mexican, *nouvelle* Mexican, church cookbook collection Mexican, and quite a few of the dishes at Del Taco, a fast-food Mexican joint.

The Mexican shelf of my cookbook collection reflects my wide-ranging tastes. Each of the books has some particular strength or focus. Any one of them would make a good holiday gift, or enable you to cook good Mexican food. But you may find that one will suit your tastes better than another.

◆ *The Art of Mexican Cooking: Traditional Mexican Cooking for Aficionados* by Diana Kennedy — This is Kennedy's latest Mexican cookbook and as per usual it is absolutely authentic, with more information than you will ever use (but not more than you will ever want to know). "Aficionado" is right. But don't be frightened. Though this book is for the more-than-casual Mexican cook, you won't need an advanced degree to cook its many terrific recipes.

◆ *The Complete Book of Mexican Cooking* by Elisabeth Lambert Ortiz — This is my personal favorite among all my Mexican cookbooks because every recipe I've ever cooked has turned out great.

It is real Mexican cooking. You can cook entire authentic meals or just find a recipe or two to add to your everyday meal rotation. The only edition currently available is a mass-market paperback — perfect for inserting into a Christmas stocking.

◆ *Sunset Mexican Cook Book and Sunset Southwest Cook Book: The New Cuisine with a Mexican-Old West Flavor* by the editors of Sunset Books and Sunset Magazine — Sunset cookbooks are always great value for the money. They are inexpensive. They have a large (8½ x 11-inch) format so they will open up flat. And they are full of useful information on techniques and ingredients. The recipes are well-tested and Sunset updates the books from time to time. I like and use both of these. The Mexican cookbook had all the recipes I wanted when I first started cooking Mexican — tortillas (remember when canned tortillas were the only store-bought possibility if you lived outside the Southwest?), tacos, enchiladas, and so on. The Southwest cookbook has a more up-to-date slant (but not too far out — it is "new" not "nouvelle"). It offers, for instance, lots of interesting things to do on an outdoor grill.

Now, for a little warm-up exercise, I offer a beef enchilada recipe adapted from my bean-and-chile-stained 20-year-old $1.95 *Sunset Mexican Cook Book*.

Rolled Beef Enchiladas

16 corn tortillas
vegetable oil
2½ cups red chile sauce (recipe below)
3 cups ground beef filling (recipe below)
1 medium onion, chopped
2 cups shredded sharp cheddar or
    Monterey jack cheese
2 cups sour cream

If you have a microwave oven, rub each tortilla with salad oil and wrap stacks of 5 to 6 in waxed paper. Microwave on high for 50 seconds, until limp and warm. The more traditional (non-microwave but higher fat) method is to lightly fry each tortilla until limp in medium hot oil.

Dip each tortilla in the warm red chile sauce. Spoon about three tablespoons of the beef filling down the center of each tortilla — sprinkle with chopped onion and a little cheese. Roll the tortilla around the filling and place flap side down in an ungreased shallow casserole. If necessary, use several pans rather than making several layers of enchiladas.

Pour the remaining sauce over the enchiladas, being careful to moisten all top surfaces. Sprinkle with cheese and bake, uncovered, in a 350° oven, until hot and bubbling (15-20 minutes). Serve with sour cream on the side. Serves five to eight.

Red Chile Sauce

> 4 ounces (8 to 10) whole dried ancho,
>   pasilla, or California chiles (mild)
> 2½ cups hot water
> ¼ cup tomato sauce
> 1 clove garlic, minced
> 2 tablespoons vegetable oil
> salt and pepper
> 1 teaspoon oregano
> ¼ teaspoon toasted cumin, ground

Toast chiles lightly in a 400°F oven until they give off a mild aroma (3 to 4 minutes). Remove from the oven, cool, and then remove and discard the stems and seeds. Cover with hot water and let stand for an hour.

Place the chiles in a blender or food processor with enough water to let you blend until smooth. Add the rest of the water and the other ingredients and blend. Simmer gently for 10 minutes, stirring from time to time.

Ground Beef Filling

> 1 pound ground beef
> 1 to 2 tablespoons vegetable oil (if needed)
> 1 medium onion, chopped
> ½ cup red chile sauce

Fry the ground beef, using the oil if the beef is lean enough to make that necessary. Break it apart as it browns. Add the onion, turn down the heat and cook until the onion is soft. Add the chile sauce and let the filling simmer gently for 10 minutes.

Our Own Traditions

The Independent
December 19, 1990

HOLIDAYS ARE INDEED A TIME to celebrate family traditions. In our affluent, literate society these "roots" are as likely to be acquired as inherited. We are no longer limited to what we have done in the past, but can choose from a range of possibilities.

My own family situation was slightly unusual: I had a wonderful stepfather and also maintained close ties with my father's family. While I never met any of my grandfathers, for a long time I had three grandmothers. I remember the first Thanksgiving with the third grandmother: I became a convert to new traditions when the creamed onions appeared on the table.

Mine was also a military family; we lived in many exotic and wonderful places, from Columbus, Georgia to Heilbron, Germany, and we took interest in the food and customs all along the way. Our holiday meals weren't place specific; these feasts took place wherever the family gathered around the table.

Each evening meal was a social occasion. We'd discuss with equal intensity the state of the family, the block or the world; the meal was an event, more often than not full of fun and humor. I inherited a love of good food and the pleasure of preparing and eating it.

What made holiday meals festive were things that took a little more effort: an entrée a little out of the ordinary, a few extra side dishes, the "good" china and silver, wine, candles and maybe a few guests at the table. The menu would probably be roast — beef, pork, or our particular favorite, lamb; roasted or mashed potatoes (gravy!); some green vegetable, probably broccoli; a selection of side dishes, maybe a Southern ham, spiced peaches, creamed onions, candied sweet potatoes; and my mother's famous "risen" biscuits *(see page 44.)* Dessert was usually apple and pecan pie.

When it comes time to lay your own festive table, strike a balance between the new and the old. Think about what you remember fondly about past family gatherings but incorporate a new recipe or two. Don't set impossible standards or try to do too much yourself. There is real pleasure in sharing the work as well as the rewards of that work.

And while you're thinking about your own festive meal, consider a donation to one of the many groups that will share the bounty with those who have less. I've heard that this year some organizations are concerned that donations will drop because the economy is slowing down; I hope all the talk of recession will make us more willing to respond where help is needed.

Creamed Onions

20 ounces small fresh pearl onions
1 cup dry white wine or vermouth, stock
or water
2 sprigs parsley
1 bay leaf
salt and pepper
1 tablespoon butter
white sauce (recipe below)

Trim the root end of each onion. Loosen their skins by immersing in boiling water for 30 to 60 seconds or by microwaving in one uncovered layer with two tablespoons of water for $2\frac{1}{2}$ minutes. When they cool down the onions should, more or less, slip out of their skins. Some will need a little help.

Cook the onions in the wine, vermouth, stock or water with the parsley, bay leaf, salt, pepper and butter. Depending on their size this will take 15 to 30 minutes. Drain the onions, discard the parsley and bay leaf, and reduce the cooking liquid to about a half-cup.

Make your white sauce (see below), gently stir in the onions, heat until all is quite hot and serve. A sprinkle of finely chopped parsley or paprika will liven up the whiteness.

I don't know what recipe, if any, Grandma Margaret followed years ago, but this recent Thanksgiving adaptation from *The Victory Garden Cookbook* by Marian Morash was my best effort yet. I specify 20 ounces of onions because pearl onions seem to be most commonly available in 10-ounce boxes. Frozen prepared pearl onions are available in some local supermarkets, but resist the temptation to save time; you just won't get the same intensity of flavor. You can prepare the onions a day in advance, make the white sauce the day of serving, and combine and reheat just before the meal. This will make enough for six to eight as a side dish.

White Sauce

2 tablespoons flour
2 tablespoons butter
1 cup liquid (about ½ onion cooking liquid
   and ½ milk)
¼ cup heavy cream

Melt the butter over a medium low heat. Stir in the flour and cook for a couple of minutes stirring constantly. Adjust the heat so that while everything is bubbling there is no danger of it turning brown.

Incorporate the liquid. One method is the gradual: letting each addition heat up in the pan, then stirring madly with a wire whisk to incorporate it thoroughly before adding the next bit. Another method is to preheat the liquids just to boiling and add it to the roux (cooked butter and flour mixture) all a once, whisking all the while. Whichever method you choose, simmer the sauce gently for minute or two before stirring in the cream and tasting for seasonings.

Tim McDonough remembers —

Helen was a conspirator, and probably a charter member, in the annual mixture of nostalgia and hoop dreams known as the Monkeytop Memorial NCAA Tournament Basketball Pool. Like the Regulator Bookshop and like bridge, the Pool played right into Helen's joys — people and ideas, gravitas and foolery.

HHW was a most loyal scorer of entries, not only at the raucous donut-fueled Saturday mornings but for the quiet off-nights when she might be the only volunteer, still ready with quips and puns and insights into basketball, pool strategy, and the human condition. She always warmed a seat at Pool Central for the Finals.

In 1997 as her Blue Devils took a dive in the second round, Helen faded from the early leader board but came on strong near the end, blasting out of the pack to finish one measly pool point out of second place. A new "So Close" category was created for the occasion, and she reveled in simultaneous congratulations and condolences.

Her last dip in the Pool was 1998, the (possible) silver anniversary, for which her first round submission came via e-mail and closed "Hoopfully yours, Helen."

The Food of Love

The Independent
February 28, 1991

AH, LOVE! YOU NEVER KNOW what it'll inspire. You spot a friend in a store he's never ventured in before, closely questioning the butcher or fishmonger about freshness or the right cut. You turn the corner and see him in consultation with the wine merchant, a bunch of flowers in hand. Who's he having over for dinner tonight?

Love has been the motivation for many a fine meal. Although it can be romantic to go out to eat, there really is nothing quite like a meal prepared for and with someone you love. It can be especially seductive when it's unexpected, when you surprise your intended with your culinary talents. I remember one evening that started with spur-of-the-moment crepes . . .

I offer a menu here for lovers that consists of out-of-the-ordinary food well within the realm of a modestly outfitted kitchen.

You'll start with an interesting cheese and some crackers to nibble on while you and your true love get busy in the kitchen. The main course is Dou-ban Yu (Fish with Hot Sauce and Spices), boiled rice and Cold Cucumbers, Chinese Style. For dessert, I suggest a good bakery brownie or chocolate cake with vanilla or coffee ice cream (chocolate and love just seem to go together). Or end the meal very simply with a small cup of strong hot coffee and a few superior after-dinner mints.

Don't wait until the last minute to start shopping. You may need to make a trip to a specialty store if your usual supermarket doesn't stock Chinese hot bean sauce. For cheese, go to a store with a decent cheese department so that you may sample a few before you make up your mind. Don't get cute with the crackers — too many "flavor enhancers" will overwhelm the cheese.

Plan a stop at a market where someone in the wine department knows what's on the shelves, and solicit advice on a good wine to go with a hot Chinese fish dish. (Champagne is always festive and romantic, and a dry champagne will stand up well to the hot, garlicky fish flavors.)

Buy the fish the day you are going to cook it. Chat with the fish seller and ask exactly how fresh the fish is, or if it has been frozen, how long it has been thawed. Sniff it — good fish smells like fish and not in any way unpleasant.

Start the meal preparations by chilling the champagne. Then marinate the cucumbers. Remove the cheese from the refrigerator — the flavor will improve when it warms a little and softens. Set a romantic table. Flowers and candles encourage an appropriate mood; cloth napkins and pretty wine glasses can't hurt. When you are ready for dinner, wash and drain the rice, then start it cooking. Lastly, prepare the fish. Enjoy the meal; how you spend the rest of the evening is up to you.

Dou-Ban Yu

¾ to 1 pound firm white-fleshed fish fillets, thick rather than thin
½ to 1 cup peanut oil
2 tablespoons finely chopped fresh ginger
1 tablespoon finely chopped garlic
1 to 2 tablespoons hot bean sauce (depending on its strength and your taste for hot flavors)
3 green onions, chopped

MARINADE:
1 tablespoon rice wine, dry sherry or dry white wine
2 tablespoons soy sauce

SEASONINGS:
2 teaspoons cornstarch mixed with
    4 teaspoons water
1 cup fish stock or water
2 tablespoons soy sauce
3 tablespoons rice wine, dry sherry or
    dry white wine
1 teaspoon sugar

Score the skin side of the fish lightly with a sharp knife by making shallow slashes about ¾ inch apart. Mix the marinade ingredients, pour over the fish. Let it sit while you prepare the rest of the ingredients but turn it a couple of times to let both sides absorb flavor.

Mix the cornstarch with the stock or water in a cup or small bowl; then stir in the rest of the seasonings.

Using a wok or a skillet just large enough to hold the fish, heat enough oil to come about half way up the fish. Use a moderately high heat. Fry the fillets for 2 to 3 minutes per side, turning gently once, until brown and tender. Remove, drain away all but 4 tablespoons of the oil, and place the fish on a hot serving dish.

Reheat the pan and add the ginger and garlic to the reserved oil; stir fry briefly. Add the hot bean sauce and stir until well mixed with the ginger and garlic. Stir the seasonings and add to the pan. Bring to a boil; simmer until thickened. Add the green onions and pour over the fish.

This is adapted from *The Good Food of Szechwan* by Robert A. Delfs. (I surmise from the number of stained pages that this is one of my favorite Chinese cookbooks.)

Boiled Rice

½ to ¾ cup rice
twice as much water (1 to 1½ cups)

Rinse the rice well to remove the surface starch. This will keep it from becoming a gluey mess.

Bring the water to a boil; slowly pour in the rice. Stir once and bring back to a boil. Simmer briskly until the water level drops to just above the rice. Cover tightly and turn the heat down as low as possible. Check at about 15 minutes. It is done when the liquid is gone and the rice is cooked through but not mushy. Fluff up with a fork just before serving.

If the water disappears before the rice is tender, add a tablespoon or two, re-cover and continue cooking. If the rice is cooked before the fish is ready, turn off the heat, keep the cover on tightly and set the pan in a warm spot. It should keep for 15 to 30 minutes, depending on the prevailing winds. If it seems you absolutely cannot cook rice without ruining it, try cooking it like pasta in lots of briskly boiling water until it is almost tender (about 12 to 15 minutes). Drain it briefly and put in a tightly covered pan over the lowest possible heat or in a very low oven for a few minutes to finish it off.

Cold Cucumbers, Chinese Style

1 large or 2 medium cucumbers
2 tablespoons soy sauce
2 tablespoons rice or white wine vinegar
2 tablespoons vegetable oil (I prefer peanut oil)

Slice the unpeeled cucumbers as thinly as you can and still retain your sanity. If the cucumbers have been waxed, peel them. Mix the slices with the marinade and store in the refrigerator. This simple salad is at its best within a couple of hours, after the flavors have mingled but while the cucumber still remains somewhat crisp. Serve with a slotted spoon.

Serves two generously. Adapted from Helen Brown's *West Coast Cookbook*. This is not the Helen Gurley Brown of Cosmopolitan fame. I like to think that Helen Brown's food ideas have done more for romance that H. G. Brown's *Sex and the Single Girl* ever could.

A Jug of Wine, a Loaf...

The Independent
April 3, 1991

HERE'S PROOF THAT WE in *The Independent* Test Kitchens respond to reader requests. A new father recently asked for "one-handed" recipes — for foods that can be tended while minding the baby.

I suggest meat loaf. OK — you will have to put the baby down to put the meat loaf together. But if you can find just 15 minutes or so to devote to dinner preparation, meat loaf is a wise investment of time. Once it's in the oven, you're free for other pursuits; the only attention required is to pull it from the oven when it's done. It's good hot, warm or cold so if dinner gets postponed, it won't be ruined. Extra meat loaf can be reheated or turned into hearty sandwiches for days.

And don't worry about getting behind trendwise. Meat loaf is all the rage. Fashionable diners and cafés have it on the menu, and several recipes graced the *New York Times Sunday Magazine* earlier this winter.

My favorite meat loaf recipe is adapted from Robert Carrier's *Great Dishes of the World,* which I acquired in England in 1968. (I've tried to find a copy for a friend, but it is not available anymore.) Carrier is an American who settled in Europe after World War II and made a career of food — cookbooks, restaurants, department-store cooking boutiques. He describes meat loaf to his English readers as a meatloaf paté and first cousin to the hamburger.

There are two points requiring attention when making meat loaf. The first is selecting the meat.

It need not be an expensive cut, but it should not be too fatty. Ground chuck or round are good choices. You may need to grind the pork yourself. Trim the meat and either use an old-fashioned meat grinder or process small batches of 1-inch cubes in a food processor using short pulses.

The second matter to consider is the starchy filler. You need something to help hold things together, but as a co-worker of mine pointed out, you can easily add too much. The usual choices are soft bread crumbs soaked in a liquid and squeezed to a pulp, dried bread crumbs, crackers or oatmeal. A light touch is essential.

To accompany meat loaf, I suggest mashed potatoes. I've adapted the recipe from *Mrs. Witty's Home-Style Menu Cookbook*. Helen Witty's break-through is mashed potatoes that can be started in advance and finished when you are ready to sit down and eat. You will need a food mill or potato ricer to accomplish this, but it is worth the modest investment of time and money. Electrical methods are not really satisfactory because it's all too easy to develop the gluten and end up with a sticky mass. By contrast, the recipe here produces terrific mashed potatoes.

American Meat Loaf

> 1¼ pound ground beef
> ¾ pound ground pork
>   (or use 2 pounds ground beef)
> 1 small onion, finely chopped
> 1 celery rib, finely chopped
> 2 cloves garlic, finely chopped
> 2 tablespoons olive oil
> 1 tablespoon butter
> ½ cup red wine
> 2 slices bread
> 1 teaspoon salt
> freshly ground black pepper

> pinch of ground allspice
> ½ teaspoon thyme
> 2 eggs, beaten
> 1 bay leaf

Sauté the onion, celery and garlic in the oil and butter until transparent. Add the red wine and simmer gently for five minutes.

Trim the crusts from the bread, dice, and add to wine mixture. Let this soak for a moment, then pour this mixture over the ground meats. Mix well and season with salt, pepper, allspice and thyme. Add the beaten eggs and mix well once again. If you wish to test the seasonings, fry a small patty and taste. Pat into a loaf shape and place in a baking pan. Put the bay leaf on top and bake for about an hour in a 350°F oven. It is done when the juices run clear rather than pink, or when internal temperature is about 160°F.

Serves six to eight. Carrier suggests serving it with tomato sauce, chili sauce, sour cream, hot curry sauce or red wine sauce *à la bordelaise,* though I think it's just fine solo. If you're not tending a baby, by all means make your favorite tomato sauce from scratch. Red wine sauce *à la bordelaise* is not in my repertoire, but a simple deglazing of the pan with wine after removing the loaf and pouring off the fat is easy and delicious.

Mashed Potatoes

> 8 medium-large baking potatoes
> 1 cup, at least, milk
> salt and pepper to taste
> unsalted butter (a large dollop)

Peel and halve the potatoes and boil them gently in salted water until fork tender, but not soggy, 20 to 30 minutes.

Drain the potatoes and immediately put them

through a food mill (using the medium disk) or a potato ricer into the now dry cooking pot.

Do not touch the light heap of potato pulp until you are ready to proceed with dinner. It can wait, up to an hour, covered with a cloth.

Set the pot over low heat, pour in about half the liquid and vigorously stir the potatoes as they heat with a whisk or slotted spoon. Beat in more liquid until the consistency pleases you but make sure the potatoes get very hot. Add salt, pepper and butter, to taste.

Serves six. Mrs. Witty points out that you can vary this recipe along the healthful-decadent continuum to suit yourself by your selection of cream or milk and the quantity of butter. I use two percent milk and a large dollop of butter, because I like the taste of butter rather than the richness of cream.

Georgia on My Mind

The Independent
June 21, 1991

THERE'S NOTHING LIKE A REAL-LIFE social studies lesson, especially when it combines history, geography, current events — and food.

I was recently introduced to cooking as it's done in Georgia — not Athens, but Tbilisi — when I joined a group helping chef Tengiz Chiguinadze prepare a Georgian meal for visiting Georgians and their American hosts from the United Church of Chapel Hill. Until this event in April the main thing I knew about Soviet Georgia was that it was Stalin's birthplace and that its inhabitants had recently declared independence from the rest of the USSR. What I knew nothing about was their exhuberant style of cooking: highly flavored, spicy and often hot; just the sort of food I love.

Things were already underway when I arrived at the Wellspring Grocery kitchen in Chapel Hill, and I was immediately hit by wonderful spicy smells — garlic, turmeric, fenugreek, cumin, caraway, coriander (fresh leaves as well as ground seeds). The aroma was somewhere between Middle Eastern and Indian foods, reminiscent of Georgia's location on the map.

The helpers were both Georgian and American; the Georgians, knowing Chiguinadze's fame as a chef, were very excited. He demonstrated for us both his culinary and organizational skills, speaking some English. There were a couple of trilingual Georgians helping, but many of us spoke neither Russian nor Georgian. This was no problem; he kept us all busy chopping hot peppers, slicing eggplant for stuffing, grinding garlic and walnuts, stirring, kneading dough, stuffing dumplings. It was all fun — I only wish I had the language skills to better appreciate his sense of humor.

The food was superb: marinated mushrooms; a salad with chunks of tomato and cucumber, slices of sweet green peppers, chopped green onions, jalapeño peppers and parsley (both stems and leaves); Badrijani Nigvzis Satenit — cooked eggplant stuffed with a hot and spicy walnut puree; Satsivi — chunks of chicken breast mixed with a deep yellow ground-walnut sauce flavored mainly with turmeric and fenugreek; and Khinkali — juicy, meat-stuffed pasta dumplings.

As a result, these days I am not only more likely to notice news items about things like Zviad Ganisakhurdia's recent election as president of Georgia, I'm also on the lookout for Georgian recipes.

After rejecting my only Russian cookbook as worthless for Georgian cooking, I discovered a regional Russian cookbook, *Please to the Table* by Anya von Brenizon and John Welchmail. The spicing is a little timid compared to Chiguinadze's lavish hand, but taking that into account, I have been pleased with the things I have tried.

Satsivi (Chicken with Walnut Sauce)

2 pounds chicken breasts, with bone
I quart chicken stock

SAUCE:
2 cups walnut pieces
5 large cloves garlic, coarsely chopped
I bunch fresh cilantro, stems removed
I small dried red chili pepper, chopped
½ teaspoon coarse (kosher) salt
2 tablespoons unsalted butter

2 large onions, finely chopped
I tablespoon all-purpose flour
4 cups hot stock from cooking the chicken
2 large egg yolks
¾ teaspoon sweet Hungarian paprika
¼ teaspoon cayenne pepper, or more to taste
½ teaspoon ground fenugreek
¾ teaspoon ground coriander
small pinch of ground cinnamon
I teaspoon ground turmeric
½ teaspoon dried tarragon
salt to taste
3 tablespoons white vinegar
walnut pieces to garnish
cilantro sprigs for garnish

Rinse the chicken well, place in a saucepan and cover with chicken stock. Bring to a boil and skim off any foam that rises to the top. Simmer, covered, until the chicken is done, about 30 minutes. Remove the chicken and set aside 4 cups of the stock for the sauce.

When the chicken has cooled, remove skin and bones and shred the meat into medium-sized pieces. Grind the walnuts, garlic, cilantro and chili pepper with the coarse salt in a food processor.

Soften the onions in melted butter for 8 to10 minutes. Stir in the flour and cook, stirring, for another minute. Gradually stir in the chicken stock and simmer for 5 minutes. Turn the heat down to low and gradually add the ground walnut mixture, stirring. Let simmer for 3 to 4 minutes.

Whisk the egg yolks in a small bowl, then stir in about a ladleful of the simmering mixture to warm them. Whisk the yolks into the sauce. Add all the spices, the tarragon and salt and let simmer without allowing the sauce to boil, about 10 minutes. (Use the lowest heat you can manage, stir often and watch for signs that the egg yolks are scrambling.)

Add the shredded chicken to the sauce and stir to coat. Cool to room temperature, cover and refrigerate several hours or overnight. To serve, remove from the refrigerator about 20 minutes before serving. The sauce will have thickened considerably. Carefully stir and place in a large serving bowl, garnish with walnut pieces and cilantro sprigs.

Serves four or five. Adapted from *Please to the Table.* The main difference is more robust spicing. This would be an excellent dish for a cold buffet.

Badrijani Nigvzis Satenit (Eggplant Stuffed with Walnuts)

1 medium-large eggplant, sliced lengthwise, into 3/8-inch thick slices
1 teaspoon coarse (kosher) salt
1 cup walnut pieces
2 large cloves garlic
4 sprigs fresh cilantro
1/2 teaspoon hot Hungarian paprika
1/2 teaspoon turmeric
5 tablespoons water
3 tablespoons finely chopped onion
1/2 small rib celery, finely chopped
2 tablespoons tarragon vinegar
1/4 cup finely chopped basil
3 tablespoons finely chopped parsley
salt and pepper, to taste
1/3 cup olive oil
To garnish: cilantro sprigs, red onion rings, pomegranate seeds

Sprinkle the eggplant slices with coarse salt and let them drain in a colander for at least 1/2 hour. Meanwhile, grind the walnuts, garlic, cilantro, paprika and turmeric thoroughly in a food processor. When the mixture starts to resemble walnut butter add the water and process briefly again. Add the onion, celery, vinegar, basil, parsley, salt and pepper to taste and process briefly to combine.

Using a large skillet, sauté the eggplant slices in the olive oil. Cook until they are limp and just beginning to brown. Drain on paper towels. When cool enough to handle, spread each slice of eggplant generously with the walnut mixture. Roll up and place on a serving platter. When they are all done, cover and refrigerate for several hours or overnight. Garnish with cilantro, red onion rings or pomegranate seeds before serving. Serves four and is also adapted from *Please to the Table.*

Heat Wave Cooking

The Independent
August 7, 1991

THE DAY THE RECENT HEAT WAVE BROKE, I attended a potluck supper. We spent much of the evening on the porch admiring the rain and feeling less cranky than we had for days. The main course was Thai ribs, cooked on the grill (an admirable strategy on a hot day: Keep the heat outside). Other offerings included two fruit salads — one sweet, one savory (more strategy: Don't cook at all); pasta salads (cook early in the day); *spanikopita* — Greek spinach, cheese and phyllo-pastry pie (cook beforehand and serve at room temperature); and a hot Thai cabbage dish (eat hot peppers, break out in a sweat and feel cooler — a technique that doesn't work for me, as I feel hotter when I sweat, but some swear by it).

Even those of us who deal with heat waves by moving from air-conditioned site to air-conditioned site were loath to do much cooking during the spell. I initiated a rotating salad scheme preparing a new cold dish each day. Potato salad appeared the night after the last of the pasta salad had gone; cucumbers in sour cream followed green beans in yogurt dressing.

Chicken became a standby. Boneless or bone-in pieces cook quickly and are easily transformed into salads, burritos or stuffings for pita bread. Chicken can be baked, steamed, poached or microwaved, depending on which appliance is free — and will radiate the least heat into the room. When cool enough to handle and any bones or skin are removed, the meat can be shredded or torn into bite-sized pieces and tossed with a dressing.

I experimented with chicken salad, starting with vegetable or fruit additions: apples, mangoes, grapes, pecans, onions, celery, sweet and hot peppers, water chestnuts, snow peas. I used fresh herbs: cilantro, dill, basil and mint.

The dressing of choice was mayonnaise-based, seasoned to taste with curry powder, chili powder, garam masala, chutney, salsa or tahini. If it seemed too thick, I added a bit of milk, lemon juice, vinegar or water. A little minced garlic never seemed to hurt. Simplicity produced the best results: one to three items from the vegetable-fruit group, and one strong seasoning or chopped fresh herb.

My next variation will probably be chicken (or I might try turkey) with avocado and jicama chunks dressed with a cooked, pureed tomatillo, sour cream, fresh cilantro and lime juice. Or maybe peeled grapefruit chunks would be better than avocado. You get the idea: Look in the cupboard, at the farmer's market, or in the garden, and try combinations that sound promising.

I offer two recipes to add to your hot weather repertoire. The first is adapted from Ken Hom's *Quick & Easy Chinese Cooking.* I like this book for the summer, as many of the recipes require short cooking times and are served cool or lukewarm. The second recipe is adapted from Darra Goldstein's *A Taste of Russia.*

Quick Chinese Chicken Salad

¾ pound chicken breasts
2 teaspoons salt

SAUCE:
1 garlic clove, peeled
1 slice fresh peeled ginger
2 green onions, green tops removed
2 teaspoons chili bean paste
2 teaspoons dark soy sauce
1 teaspoon sugar

2 teaspoons white rice vinegar
2 teaspoons sesame paste or peanut butter
½ teaspoon salt
½ teaspoon freshly ground black pepper
2 teaspoons toasted sesame oil

Barely cover the chicken with water, add the salt, bring to a simmer and cook until just done. This may be as soon as 10 minutes after the liquid begins to simmer, depending on the thickness of the chicken. Turn off the heat and let cool while you prepare the sauce. The chicken will be moister if you have time to let it cool in the liquid.

Put all the sauce ingredients into a blender or food processor and blend well. When the chicken is cool, remove any skin. Shred the meat and toss with the sauce. Serve immediately.

Serves two to four. Hom serves it on a bed of shredded iceberg lettuce that has been tossed with a little white rice vinegar. Though leftovers are good the next day, these Chinese chicken salads are at their best right after the chicken has been combined with the sauce so do the final mixing just before serving.

Cucumbers in Sour Cream

2 cucumbers
1 cup sour cream
2 to 3 tablespoons cider vinegar
2 tablespoons snipped fresh chives
2 tablespoons snipped fresh dill
freshly ground white pepper to taste
2 teaspoons salt

If the cucumbers have been waxed, peel them, otherwise, just wash them well. Slice the cucumbers very thinly and pat them dry with paper towels.

Mix together the remaining ingredients, adding the vinegar to taste. Stir in the cucumbers. Let stand at room temperature for 30 minutes before refrigerating. Serve well chilled. Serves four to six.

Jingle What?

The Independent
October 2, 1991

I'VE JUST RETURNED FROM a wedding on the coast of Maine where I was reminded that Native Americans aren't the only Americans whose rituals redefine and reinforce family ties. The brightly colored leaves on the trees and frost on the roof of the shed next door turned my mind to our upcoming cold weather. That combination of family and winter increased my urge to bring up Christmas.

I want to point out a couple of special foods that will not be possible this holiday season if you don't attend to them soon. The first is Christmas pudding, which is greatly improved by a one-to-three-month interval between the first steaming and its appearance at the table. Don't assume that if you don't like fruitcake you won't like Christmas pudding. I am lukewarm about fruitcake, but I love Christmas pudding — it is served warm, the texture is looser and the flavor is stronger and more interesting. Because one of the traditional ingredients, freshly grated beef suet, is not only artery-hardening but extremely difficult to obtain, I offer a version from *Linda McCartney's Home Cooking* which uses vegetable shortening, butter or margarine, so you can select your own degree of saturation from the animal or vegetable kingdom. Make two puddings: one to keep and one to give away.

The herb-growing season is coming to an end, so the second item of business is to urge you to consider making presents now that call for fresh herbs. *Country Fresh Gifts: Recipes and Projects From Your Garden and Country Kitchen* is full of good gift ideas. Many are suitable for procrastinators (candies, cookies, potpourri and more), others need to age a bit (liqueurs), and some you need to start during the proper season (jams, jellies, dried flowers and the fresh-herb preparations). If you like to make gifts or even think about making gifts, I recommend this book.

My last gift suggestion is to search out a cookbook that will remind the recipient of some place dear to his or her heart. A friend who grew up near Philadelphia might like *Main Line Classics* by The Junior Saturday Club of Wayne, Penn.; and a friend of Cherokee heritage could appreciate *Pow Wow Chow* by The Five Civilized Tribes Museum of Muskogee, Okla.

Linda McCartney's Christmas Pudding*

1 cup raisins
1 cup sultanas (golden raisins)
1 cup currants
3 ounces candied citrus peel, chopped
   (see page 102)
rind of one lemon, grated
1 cooking apple, peeled and grated
⅔ cup plain flour
¼ teaspoon mixed spice
¼ teaspoon ground nutmeg
¼ teaspoon ground cinnamon
1 cup soft bread crumbs
6 ounces vegetable shortening, butter
   or margarine
1¼ cup sugar
4 tablespoons brandy, sherry or fruit juice
juice of ½ lemon
3 eggs, beaten
2 tablespoons honey
pinch of salt
¾ cup walnuts, chopped
¾ cup Brazil nuts, chopped
¾ cup almonds, peeled and chopped

For a more traditional Christmas Pudding with suet, see page 15.

Grease two 1-quart pudding steamers (heat-proof bowls with a bit of a lip will do nicely if you don't have an old-fashioned lidded steamer). Place two saucepans large enough to hold your containers over a low heat and fill half full of water.

Mix the dried fruits with the candied peel, lemon rind and grated apples. Your hands are the best mixing tool throughout this recipe.

Mix the flour, spices and bread crumbs together and add the shortening or butter. Mix this well, then add to the fruit. Mix well; add the rest of the ingredients and mix again.

Put the mixture into the pudding steamers, cover with greaseproof paper (kitchen parchment or waxed paper can be substituted) and a damp cloth. Tie around the lip of the bowl with a piece of string or put the lid on the steamer. Arrange the ends of the cloth on top of the bowl or steamer so they won't drag in the water, and place the puddings into the saucepans to steam them. The water should gently bubble, and the level should be just below the lip of the bowl. Steam for 5 to 6 hours. You will need to maintain the water level by topping up with boiling water from time to time.

Cool the puddings, remove the cloth, cover tightly with aluminum foil and store in the refrigerator until you're ready to re-steam for 1 to 2 hours and serve. For a spectacular end to Christmas dinner, pour on a tablespoon of brandy, light it carefully and quote Tiny Tim as you carry it to the table. Hard sauce or brandy butter are traditional accompaniments, but I like whipped cream, flavored with a bit of brandy, best.

Helen may have fooled some people with that quiet smile of hers, but to us she was *The Queen of Darkness*.

We were a grab-bag of card players who gathered every week at some Durham watering hole to play bridge until the establishment closed. Not closed for the night; closed for good. In less than a decade, our self-styled Group of Doom saw the demise of Halby's Deli (twice), Seventh Street, and Catherine's. Fearing we might blight the entire local restaurant scene, we switched to playing in each other's houses.

Helen joined the group in the mid-90s through a friend of hers from undergraduate years at Duke. Our card etiquette also had an undergraduate flavor: drinking and table-talk were not unknown; kibitzing was encouraged; and a played card could be hastily retracted before the next player covered it. Duplicate play and elaborate conventions were avoided — who could keep track of them?

Helen probably could. She easily remembered which cards had been played, and she always knew what another player's bid meant — or should have meant. Most importantly, she could plan the play of a hand. "A bad plan is better than no plan," one of us would say after some narrow escape. Helen always had a plan, and it was never a bad one. If a contract could be made, she made it — swiftly, calmly and confidently. Then she'd take a sip from her drink with a modest yet satisfied smile.

But it was on defense that Helen showed her true colors. When she defeated an opponent's contract, her smile got bigger and her face glowed with the satisfaction of a child who'd snatched a rival's favorite toy. It was on one such occasion that Dave Hewitt, with mock-anger and

not-so-mock exasperation, said, "Helen, you are *The Queen of Darkness*."

The name stuck. From then on, Helen was the monarch of defensive play — particularly when that play was unexpected, devastating, and a little bit sneaky. Even today, whenever two partners find a contract-destroying cross-ruff, or a defender drops an overlooked trump for a down-one set, it feels like *The Queen of Darkness* is in the room. It's the quiet ones you have to watch out for, isn't it?

Kwanzaa Fest!

The Independent
November 27, 1991

NEED SOME IDEAS for this year's Kwanzaa celebration? Or maybe you don't know much about this event that many African-Americans enjoy Dec. 26 until New Year's Day. In either case, you should check out Eric V. Copage's wonderful new book, *Kwanzaa: An African-American Celebration of Culture and Cooking.* It's a resource full of ideas, readings and recipes designed to stimulate anyone who's planning an event for Kwanzaa. The book is also an ongoing project, including an invitation to its readers for contributions for the next edition.

Kwanzaa was created a little more than 25 years ago by Maulana Karenga, who synthesized elements from many African harvest festivals and named it with a Swahili word meaning "first fruits of the harvest." It's been evolving and spreading ever since. Copage describes it as providing ritual, structure and climax in order to share the joys of being black. He's a father, and his book reflects a family focus within the larger community.

The sections of text are organized by the seven principles of Kwanzaa — unity, self-determination, collective work and responsibility, cooperative economics, purpose, creativity and faith. Stories, poems and bits of recent and ancient history illustrate them, from proverbs and folk tales to *The Autobiography of Malcolm X,* and can be read aloud to foster discussion.

The recipes come from wherever Africans have cooked and eaten — Africa, the Caribbean islands, Brazil, the Southern United States and so on. The exuberant and often spicy food is celebratory, to be shared with family, friends or at larger gatherings.

There are dishes for every course, including good party beverages (many without alcohol). I'm going to try the Peanut Butter, Sweet Potato and Winter Squash Soup; one of the Brazilian dishes; and the Charleston Crab Spread next.

Interesting sidebars on almost every recipe page offer further information about the dish, often from the contributor. The book's design is very attractive with woodcuts reminiscent of African textiles decorating most pages. All in all, it's a delightful book. Here are a couple of recipes I've adapted to tempt you.

Chicken & Groundnut Stew

> 2 tablespoons olive oil
> 9 chicken thighs (about 3 pounds)
> 2 medium onions, chopped
> 2 garlic cloves, minced
> 1 teaspoon curry powder
> ½ teaspoon dried thyme
> 2 bay leaves
> ½ teaspoon salt
> ½ teaspoon cayenne pepper, or to taste
> 2 8-ounce cans tomato sauce
> 2 to 3 cups chicken stock
> ¾ cup unsalted sugarless chunky peanut butter

Heat the oil in a 5-quart Dutch oven. In batches, add the chicken and cook over medium-high heat, turning often, until browned on all sides, about 6 minutes per batch. Transfer the chicken to a plate and set aside.

Add the onions to the Dutch oven and cook, stirring, until lightly browned, about 5 minutes. Then add the garlic, curry powder, thyme, bay leaves, salt and cayenne. Stir for 1 minute, and then stir in the tomato sauce.

Return the chicken thighs to the Dutch oven, add enough chicken stock to just barely cover the chicken and bring to a simmer. Reduce the heat to medium-low, cover tightly and simmer until the chicken shows no sign of pink at the bone when prodded with the tip of a sharp knife, 30 to 45 minutes.

In a small bowl, blend the peanut butter with about one cup of the cooking liquid. Stir this mixture back into the sauce and cook until heated through, about 2 minutes. Serve immediately.

Serves six to eight. I was attracted to this recipe because it uses my favorite piece of chicken, the succulent thigh. I recommend chunky peanut butter rather than smooth for a more interesting sauce texture.

Fresh Greens & Apples with Curried Yogurt Dressing

> 2 tablespoons cider vinegar
> 1 teaspoon curry powder
> ¼ teaspoon salt
> ⅛ teaspoon freshly ground pepper
> 6 tablespoons vegetable oil
> 6 tablespoons plain low-fat yogurt
> 2 teaspoons chopped fresh chives or
>   ¾ teaspoon dried
> 1 head red-leaf lettuce, rinse, dried and torn
>   into pieces
> 2 medium tart apples, such as Granny Smith,
>   cored and cut into ¼ inch slices

In a small bowl, whisk the vinegar, curry powder, salt and pepper until blended. Gradually whisk in the oil. Using a wooden spoon, stir in the yogurt and the chives. (Use dressing immediately or it may curdle.)

In a large bowl, toss the lettuce, watercress and apples together. Add the curry dressing, toss well and serve immediately.

Serves six.

Say It With Cauliflowers

The Independent
January 15, 1992

WHILE ONE CAN ARGUE any food that goes well with hollandaise sauce possesses a certain allure, cauliflower is not exactly glamorous. Part of its less than exciting reputation may be because, like other members of the cabbage family, improper handling can produce unpleasant odors. But this can be avoided.

The fresher the cauliflower, the better the taste. Examine the head closely. The mass of tiny undeveloped flower buds that make up the curd should be creamy white and unblemished. Reject the cauliflower if the head has brown spots or has been trimmed to remove them. Any leaves attached should be green — not brown, yellow or withered. Take a whiff, it should smell fresh and only faintly like a member of the cabbage family. Small heads are usually neither younger nor more tender than large ones, so buy the size you need based on the number of diners.

Cauliflower will keep for two to three days in the refrigerator; the flavor will deteriorate if you try to store it much longer.

To prepare the whole head for cooking, first trim away any leaves and even off the stem. Rinse it well; if you suspect insects, soak for 20 minutes in cold salted water to drive them out. Separating the head into flowerets saves some cooking time and enables them to cook more evenly. Divide the larger ones to achieve uniform stem thickness. If you want to dress a whole head for a fancier presentation, use a smaller cauliflower.

The three methods I most often use for cooking cauliflower are steaming, simmering and microwaving. Many recipes suggest adding lemon juice or milk to the cooking water to avoid discoloration but, personally, I don't perceive the creamy color of cooked cauliflower as discoloration.

Cooking time depends on the size of the flowerets or the mass of the whole head. Steamed flowerets will take from five to 15 minutes; boiled, from five to 12 minutes, and microwaved from two minutes (about ⅔ cup) to 11 minutes (6 cups). A whole head will steam in 10 to 25 minutes or boil in 10 to 20 minutes. Start checking after the minimum time; the cauliflower should be cooked but retain a little crunch. Avoid mushiness.

Drained cauliflower can be simply dressed with butter, lemon juice, breadcrumbs or grated cheese. If you're feeling fancier make a cheese sauce or some hollandaise. Sauce maltaise (a hollandaise variation with orange juice) is great with cauliflower.

In *The Victory Garden Cookbook,* Marian Morash suggests two columns worth of terrific simple "finishes" for cooked cauliflower. This book may seem expensive, but when you calculate the price per useable idea you realize what a bargain it is. It's full of invaluable information for the vegetable cook, from choosing a prime specimen to storing it properly and cooking it with the care it deserves.

I offer two possibilities for cauliflower. The first is Indian and demonstrates how well this vegetable stands up to hot and spicy treatments. While researching my recent food piece on English cheeses I was intrigued by a reference to "proper English Cauliflower Cheese." Unfortunately the writer did not explain further, nor provide a recipe, so I have spent about a month reading about and trying out various possibilities. My conclusion is

that while cooked cauliflower, sprinkled with cheese and popped into a hot oven until the cheese melts is a good simple way to combine cheese and cauliflower, the full-dress gratin recipe below is really better. Other cheeses can be substituted, but do try it at least once with the classic Gruyère-parmesan combination.

Cauliflower Curry

¼ cup vegetable oil
1 medium cauliflower, separated into flowerets
2 medium red potatoes, peeled and cut into chunks
¼ teaspoon cumin seeds
2 green chilies, seeded and finely chopped (optional)
¼ teaspoon grated fresh ginger
1 teaspoon ground cumin
1 teaspoon turmeric
¼ teaspoon garam masala or freshly grated black pepper
1 teaspoon salt
½ cup water

Using medium-high heat, fry the cauliflower pieces in the vegetable oil until they start to brown. Do this in several batches if necessary to avoid crowding the pan.

Set the cauliflower aside and fry the potatoes until they, too, start to brown. Add the cumin seeds, stir and fry for a minute. Now add the chopped chilies, grated ginger, ground cumin, turmeric, garam masala or pepper and salt. Stir and fry for a minute or so more. Now add the water and when it boils, add the cauliflower. Cover and simmer briskly, stirring once or twice during the cooking time and adding more water if the pan threatens to dry out. The potatoes and cauliflower should be tender in about 8 to 10 minutes. Check for seasonings and serve.

This is one of my favorite vegetable dishes and is adapted from *The Home Book of Indian Cookery* by Sipra Das Gupta. The original recipe calls for the addition of fresh or frozen peas, but I prefer the potato-cauliflower combination. If you own any Indian cookbook, it probably contains a recipe for some variation on this dish, as well as several other delicious ways with cauliflower.

Cauliflower au Gratin

1 medium cauliflower, separated into flowerets

MORNAY SAUCE:
2 tablespoons butter
2 tablespoons flour
2½ cups liquid — half cauliflower cooking liquid and half milk or light cream
½ cup grated Gruyère cheese
2 heaping tablespoons grated parmesan cheese
salt and black or cayenne pepper to taste
1 further tablespoon grated Gruyère cheese
2 tablespoons bread crumbs
1 tablespoon melted butter

Cook the cauliflower pieces until just barely done. Drain them, saving the cooking liquid for the sauce.

Make the cheese sauce: Melt the butter. Add the flour and cook for three minutes, stirring constantly. Add the liquid — all at once, if hot; in four to five lots, bringing to a boil and stirring between each addition, if cold. Let the sauce barely simmer for 3 to 5 minutes. Add the cheese and stir until it melts. You may need to keep the heat on under the sauce until the cheese starts to melt but turn the heat off before the sauce boils again. Taste the sauce and season with salt and pepper. You may not need any salt because the cheeses may add enough for your taste.

Put a thin layer of the sauce in an ovenproof dish. Arrange the cauliflower on top and pour over the rest of the sauce.

Sprinkle with the reserved grated cheese and the bread crumbs. Drizzle on the melted butter. Place in a 425°F until heated through and just starting to brown on top. This will take from 15 to 30 minutes, depending on how long the dish sits before going into the oven.

Serves four to six, depending on what else is on the menu. It is just fine as the main course with a big crisp salad and some good bread.

Feeding the Family

The Independent
April 1, 1992

FROM WHAT I HEAR there are two sorts of kids at the table: those who will try anything and those who will try nothing. The second group's approved dinner items are more likely to be fish sticks, unsauced pasta, pizza and hot dogs than items from some nutritionist's basic four food groups. This presents problems for parents who want to enjoy dinner without becoming mealtime heavies, insisting that certain foods be consumed or worrying about their children's ability to thrive on a limited diet. I consulted with several parents for this article and got some helpful suggestions.

A parent's choices can be broadened by paying attention to what a picky eater eats outside the home. My nephew Tom, for example, is not interested in anything new unless it's presented in light of what he's eaten and liked before. Maybe because of peer pressure he's a little more adventurous at school, so my sister has been able to add tacos to the home menu. Pizza is a universal favorite, and with partially baked or refrigerated dough available, it can easily be made at home.

When Margaret Stewart's family eats out, her three daughters are as interested in a good salad bar as a good dessert selection. This spills over at home — they have a salad with almost every dinner. Margaret is a health professional and tries to encourage good nutrition by providing information — for example, which items in the salad bar are high or low fat — to help her family make good choices. At home she cooks a single menu but includes at least one item that each person will like. She doesn't mandate portion size but encourages everyone to have at least a little of each dish.

By getting your kids involved in planning and preparing the dinner, they are more likely to eat what ends up on the table, plus they can be a big help. At the Campbell house, Lee and Ewan are responsible for one night in the dinner rotation. Lee told me they usually cook something boiled, frozen or canned; favorites include hot dogs, chicken nuggets, broccoli or cauliflower. They recently expanded the repertoire to include frozen French fries. They add items to the grocery list and sometimes help with the shopping.

If parents look for common ground — foods that both you and your kids like — you'll feel less like a short-order cook and save precious energy. Dawn Freer says that since the birth of her second child just over a year ago, her 6-year-old daughter is the biggest influence on what's for dinner. Dinner is usually very simple. She can hardly wait for Catherine to begin appreciating items cooked in flavored sauces. Dawn also pointed out that nutrition information flows both ways nowadays: Kids are growing up "green," knowing a lot about what's good for them and the planet and sometimes disconcertingly — you.

Most of the people I talked to let their kids eat as much of well-liked but healthy foods as they want and try not to worry about the absolute refusals. Lee Campbell says he doesn't like vegetables much, but he will eat at least one a day. He likes fruit so he eats two or more a day. Another friend says her kids won't touch any vegetables at all — not even raw or in salads, which seems to be the only way vegetables get eaten in many homes. Her kids love fruit; she expects that will sustain them until their tastes broaden a bit. Others will eat vegetables in soup that they refuse to look at in single portions on the plate.

One other tip: Don't forget that for a hungry, cranky kid, a microwave's ability to heat something quickly is a big help. The microwave also can be a fast and safe way for kids to do some of their own cooking. Tom Campbell says his kids became expert long before he did on just exactly how many seconds a particular size of frozen bagel would need to thaw.

There are a couple of cookbooks that look very helpful in terms of feeding children, including *Jenifer Lang Cooks for Kids*. Lang is a food professional who found mealtime was drastically altered when she became a mother. She was surprised by how much less time and energy she had for cooking. Her book contains some great easy recipes and lots of practical suggestions. One valuable, if slightly sneaky tip, is to prepare soups with recognizable chunks of well-liked vegetables floating in a puree which might include unnamed vegetables that your children don't think they like. The recipes are clearly marked with symbols as to preparation time, whether the recipe can be doubled or frozen, and whether adults as well as children will like the finished product. The book seems especially good for new parents who feel stifled because there is not much call for the pre-children menus.

For a family with children old enough to get interested in cooking, I'd recommend *Betty Crocker's New Boys and Girls Cookbook*. These recipes were tested on real families, and the book includes some of their comments with many of the dishes. It is well organized with good safety tips and clear instructions — including an ingredient list, a utensil list, step-by-step procedure and instruction on when to get adult help. When appropriate, the recipes include alternative microwave instructions. Not only can a child cook from this book; an adult who's tired of the same old menus can get some new ideas.

The book can also help you organize kitchen assistants. For instance, someone could follow the recipe for Oven Fries while you flip burgers. The special occasion chapter is very good and includes a couple of dishes I loved to cook when I was a kid, such as Upside-Down Pineapple Cake. I'm hoping for a Big Burger Cake on my next birthday. (I wonder if I'll feel the same about Penuche Frosting as I once did).

A third possibility is *Let's Eat In: Quick and Delicious Weekday Meals* by Brooke Dojny and Melanie Barnard. It's full of good recipes that appeal to children and adults alike. Maybe it reminds me of what my mother often served at those everyday family dinners I so fondly remember, but the more I use it the more I like it; that's why I've recommended it so often.

For further inspiration, swap favorite recipes with friends — real food that has been eaten by real people. You might come up with some new family favorites. The recipes that follow include some from the aforementioned books as well as several given to me by the people I talked to when gathering information for this article.

Margaret Stewart's Refrigerator Bran Muffins

**2 cups boiling water poured over
   2 cups All-Bran cereal
1 cup Crisco
3 cups sugar
4 beaten eggs
1 quart buttermilk
5 cups plain flour
5 teaspoons baking soda
1 teaspoon salt
4 cups All-Bran**

Feeding the Family

Cream shortening and sugar. Add eggs, butter-milk and scalded bran. Sift flour, salt and soda and add all at once. Fold in bran until moistened.

This can keep in a gallon jar in the refrigerator for up to a month.

Bake muffins at 375°F for 20 minutes. You can vary the muffins by adding nuts or raisins to the basic batter.

Carol Wills remembers —

Helen held an informal open house for knitters every other week — rain or shine, sleet or snow. Usually there were five or six of us on any given knitting evening, showing off our current projects and sharing with each other the news of our lives.

All of us were avid readers, and Helen kept us up-to-date on all the great books that were coming into the Regulator Bookshop. She especially kept up with all the books and magazines on knitting, as well as the best of the new cookbooks and mysteries. She was the authority that we all turned to whenever there were knitting prob-lems, because she had experimented with all sorts of yarns and patterns and was never afraid to try something new.

Helen set the tone: All the talk was kind; all the lis-tening was supportive. Halfway through the evening, she'd go out to the kitchen and make a pot of tea. Often there were cookies, too. And such was the environment that Helen created that we always left her house feeling that we had taken part in an edifying ritual. We were confirmed in our creativity, recreated in our femininity and bonded in friendship. That was Helen's magic, and that is her legacy to us.

Liz Whiting's Chicken Fajitas

1 package fajita seasoning
water or white wine
1 to 1½ pounds boneless chicken breast or thigh
cooking oil
1 green bell pepper
1 red or yellow pepper
1 to 2 yellow onions
1 package flour tortillas
sour cream
1 avocado
salsa, prepared

Mix fajita seasoning as directed, or substitute wine for water. Slice chicken into ¼-inch strips. Marinate chicken in seasoning while you prepare the other ingredients. Clean and seed peppers. Slice into ¼-inch strips. Peel and halve onions, slice coarsely.

Heat two medium skillets. Add one to two tablespoons cooking oil to the first skillet. When hot, but not smoking, add vegetables. Stir until well mixed. Cover and steam on medium-low setting until starting to soften (5 to 10 minutes).

Heat oil in second skillet, then add chicken and sauté quickly (3 minutes) over medium-high heat. Heat tortillas according to package. Assemble by spooning 2 tablespoons of each mixture into tortilla and roll. Serve with a dollop of sour cream, a slice of avocado and salsa to taste. Allow two fajitas per adult or hungry child.

Susan Naumoff's Chicken Livers & Rice Casserole

½ to 1 pound chicken livers
flour
salt and pepper
margarine
⅓ to ½ cup raw white rice
1 can cream of chicken or cream of
    mushroom soup
milk

Cut livers in half or smaller. Dredge in seasoned flour (salt and pepper). Sauté in margarine. At the same time cook rice separately (two parts water to one part rice).

Mix cooked livers, cooked rice and canned soup together. Adjust seasonings to taste. Place in greased casserole. Pour a little milk over the top, poking in casserole to let it sink in and just show over the top. Bake uncovered at 350°F for about a half hour. Serve with green peas and/or salad.

From Peanuts to Soup

The Independent
July 8, 1992

FIVE HUNDRED YEARS AGO Columbus arrived in the "New World." People love to celebrate milestone anniversaries, but this one is proving a little awkward. Realists point out that he didn't really know where he was or what he had stumbled upon. Scandinavians quibble about his being the first European. Others wonder about the "discovery" of lands already populated by many groups, nearly all of whom suffered as the Europeans took control.

Culinarily, however, we can celebrate: dinner got better all over the world. *Blue Corn and Chocolate* is a cookbook by Elisabeth Rozin that provides an appreciation of this bounty. It's full of terrific recipes using plants and animals native to the New World: potatoes, tomatoes, sweet and hot peppers, chocolate, turkey, squash, beans and peanuts.

The peanut is the perfect example of this dissemination. Though a 100,000-year-old peanut fossil has been discovered in China, culinarily, it originated in Brazil and spread through Central America. Early conquistadors took it east to Africa and west to Indonesia where it traveled through Asia. It came back to North America from Africa with slaves because it was inexpensive, easy to grow and a source of good nutrition.

Though peanuts share some characteristics with nuts, they are actually legumes, close relatives of peas and beans (pea-nut, get it?). They are also known as groundnuts because after flowering, the plant bends over, the pods are buried in the ground and the seeds develop within the shells. Though peanuts are high in fat, it is unsaturated fat, and they are rich in protein.

About half the current American crop goes to make peanut butter (one of the few uses for the peanut not discovered by George Washington Carver, who pushed peanuts as a replacement crop for cotton in the South). Peanut butter was developed in 1890 and touted as a health food at the 1904 St. Louis World's Fair.

To discover more recipes using peanuts, look into books featuring Central and South American, Indonesian, African or African-American cooking. The many new books on cooking with hot peppers often feature good peanut recipes as well.

Peanut Sauce with Greens

    ½ pound fresh greens (kale, collards, mustard
        greens, broccoli rabe)
    1 medium onion, coarsely chopped
    2 large cloves garlic, very finely chopped
    2 tablespoons oil
    1½ teaspoon curry powder
    2 cups canned crushed tomatoes or
        tomato sauce
    2 tablespoons peanut butter
    ¼ to ½ teaspoon crushed dried peppers
    ½ cup unsalted roasted peanuts, coarsely
        chopped

Wash the greens and drain thoroughly, chop coarsely. In a large skillet sauté the onion and garlic in the oil over moderate heat until the onion is just beginning to wilt. Stir in the curry powder and sauté a few minutes more. Add the tomatoes, mix well, and cook over low heat for about 15 minutes. Stir in the chopped greens and cook for 10 minutes. Add a little water if necessary.

Stir in the peanut butter until it is smooth and well blended, then add the hot peppers. Taste for salt and hotness, adding a bit more salt and hot

peppers if necessary. Stir in the chopped peanuts. Serves four to six over cornmeal mush, rice or cheese grits. I've adapted this recipe, one of my favorites, from *Blue Corn and Chocolate.*

Peanut Dressing

    1¾ cups roasted peanuts
    2 tablespoons vegetable oil
    2 garlic cloves, finely chopped
    3 medium shallots (or ½ small onion) finely
        chopped
    2 cups water
    ½ teaspoon ground red (cayenne) pepper
    ½ teaspoon salt
    2 teaspoons dark brown sugar
    fresh ground black pepper
    4 to 5 teaspoons lime or lemon juice

Grind the peanuts as finely as possible in a food processor or blender.

Heat the oil in a small pan and fry the onions and shallots over high heat, stirring constantly, until they start to brown. Add the water, red pepper, salt, sugar and ground peanuts. Stir and bring to a boil. Simmer for 15 to 20 minutes, stirring from time to time, until the sauce has thickened. It should be no thicker than a creamy salad dressing.

Remove from the heat and let the dressing cool a little. Add the black pepper and lime juice. Taste and add more lime juice if you'd like it a bit sharper.

This Indonesian recipe is adapted from Madhur Jaffrey's *Far Eastern Cookery.* I have tried it both ways she suggests: on grilled chicken and as a dressing for a vegetable salad composed of both raw and crisply cooked vegetables (potatoes, green beans, carrots, cauliflower, bean sprouts, cucumbers are a few possibilities). This quantity will be plenty for four people and the dressing keeps well for several days in the refrigerator.

African Peanut
Chicken Soup

- 2 medium onions, chopped
- 2 large sweet red and/or green peppers, seeded and chopped
- 3 to 4 cloves garlic, crushed
- 2 tablespoons vegetable oil
- 28-ounce can Italian-style tomatoes, with juice, coarsely chopped
- 8 cups chicken stock
- ¼ teaspoon black pepper
- ¼ teaspoon crushed dried red peppers
- ½ cup rice
- 1 to 1½ cups diced cooked chicken
- ⅔ cup unsalted peanut butter

The recipe calls for "no salt" peanut butter but you can used salted, depending on the saltiness of your other ingredients (chicken stock, tomatoes).

In a large heavy pot sauté the onions, the fresh peppers and the garlic in the oil over moderate heat until the onions are just beginning to brown.

Add the tomatoes, the stock, the black and dried hot peppers. Simmer, uncovered, over low heat for about one hour. Add the rice and the chicken and simmer for another 10-15 minutes, until the rice is tender. Stir in the peanut butter and whisk it until it is completely dissolved and smooth. Taste for salt and hot pepper, adding more if necessary. Serve hot. Serves eight to 10. Adapted from *Blue Corn and Chocolate*.

Summer's Bounty Year 'Round

The Independent
September 2, 1992

"The modern world seems to have no notion of preserving different things side by side, of allowing its proper and proportionate place to each, of saving the whole varied heritage of culture. It has no notion except that of simplifying something by destroying nearly everything."
– G.K. Chesterton, *All I Survey,* "On Love"

THIS TIME OF YEAR I am often tempted into my kitchen by the abundance of good seasonal produce, and generally put up a few jars of jams, chutneys, pickles or sauces. Necessary errands can be run or the house cleaned later on — like next winter — with strength garnered from a hearty breakfast of pancakes covered with my own blueberry syrup. In addition to the bounty of my four blueberry bushes, my young apple tree has produced what might accurately be labeled its first crop, so I've been busy.

Traditionally, people have preserved food for a couple of reasons. They wanted a product at some future time — i.e., winter came and fewer foods were available. Or, they had an abundance of some fresh ingredient to use up before it spoiled. Nowadays these reasons still apply, but most of us who put foods up are as likely to be interested in the quality of the finished product as anything else. We don't need to compromise on the quality of ingredients in order to turn a profit. When we lift the lid of a Mason jar next winter we can savor the Proustian rewards of having spent a hot summer's day in the garden picking ripe tomatoes.

In the old days a cook needed to be opportunistic, going to work when the ingredients were in their prime, spending long, hot hours over the stove and putting up vast quantities in order to fill the larder and stave off hunger through the lean months. This summer I have been inspired by a different perspective, found in *Preserving Today* by Jeanne Lesem.

It is full of recipes for jams, jellies, chutneys, relishes, pickles, confections and the like; most are quickly and easily done. Batch size is less than gargantuan, a bonus when considering the small amount of cupboard space that passes for the modern larder and the decreased number of diners around the family table these days.

Lesem covers basic techniques, including safety steps and tips for using the microwave to quickly cook ingredients. She points out when you can stop a recipe and proceed at a later time — like freezing a fruit puree to make a jam or syrup when more convenient. The recipes I've tried have been delicious.

Beginners or very enthusiastic gardeners might want to acquire one of three currently available basic manuals: *Keeping the Harvest* by Nancy Chioffi and Gretchen Mead; *Putting Food By* by Janet Greene, Ruth Hertzberg and Beatrice Vaughan; and *Stocking Up* by Carol Hupping and the Staff of the Rodale Food Center.

Each provides thorough information, covering equipment selection and use and techniques for canning, freezing, brining, drying and root-cellering. They all address nutrition, taste and safety (from sterilization to detecting spoilage), and they have been revised to reflect the current U.S. Department of Agriculture guidelines.

"Gifts-from-your-kitchen" cookbooks are another good source of recipes for chutneys, jams, pickles and the like. You may need to consult a standard reference in conjunction with one of these books because they are often long on imaginative recipes and short on technique.

If you are new at canning I'd suggest selecting a batch size that matches your needs because multiplying or dividing ingredients can drastically alter a recipe's timing. Once you get some experience you'll be able to recognize the proper thickness for fruit butter or chutney or when to do a gel test for jams and jellies.

Because a couple of the following recipes call for sterilized jars, here's how to do that: Place clean jars in boiling water so they are completely covered with an inch or two of water to spare. A rack or folded dish towel on the bottom of the pan will prevent possible cracking from direct heat on the bottom of the pan. Boil for 10 minutes. Remove from the hot water as you are ready to use each jar. Follow the manufacturer's instructions for sterilizing the lids (usually they tell you to cover the lids and rings with boiling water and let them sit until you are ready to use them).

Apple Butter

2 pounds apples
6-ounce can frozen apple juice concentrate,
thawed, or ¾ cup boiled apple cider
(start with 1½ cups, boil down by half)
sugar or maple syrup (optional, to taste)
ground cinnamon, ginger, mace or coriander
(optional, to taste)

Peel and core the apples and puree them in a food processor with the thawed apple juice or the concentrated cider. Empty the puree into a 2-quart slow-cooker and cook covered, on high, for five to eight hours or until very thick. Taste for sweetness (varies greatly with apple variety) and add sugar or maple syrup, if desired. If this thins down the butter, re-cover and continue cooking until thick.

Stir in the spice or spices of your choice, starting with a quarter-teaspoon and tasting between additions. (Be hygienic; don't stir with a spoon that's been in your mouth.) Divide among hot, sterilized jars or freezer containers, cool, cover tightly, label and refrigerate or freeze. Keeps at least one month in refrigerator, or six months or more in a freezer.

Makes about two half-pints. Adapted from *Preserving Today.* My batch took only five hours, and I turned the heat down to medium after two when most of the liquids had evaporated, because I was nervous about the apple puree sticking and burning. If you are using a larger cooker you may need to increase the batch size to meet the manufacturer's fill requirements.

The beauty of the slow-cooker method is that while you should check on the batch from time to time, you don't need to hover over the pot, stirring constantly as with other methods. The flavor of my batch was like apple butter I've previously made the old-fashioned, intensive-care way.

Blueberry Syrup

5 cups blueberries
1 cup plus 2 tablespoons sugar
½ cup plus 2 tablespoons water
1 teaspoon freshly squeezed lemon juice

Combine the berries, sugar and water in a medium-sized heavy saucepan over medium high heat and bring to a boil, stirring. Adjust the heat so the mixture is boiling gently, and continue cooking, stirring occasionally, until the berries pop

and look somewhat shriveled, about 10 minutes. Stir in the lemon juice and remove from the heat.

For refrigerated storage (two to three weeks): Allow the syrup to cool, then ladle into jars. Cover and refrigerate. For longer storage: Ladle the hot syrup into sterilized canning jars. Seal the jars, following the lid manufacturer's instructions, and process for 10 minutes in a boiling-water bath.

Makes three pints. Adapted from the *Farm House Cookbook* by Susan Herrmann Loomis. The book is a record of Loomis' trips through the farmlands of America collecting recipes while researching how some modern American food is produced. Loomis credits Nate Pennell of Machias, Maine, with this recipe. The preserving chapter, "A Full Larder," has many tempting recipes.

Quick Dill Slices

about 1½ pounds unwaxed cucumbers
1 tablespoon salt
several sprigs fresh dill, or about 2 teaspoons dried dill weed
white wine vinegar, cider vinegar, or rice wine vinegar (about 2 cups)

Slice cucumbers thinly with a food slicer or processor. Layer cucumber slices with salt in a colander, and cover with a plate weighted with a heavy can or jar. Let stand about one hour. Rinse to remove excess salt, drain well and layer with the fresh or dried dill in a sterilized jar or dish you can cover tightly. Cover with vinegar and refrigerate.

Makes about a quart. This is a long-lasting version of wilted cucumbers adapted from *Preserving Today.* The author says they keep indefinitely in the refrigerator and get milder as time passes.

Spiced Apple Slices

6 cups sugar
2 cups vinegar
4 sticks cinnamon in small pieces
2 teaspoons whole cloves
5 pounds firm apples, peeled, cored,
  and sliced thickly

Boil sugar, vinegar and spices; add apples and simmer uncovered until they are tender but not broken. Pack into hot, sterilized pint jars, leaving a ½-inch head room, and process in a boiling-water bath for 10 minutes.

Adapted from *Keeping the Harvest*. Yields 3 to 4 pints.

The Magnetic Church Key: Not Just a Simple Twist-Off Fate*

The Independent
October 7, 1992

ONCE UPON A TIME, many years ago, bottle- and can-openers were necessities. Now, depending on your usual brand of beer, the necessity may not be absolute. Technology has provided nearly foolproof tabs on the tops of cans and twist-off caps on most bottles. I lived in Europe when this change took place; I still remember being amazed upon my return to the States when the best banjo player I ever knew casually opened a bottle with his bare hands and no one present showed the slightest bit of interest.

Technology aside, the old-fashioned church key is still quite a useful gadget. You can flip off the caps that aren't twistable. You can cut down on wear and tear on your palms with the caps that are.

Form and function intersect with the magnetic church key. Your cold beer is right there in the fridge; your opener is right where you need it: stuck to the outside of the door, preferably at eye level, ready for use. No more rummaging around in cluttered kitchen drawers or trying to retrace your life to the point where you last opened a bottle.

*Following the likes of the Williams-Sonoma catalog, the **The Independent** briefly ran sidebars in the food and gardening section about the latest in kitchen gadgets. When HHW was asked to recommend a useful tool, she opted for the retro-gadget, as we might have predicted. — ed.

Styles range from the strictly utilitarian to those with some decoration in the event that design coordination on the front of your fridge is an important consideration.

An argument could be made that this is the only refrigerator magnet I'll ever really need, but I'm not sure I could give up my guitar-shaped Elvis swizzle stick.

Dawn Freer remembers —

Helen was wildly messy in the kitchen. When we lived in the little house at Monkeytop, we had lots of dinner parties. I think it was our main form of entertainment. I remember long nights sitting and talking over the remains of another one of Helen's incredible meals. But when she cooked, she went in with abandon — no thought of tomorrow. It took every pot and every utensil — and she had a utensil for every possible need: mushroom brushes, heavy sauté pans, copper pans for whipping up cream (chilled to just the right temperature, of course), olive pitters, parmesan cheese graters (as opposed to graters for other cheeses). The kitchen was tiny, and she achieved marvelous stacks of dirty dishes. Well worth it, of course.

The Culinary Poets

The Independent
November 4, 1992

GOOD COOKING REQUIRES both prose and poetry. By prose I mean something like *Joy of Cooking* or, more elegantly, Child, Bertholle and Beck's *Mastering the Art of French Cooking.* These are basic references, books that cooks turn to when they need the correct information about an ingredient, a recipe, a technique.

When I talk of poetry I refer to the food writers who have put us in touch with our own cooking souls. The best of these poets don't chain us to their own recipes or rules but rather free us to map out and explore our own imaginary cooking landscape.

For some cooks, the poet is Richard Olney with his exacting but inviting ideas about French cooking. For others it's Craig Claiborne or James Beard, with their omnivorous, and often American, enthusiasms; Bill Neal, writing elegantly of both high and low Southern food; Mollie Katzen, out with the first *Moosewood Cookbook* just as many were longing for new ideas for meatless meals; Alice Waters, who inspired countless restaurateurs as well as home cooks when she revealed ideas behind Chez Panisse; or M.F.K. Fisher, who encouraged contemplation of the proper place of pleasure — especially culinary pleasure — in life.

For me, the poet has been Elizabeth David. She perfectly satisfies my culinary reading needs by taking me somewhere interesting and giving me the ability to cook a good meal when I get back. If I could only have one cookbook, it would be her *French Provincial Cooking.* If I could have only one book of essays, I'd take *An Omelette and a Glass of Wine.* I could cook and read happily for years to come.

When I acquired her books while setting up my first kitchen, I encountered ideas that seemed odd at the time but have since become deliciously incorporated into my daily routines — such as salad after the main course and on the same plate. She introduced me to foods I'd never eaten — zucchini, turnips or various odd organs from the insides of animals. She showed me new ways with foods I'd always resisted — carrots, eggplant and fish.

David encouraged my appreciation of simplicity. Though many soups require a good stock as a base, there are other wonderful soups in which water is the liquid and anything more would overwhelm the balance. While lettuce tossed with olive oil, wine vinegar, a scrap of salt and ground pepper is a delightful salad, it is important to pay attention to the details: The lettuce should be a flavorful variety, fresh, clean and dry. The olive oil and vinegar should be tasty and in balance with each other. The pepper should be freshly ground. David quoted a maxim, *Faîtes Simple,* and asked, "Does a Paris milliner put lace trimmings on a fur hat?"

She stressed being sensible. Maybe I couldn't make a real bouillabaisse unless I could shop in the fish markets along the Mediterranean (preferably Marseille). But that should be no impediment to making wonderful fish soups with the fresh ingredients available to me almost anywhere else in the world I happened to be.

I knew I could trust her. When Elizabeth David said oxtail could be difficult to eat but the flavor would be worth it, I was willing to try Stewed Oxtail with White Grapes. She not only described the right instant to remove the skillet from the heat when preparing black butter, but said Skate with Black Butter is such a perfect combination one doesn't really need other recipes for skate.

David, once accused of "criticizing everything, enjoying nothing," replied by characterizing her essays in *An Omelette and a Glass of Wine* as being "about good food, good wine, good cookery books. Those pleasures I did my best to express to my readers in lively terms."

Both Elizabeth David and M.F.K. Fisher died this year and we have lost two of our finest culinary poets. Their writings will continue to remind me not to search for the lost perfection of some past golden age but to approach the culinary present with similar gusto and discernment as I ferret out my own cooking pleasures.

Cook's Choice:
Exotic Mushrooms Stored in Oil

The Independent
December 1, 1993

IF AUNT AGNES' HOLIDAY PRESENT had been edible, you wouldn't have to move that 4-foot statue of Cortez from the attic to the front hall before she arrives next month. A gift of food is enjoyed when consumed and, serendipitously, does not need to be stored or dusted.

The best food gifts are usually somewhat extravagant. This does not mean you must have a big budget — although a rare or more expensive version of something the recipient likes makes a wonderful present. Those on your gift list who don't have the time or the savvy to make their own will find tins of homemade holiday treats a true extravagance.

Luckily, there are many gifts — like fancy mustards, marinated goat cheeses, or jars of spiced olives that don't take 300 ingredients and three days to make. When I'm considering the possibilities, I look for something useful but outside the person's usual experience.

One of my most successful gifts in recent years was dried mushrooms in olive oil. Choose an exotic and flavorful type of dried mushroom (porcini or shiitaki, for example), good quality olive oil and suitable containers (try half-pint or pint mason jars, or attractive mustard or olive jars).

Make sure the jars are scrupulously clean, fill them loosely with mushrooms, pour in olive oil to cover, and screw on the lids.

This is a double present: the dried mushrooms, which can then be drained and used as usual; and the mushroom-flavored olive oil, increasing in intensity as time passes, delicious for cooking or in salads. Make up an extra jar for yourself.

The Fungus Among Us

The Independent
April 6, 1994

M Y FIRST ENTHUSIASTIC ENCOUNTER with a mushroom was in a Chinese restaurant. Chicken with Black Mushrooms was a revelation of flavor and texture after a childhood of meals spent pushing the (usually canned) variety to one side of the plate, and wondering in just how many dishes cream of mushroom soup could appear.

I have since made up for lost time, eagerly sampling any new variety of mushroom that crossed my plate, wild or cultivated. While I'm not a gatherer, I have gratefully feasted on the fruits of others' labors.

And fruit is the right word. A mushroom is the fruiting body of mycelium, a fungus that has probably been human food as long as there have been humans. Think gratefully of those who lost their lives in search of the edible varieties.

While shiitake mushrooms have been culti-vated by the Japanese for 2,000 years, and *aquaricus bisporus* (common button mushrooms) have been produced and sold in the West since the 18th century, it is only recently that many other edible varieties have been successfully cultivated and commercially available.

These days we mushroom fanciers are in luck. White button mushrooms, of course, are available in supermarkets everywhere; the slightly more flavorful brown button crimini (or cremini) are frequently seen in produce sections; and some of the less ordinary cultivated types (mainly shiitake and enoki) appear in specialty groceries and "gourmet produce" sections of some of the big supermarkets. The rare sorts cost more than the white buttons, but their deeper flavors and interest-ing textures are worthwhile.

An even wider selection is available if you're willing to plan ahead. Some gourmet groceries will special order cultivated portobello and shiitakes and other cultivated mushrooms (oyster, white trumpet, hen-of-the-wood, to name just three) and — in season — many different wild varieties (morels, porcini or cèpes, chanterelles and others).

While a few of the wild types become available in the spring (notably morels, in late April) many more are available in the fall. Call to find out what's available and at what price.

Select mushrooms carefully for best flavor. Fresh mushrooms should be "pristine": whole, unblemished, dry and not discolored. They may smell a little earthy, but the scent should be pleasant and they should not be slimy.

Store them in the refrigerator wrapped in paper, not plastic. Paper will keep moisture in while still allowing breathing room. In general, mushrooms are very perishable, and you should use them promptly.

When you're ready to cook, it's time to clean your mushrooms. Loose soil can be wiped away. As for washing them, some cookbooks warn that mushrooms will become waterlogged, but in *The Curious Cook: More Kitchen Science and Lore,* scien-tifically-minded food iconoclast Howard McGee points out that they are already 90 percent water. He soaked mushrooms in water for five minutes to compare the pre- and post-soaked weights. McGee found that a half-pound absorbed less than one-and-a-half teaspoons total water. So if wiping isn't getting the job done, don't hesitate to rinse.

If you have more mushrooms than you can use, sauté the extras briefly and freeze them. Use them within a month. Still, the flavor and texture will not be as good as fresh. Both *The Mushroom Feast* and *The Edible Mushroom* give instructions for drying mushrooms.

Depending on the growing conditions, wild mushrooms may contain a lot more water than cultivated varieties. Therefore, pay attention to liquid levels as your recipe progresses: You may want to remove some or boil it down a bit so the finished dish won't look like soup. Conversely, you may need to add liquid when substituting cultivated for wild mushrooms in a recipe.

If you're using wild mushrooms, make sure you know what you've got. There are only a few lethal mushrooms, but there are many that either don't taste very good or can make you sick. There's no reason to be frightened of reliable mushrooms and many delicious reasons to seek them out.

Almost any cookbook will have mushroom recipes, but because mushrooms are prized in the French, Italian and Chinese cuisines you are likely to find especially good ones in those ethnicities' cookbooks. The following recipes will work with even common button mushrooms, but are made special with the more flavorful cultivated and wild sorts.

Mushroom Sauce with Pasta

8 ounces mushrooms
1 tablespoon lemon juice
1 small onion or shallot, chopped
1 large clove garlic, chopped
4 tablespoons butter
2 tablespoons olive oil
½ to ¾ cup finely chopped parsley
salt and pepper
1 clove garlic, peeled and smashed
½ pound pasta

Clean and trim the mushrooms, slice thinly and sprinkle with lemon juice. Cook the onion and garlic gently in the butter and oil until they soften without browning. Add the mushrooms and parsley, raise the heat slightly and cook for another 10 minutes. The time will depend on the type of mushrooms being used. They should still have a little bite to them. The mixture should be moist but not swimming in liquid. Season with salt and pepper.

Add the remaining clove of garlic to the pasta cooking water and cook the pasta until just done. Mix the sauce and pasta and serve.

Serves two to three. The original recipe calls for egg pasta shells but this simple, flavorful sauce is good with most pasta as long as they are not so fine that they soak up all the sauce and clump together.

Mushroom Caviar

1½ pounds fresh mushrooms, porcini (cèpes), portobello or crimini preferred
4 tablespoons olive oil
1 medium onion, chopped
2 to 3 cloves garlic, chopped
3 tablespoons mayonnaise
2 teaspoons fresh lemon juice
2 tablespoons fresh dill, finely chopped
salt and pepper

Clean and trim the mushrooms. Separate the stems from the caps and coarsely chop both. Heat 3 tablespoons of the oil in a large skillet over medium heat. Add the mushrooms and cook and stir until they begin to throw off their liquid. Turn up the heat and continue until most of the liquid has disappeared and the mushrooms are lightly browned, 10 to 12 minutes. Remove the mushrooms and set aside. Heat the remaining tablespoon of oil in the same skillet and sauté the onion until golden, about 15 minutes.

Combine the mushrooms, onion and garlic in a food processor and process until minced but not pureed. In a large bowl, combine the mushroom mixture, mayonnaise, lemon juice, dill and salt and pepper, to taste. Let the mixture stand at room temperature for an hour. Taste and adjust the seasonings, adding more lemon juice if desired.

This recipe is one of a number of Russian vegetable "caviars" adapted from *Please to the Table,* by Anya von Bremzen and John Welchman. It has a complex and interesting flavor and is good as an hors d'oeuvre with toast or black bread. Leftovers will liven up sandwiches (I can vouch for a combination of ham, sprouts and mushroom caviar) or a baked potato.

Cèpes Baked with Garlic & Olive Oil

1 pound cèpes (porcini)
2 cloves garlic
several sprigs parsley
salt and pepper
olive oil

Slice the stalks of the clean mushrooms off even with the caps and set them aside. Salt the stalk side of the caps lightly and let them drain for one ½ to 1 hour. Chop the stalks finely with the garlic and parsley.

Preheat the oven to 350°F. Put a thin layer of olive oil on the bottom of a deep ovenproof dish. Dry the mushroom caps and layer them in the dish, sprinkling each layer with the garlic, parsley and stem mixture, drops of olive oil, and pepper. Cover the dish and bake for approximately 30 minutes. The actual time will vary with the size and age of the mushrooms; if they are not done after 30 minutes check at 10-minute intervals. Pay attention to the liquid level and adjust if necessary.

Serves four. Adapted from Jane Grigson's *Food with the Famous.* Serve with plenty of good bread.

Books for the Fungiphile

COOKING

The Mushroom Feast by Jane Grigson — for those who gather mushrooms in the wild as well as the supermarket aisles. Contains many wonderful recipes for North American and British varieties — both rare and common. With literary and scholarly writing, the book is as delightful in the reading as the mushrooms in the cooking.

The Edible Mushroom: A Gourmet Cook's Guide by Margaret Leibenstein — covers buying, preparing, cooking and preserving fresh wild mushrooms. Includes specific instructions and recipes for most of the mushrooms, dry and fresh, you are likely to be able to buy.

GROWING

Growing Gourmet and Medicinal Mushrooms by Paul Stamets — resembles a good high-school science book with clear, in-depth instructions for growing mushrooms. Includes a very useful bibliography.

GATHERING

Mushrooms Demystified: A Comprehensive Guide to the Flesh Fungi by David Arora — clear, witty and thorough. Arora describes, illustrates or mentions 2,000 species found in North America. Contains an unusual expression of gratitude to his wife, who "did not type a single word of the manuscript nor provide countless hours of selfless assistance."

A Field Guide to Southern Mushrooms by Nancy Smith Weber and Alexander Smith.

The National Audubon Society's *Field Guide to North American Mushrooms.*

East Meets West: Cooking Chinese Style

The Independent
February 8, 1995

CHINESE FOOD. Most of us eat it, but do many of us cook it at home? If you've been afraid to try because you think it's too complicated, or that the only way to achieve authenticity is to make your kitchen a smoky, stir-fried mess, take heart. There are plenty of Chinese dishes that are a least as easy as what you've planned for tonight — if you're not stopping at a Chinese take-out on your way home.

The main reason to try cooking Chinese-style is flavor: Chinese food is very good. The second reason is variety: It's different from the food you're used to (unless your family is Chinese). And it is healthy: In contrast to our middle-class American food traditions, Chinese cuisine offers a more healthful ratio of meat to non-meat ingredients — which means less saturated fat.

Although a recent, highly publicized analysis of Chinese restaurant dishes revealed appalling amounts of fat, at home you're in control. You can limit the fat — both in your choice of ingredients and in the quantity of oil when stir-frying. And when "velveting" meat (a preliminary to stir-frying — the marinated meat is fried to firm up its texture and create a nice coating), you can do it in simmering water rather than deep fat.

As for utensils, don't be put off, thinking you will need a lot of special tools to cook Chinese style. All you really need is a wok or a big skillet, a good knife, a sturdy cutting board and a saucepan with a lid for cooking rice. These things are useful no matter what style of food you are preparing.

Your wok should be thin enough to respond rapidly when you alter the heat, but thick enough that oil won't burn the instant you add it. Forget electric woks (I've heard there are some decent high-powered electric woks, but I've never seen one).

A large wok is a very efficient tool, with its curved shape enabling good control of heat as you stir foods around and up its sides. It will cook quantities suitable for the solo diner or a large family. A 14-inch wok is large enough to be useful and small enough that it won't overwhelm your stove top. But — if you prefer — a frying pan will do the trick.

If you get into cooking Chinese style, you probably won't be able to resist acquiring a few of the specialized tools that have evolved with the cuisine over thousands of years. These implements often provide elegant solutions to cooking needs.

A bamboo steamer, unlike metal, absorbs some of the moisture that would otherwise get dumped into the dish, diluting the sauce. And an oriental ginger grate pulverizes fresh ginger much more quickly and completely than you can with a knife, blender or food processor.

My favorite recently acquired Chinese kitchen tool is a narrow grater (3 by 14 inches), slightly bowed in shape and neon pink in color. It shreds superbly, survives the dishwasher and looks great hanging on the wall.

I began cooking Chinese when I moved to the United States from England and could no longer eat once a week on London's Gerrard Street. When I arrived in Durham the only consistently good Chinese food in the area was in Raleigh — a long drive for dinner.

My cooking efforts were timid at first, but knowing what I was missing kept me motivated. I have since discovered lots of dishes that rarely appear on restaurant menus (Vinegar Splashed Chicken is one of my favorites). *(See page 171.)*

There are years of pleasure ahead — though I can follow recipes successfully and even improvise a bit, there is a great deal more to learn. I am a beginner when it comes to the philosophical underpinnings at the heart of Chinese cooking — principles of complement and contrast including hot, sweet, sour, salty that have shaped this cuisine for thousands of years.

The following are a few keys to making home Chinese cooking more authentic. Though it took me a while to realize them, I'm happy to give you a head start.

◆ *Sesame oil:* Buy the oriental (toasted) variety. It's dark in color and nutty in flavor. This ingredient is usually added last, mainly for its essential flavor.

◆ *Soy sauce:* There are two sorts — light and dark. Dark is thicker and stronger in flavor; it's called for in cooking with red meats. Light is thinner and used with chicken, fish and vegetables. For many years, I was unaware of the distinction and cooked exclusively with dark — a flavorful and interesting mistake that meant missing out on certain subtleties. Life is too short to succumb to the monotony of only one soy sauce.

◆ *Sherry:* Many older Chinese cookbooks specify sherry as a substitute for Chinese rice wine or saki. This is a mistake — even the driest of dry sherries will overwhelm other flavors in the dish. I've switched to oriental rice wine, and my Chinese cooking has improved greatly.

◆ *Sugar:* Because I don't use sugar much when cooking savory dishes, I was inclined to omit it from Chinese food. I have since learned better — the sugar isn't there to make the dish sweet, it's there as part of a balanced group of seasonings.

One last bit of advice. Don't feel compelled to cook a complete and complicated Chinese meal; you'll just be overwhelmed. Try your hand at a couple of dishes, then gradually expand your repertoire.

Here's one of my favorites adapted from Ken Hom's *Quick and Easy Chinese Cooking.* Serve it for dinner with rice and steamed broccoli.

Quick Orange-Lemon Chicken

¾ pound boneless chicken breasts
1 tablespoon peanut oil
2 tablespoons coarsely chopped garlic
1 teaspoon finely chopped peeled fresh ginger
2 teaspoons finely chopped orange zest
2 teaspoons finely chopped lemon zest
¼ cup orange juice
¼ cup fresh lemon juice
1 tablespoon light soy sauce
1 tablespoon sugar
1 teaspoon cornstarch mixed with
  1 teaspoon water
1 teaspoon chili bean paste
2 teaspoons toasted sesame oil
3 tablespoons coarsely chopped green onions

Remove the skin from the chicken and cut the meat into long strips. Blanch the chicken for 30 seconds in a pan of boiling salted water. Drain and set aside.

Heat a wok or large skillet, then add the oil, garlic and ginger. Stir-fry the mixture for 10 seconds and add the rest of the ingredients except for the chicken. Bring the mixture to a simmer, add the chicken to the wok, and cook through.

Remember that the chicken will continue to cook for at least 30 seconds after you have removed it from the wok, so be sure not to overcook it. Serve immediately. Serves two.

THE RIGHT STUFF

You can get many Chinese cooking ingredients in a regular supermarket, and even more in a specialty or gourmet store. But for the few things you just can't find, and for better brands than are available elsewhere, you'll need to shop at an Asian market. Just check out the soy sauce section in one of those markets and you'll see why it's worth the trip.

These shops are as much fun to browse as a good hardware store. Plus, the prices are low, and the proprietors typically know a lot about the items on their shelves. Most of the goods are staples with a long shelf life, so stock up.

THE GOOD BOOK

Unless the cook in your household was Chinese when you were growing up, you'll need recipes. Start with a good basic cookbook like Irene Kuo's *The Key to Chinese Cooking*. It may seem expensive, but it's the best-organized and most thorough introduction to cooking Chinese food I know.

Kuo's explanations and diagrams will make you feel as if you have your own teacher in the kitchen. You'll do things correctly from the start, learning the building blocks and how to combine them in various ways. You'll find out why certain ingredients need to be velveted and see a couple of methods of doing so. (Once you've tasted and felt the difference you won't be tempted to skip this step again.)

There are enough recipes in this book that you could cook from it every night for a long time and not get bored.

Freshly Minted Dishes

The Independent
May 3, 1995

AH SPRING! In the garden, green shoots are poking through the ground; branches of bushes are beginning to fill out with leaves. If you planned ahead, selecting vegetable and herb seeds some time ago, you're probably ready to set out the nurtured seedlings.

I have not planned ahead; in fact, these days I am not much of a gardener at all. I have two main crops. The first is blueberries, a gardening endeavor that I heartily recommend even to the lazy or allergy-plagued gardener. Just select a site with good drainage and keep the bushes watered during dry spells until the plants are well established. After that your main problems will be finding enough time to pick your crop and enough freezer space to store what you don't use fresh.

My second crop is mint. If I'm going to have only one fresh herb readily available, mint, with its cool, sweet, fresh but slightly sharp flavor, is a good one. I'm told by friends who've been to North Africa that the variety I grow, a hardy one that has survived four moves in Durham, is very like that used profusely in Morocco.

I grew up with the traditional Southern American uses of this common herb, the main one being iced tea with mint. My method of making tea, to maximize the minty taste, is to add several big healthy sprigs before the hot water. A variation, which makes a good non-alcoholic special occasion beverage, consists of equal quantities of mint tea combined with orange juice, lots of crushed ice and fresh sprigs of mint.

Then there's the other traditional Southern beverage: the mint julep. This drink is improved if you combine some of the bourbon, the sugar syrup and plenty of mint, and let it sit overnight.

The uses of mint I have come to appreciate as an adult, however, are the savory ones. I once watched a French friend throw a couple of sprigs of mint into a pot of stew with lamb, chicken and vegetables for Algerian couscous. The contrast between the sweetish mint and the spicy, hot stew was marvelous.

I have since learned that this gutsy use of mint with hot savory dishes occurs in many cuisines: Thai and Afghan cooking offer spectacular examples of mint standing up to substantial opposition such as hot peppers or strong vinegar. The Romans use mint in a similar way with vegetables, fish, salads and soups — I love the surprise when I encounter it.

I hope Elizabeth David's observation in *Italian Food* is still true today: "Anyone who has walked among the ghostly ruins of Ostia Antica will remember the haunting scent of the wild mint which rises from the ground, for one cannot help treading it underfoot."

The following are two Roman recipes calling for mint, adapted from Ada Boni's *Italian Regional Cooking*.

Stewed Artichokes

9-ounce package frozen artichokes or young fresh artichokes
1 clove garlic, finely chopped
3 sprigs mint, finely chopped
salt and pepper
2 tablespoons olive oil
1 tablespoon lemon juice
½ cup water

Arrange the artichokes in one layer in a non-corrosive pan (stainless steel, enameled or the like). Sprinkle with garlic, mint, salt, pepper, olive oil and lemon juice. Add the water and bring to a boil. Cover and cook 10 to 15 minutes for frozen artichokes, 30 to 40 minutes for fresh, until the artichokes are tender. Uncover, turn up the heat and cook briskly until the sauce has reduced and thickened. Serve two or three, hot or cold.

Canned artichokes will not work, they are already cooked and are too acidic.

Mushrooms with Garlic & Mint

1 pound mushrooms
¼ cup olive oil
2 anchovy fillets, finely chopped, or a tablespoon of anchovy paste (Italian brands are available in toothpaste-like tubes)
1 clove garlic, crushed
2 peeled, seeded and chopped tomatoes (you may substitute a good canned Italian variety; in that case use 3 or 4 because they will be smaller)
2 sprigs mint, finely chopped
salt and pepper

Clean and slice the mushrooms. Heat the oil in a skillet. Add the anchovies or the anchovy paste; cook until dissolved into the oil. Add the mushrooms, garlic, tomatoes, mint, salt and pepper. Cook over a brisk heat, stirring frequently, until the mushrooms are tender and all else has reduced to a sauce. Cultivated mushrooms will take up to 10 minutes cooking; wild may take a bit longer because of their toughness and may also give off more liquid. Serves two to four.

Cream of the Crop

The Independent
August 2, 1995

SOMETIMES THINGS WORK OUT perfectly. As I've pondered this assignment of writing about keeping cool culinarily, I've been blessed with:

1) The right weather — our first summer heat wave.
2) The right inspiration — the chapter of ice cream recipes in Melissa Clark's *The Instant Gourmet*.
3) The right equipment — a low-tech, no fuss ice cream maker.

I decided my goal was to make some frozen desserts without working up a sweat.

The easiest method is simply to freeze some concoction. The drawback with that method, however, is you end up with a frozen block. No matter how wonderful the flavor, it's likely to have all the excitement of an ice cube.

Now, if you whiz chunks of the frozen block in a food processor until slushy, the product is greatly improved. Frozen chunks of fruit — strawberries, blueberries, peaches — mixed with a small amount of yogurt and a little sugar or honey yield delicious results.

Water ices, also known as *granitas,* are only slightly more difficult. Use a well-flavored liquid, like sweetened fruit juices (all citrus varieties are outstanding), or very strong sweetened coffee or tea. Don't be shy about quantity; freezing reduces the intensity of the sweetness and the flavor.

Place the liquid in a shallow pan (a cake pan is about right for a pint). Every half-hour, as the liquid starts to freeze, stir it around to break up the ice crystals. Once it becomes slushy, serve the ice immediately, or pack it into a covered container and store it in the freezer, removing it 15 to 20 minutes before serving to soften it up.

There are various mechanical or electrical devices for making ice creams. The machines stir the mixture as it freezes, breaking down the ice crystals more thoroughly and resulting in a product that's smoother than those of the above methods.

These mechanical models include the old-fashioned hand- or electric-crank ice-cream makers that use ice and rock salt, and their simpler table-top relations that use refrigerator ice and table salt. The highest-tech (and most expensive) versions use no salt or ice; you just add the mixture and plug them in.

But there is a low-tech version of the ice-cream maker. Mine is a Donvier that I received for my birthday present a couple of years back. It consists of an insulated cylinder that you place in the coldest part of your freezer several hours or until it is solidly frozen. Then you put a mixture into the cylinder, assemble the paddle, cover and handle, and for the next 20 minutes or so turn the handle at 2- to 3-minute intervals until the mixture is semi-frozen. Store it in the freezer until it firms up, and you are ready to eat.

I admit that until recently my ice-cream maker was underused: A lot of recipes were more work than I cared to undertake on a hot summer day. *The Instant Gourmet* solved that problem with recipes consisting of two simple steps: 1) combining two to four ingredients in the bowl of an ice-cream maker, and 2) freezing the dessert according to the manufacturer's instructions.

Here are adaptations from Clark's recipes and suggestions of my own. I've been spinning off variations as fast as I can find interesting ingredients — fruit nectars, concentrated fruit syrups, frozen tropical juice concentrates and the like.

The recipes that use cream are — no surprise — creamier and can be served right out of the refrigerator. Those with yogurt or just juice freeze more firmly and are best served after 10 minutes at room temperature. These desserts are supposed to keep for up to two weeks in the freezer, but I have never had a problem with homemade ice cream lasting long enough to deteriorate.

All of the recipes make about a pint of ice cream; you can easily multiply the ingredient list if your ice cream maker holds more.

Lemon Curd Ice Cream

    1 cup heavy cream
    1 jar lemon curd

Good lemon curd is not cheap, but this is a heavenly combination and makes one of the best homemade ice creams I've ever tasted. The lemon curd provides an egg-yolk base without the work of making custard.

Grape Ice Cream

    1 cup heavy cream
    ¾ cup frozen grape-juice concentrate

A little bit of this ice cream goes a long way because it is intensely flavored and very creamy.

Quick Lime Ice Cream

    grated zest of 1 lime
    ¼ cup super-fine sugar
    1 cup heavy cream
    1 cup frozen limeade concentrate

The lime flavor is delicious and sharply refreshing. Don't omit the grated zest; it is an important element.

Peach–Honey Frozen Yogurt

    1 cup peach nectar
    2 tablespoons honey
    1 cup vanilla yogurt
    very tiny pinch of ground cinnamon

This combination has a subtle flavor and is very good with fresh fruit.

Bibliography

E<small>DITOR'S NOTE:</small> We have collected here as much current information as possible on the cookbooks mentioned in Helen's columns. Many of the editions have been revised and updated since they were first cited by HHW. Another significant batch of her favorite references are out of print and are indicated as such. We know Helen would send you to the library first to investigate the out-of-print titles before attempting to track down a used edition to purchase. However, we found that almost all of the out-of-print titles are still available through bibliofind.com or abebooks.com on the Internet.

Helen Whiting had an amazing cookbook collection that now has been dispersed among the homes of her family and many friends. Her recipe collections — gathered partially in folders for over-sized clippings and letters from friends, and the rest in one astoundingly rich assortment of index cards in a box — are ingeniously arranged by nationality of the cuisine, and in some cases by the key ingredient, such as "blueberries." The collection of recipes is a veritable United Nations of dishes. Remaining faithful to her organizational scheme, we offer this list of references from her writings:

AFRICA / MIDDLE EAST

A Book of Middle Eastern Food by Claudia Roden. Vintage Books, 1974. Paperback ISBN: 0394719484

Couscous and Other Good Foods from Morocco by Paula Wolfert. HarperCollins, 1987. Paperback ISBN: 0060913967

Kwanzaa: An African-American Celebration of Culture and Cooking by Eric V. Copage. Quill, 1993. Paperback ISBN: 0688128351

Noshe Djan: Afghan Food and Cookery by Helen Saberi. (out of print)
See also: *Afghan Food and Cookery* by Helen Saberi. Paperback, Hippocrene Books (published in July 2000)

Recipes For an Arabian Night by David Scott. Pantheon Books, 1984. Paperback ISBN: 0394722922

CHINA

Chinese Vegetarian Cooking by Kenneth Lo. Pantheon, 1974. (out of print)

The Good Food of Szechwan: Down-to-Earth Chinese Cooking by Robert Delfts. Kodansha International, 1976. (out of print)

Hunan Style Chinese Cookbook by Henry Chung. Crown Pub. 1978. Hardcover ISBN: 0517533251

The Key to Chinese Cooking by Irene Kuo. Knopf, 1977. Hardcover ISBN: 0394496388

Quick and Easy Chinese Cooking by Ken Hom. Chronicle Books, 1990. (out of print)
See also: *Ken Hom's Hot Wok: Over 150 One-Pan Wonders* by Ken Hom. West One Hundred Seventy Five, 1999. Paperback ISBN: 1884656080

ENGLAND

English Bread and Yeast Cookery by Elizabeth David. Biscuit Books, 1995. Hardcover ISBN: 0964360004

English Country Cooking at its Best by Carolina Conran. Villard Books, 1985. (out of print)

English Food by Jane Grigson. Penguin UK, 1999. Paperback, ISBN: 0140273247

Spices, Salt and Aromatics in the English Kitchen by Elizabeth David. Penguin Books, 1973. (out of print)

The Robert Carrier Cookbook by Robert Carrier. Sphere Books Limited (England), (UR#:6-111603204x-0) Offered for sale by Powells Books.

FRANCE

Cooking With Pomiane by Edouard de Pomiane. North Point Press, 1994. Paperback ISBN: 0865474818

The Cuisine of the Sun: Classic Recipes from Nice and Provence by Mireille Johnston. Random House, 1976. (out of print)

The Flavour of France in Recipes and Pictures compiled by Narcissa G. Chamberlain and Narcisse Chamberlain. London, 1962. (out of print)

French Cooking in Ten Minutes: Or Adapting to the Rhythm of Modern Life (1930) by Edouard de Pomiane, Mary Hyman (Translator). North Point Press, 1994. Paperback ISBN: 086547480X

French Country Cooking by Elizabeth David. Trafalgar Square, 1999. Paperback ISBN: 0140467890

French Provincial Cooking by Elizabeth David, Introduction by Julia Child. Penguin USA, 1999. Paperback ISBN: 0141181532

Mastering the Art of French Cooking, Volume One by Julia Child, Louisette Bertholle and Simone Beck. Random House, 1983, Hardcover ISBN: 0394533992. Paperback (1989) ISBN: 0394721780

Mastering the Art of French Cooking, Volume Two by Julia Child and Simone Beck. Random House, 1970. Hardcover ISBN: 0394401522. (Also available as a set with Volume One.)

INDIA / FAR EAST

Indian Cookery by Dharmamijit Singh. Penguin 1973. (out of print)

Madhur Jaffrey's Far Eastern Cookery by Madhur Jaffrey. BBC Books, 1989. (out of print)
See also: *Madhur Jaffrey's Indian Cooking* by Madhur Jaffrey. Barron's Educational Series, 1995. Hardcover ISBN: 0812065484. Paperback (1983) ISBN: 0812027000

Moghul Microwave: Cooking Indian Food the Modern Way by Julie Sahni. (out of print)

The Home Book of Indian Cookery by Sipra Das Gupta. Faber, 1973. (out of print).

ITALY

Essentials of Classic Italian Cooking by Marcella Hazan. Knopf, 1992. Hardcover ISBN: 039458404X

Italian Food by Elizabeth David. Penguin USA, 1999. Paperback ISBN: 0141181559

Italian Regional Cooking by Ada Boni. Crescent Books, 1989. (out of print)

MEXICO / LATIN AMERICA

The Art of Mexican Cooking: Traditional Mexican Cooking for Aficionados by Diana Kennedy. Bantam Books, 1989. Hardcover ISBN: 0553057065

Blue Corn and Chocolate by Elisabeth Rozin. Knopf, 1992 Hardcover ISBN: 0394583086

The Book of Latin American Cooking by Elisabeth Lambert Ortiz. Ecco Press, 1994. Paperback ISBN: 0880013826

The Cuisines of Mexico by Diana Kennedy. Harper Collins, 1989. Paperback ISBN: 0060915617

Complete Book of Mexican Cooking by Elisabeth Lambert Ortiz. Ballantine Books, 1992. Paperback ISBN: 0345325591

Mexican Microwave Cookery: A Collection of Mexican Recipes Using the Microwave Oven by Carol Medina Maze. Fisher Books, 1988. (out of print)

Sunset Mexican Cook Book by the Editors of Sunset Books and Sunset Magazine. Lane Books, 1974. (out of print)

Sunset Southwest Cook Book: The New Cuisine with a Mexican-Old West Flavor by the Editors of Sunset Books and Sunset Magazine. Lane Books, 1987. (out of print)

RUSSIA / EASTERN EUROPE

A Taste of Russia. A Cookbook of Russian Hospitality by Darra Goldstein. Russian Information Services, 1999. Paperback ISBN: 1880100428

The Classic Cuisine of Soviet Georgia by Julianne Margvelaslivii. Prentice Hall, 1991. (out of print)

Home Book of Greek Cookery by Joyce M. Stubbs. Faber & Faber, 1976. (out of print)

Please to the Table by Anya von Brenizon and John Welchmail. Workman Publishing Company, 1990. Paperback ISBN: 0894807536

UNITED STATES REGIONAL

Bill Neal's Southern Cooking by Bill Neal. University of North Carolina Press, 1989. Paperback (revised and enlarged edition) ISBN: 0807842559

Biscuits, Spoonbread, and Sweet Potato Pie by Bill Neal. Random House 1996. Paperback ISBN: 0679765808

Chez Panisse Cafe Cookbook by Alice Waters. HarperCollins 1999. Hardcover ISBN:0060175834

Chez Panisse Cooking by Paul Bertolli with Alice Waters. Random House, 1994. Paperback ISBN: 0679755357

Farm House Cookbook by Susan Herrmann Loomis. Workman Publishing Company, 1991. Paperback ISBN: 0894807722

Helen Brown's West Coast Cookbook by Helen Brown, Boston: Little, Brown and Co. (1952). (out of print)

Hot Links and Country Flavors by Bruce Aidells and Denis Kelly. Knopf. (out of print)
See also: *Bruce Aidells's Sausage Book: Recipes & Techniques from America's Premium Sausage Maker* by Bruce Aidells and Denis Kelly. Ten Speed Press, October 2000. Hardcover ISBN: 1580081592

Miss Ruby's American Cooking From Border to Border, & Coast to Coast, the Best Recipes from America's Regional Kitchens by Ruth Adams Bronz. Harper & Row, 1989. (out of print)

Mrs. Witty's Home-Style Menu Cookbook by Helen Witty. Workman Publishing Company, 1990. Paperback ISBN: 0894806904

The New Orleans Cookbook: Creole, Cajun, and Louisiana French Recipes Past and Present by Rima and Richard Collin. Knopf, 1987. Paperback ISBN: 0394752759

Pow Wow Chow: A Collection of Recipes from Families of the Five Civilized Tribes: Cherokee, Chickasaw, Choctaw, Creek and Seminole. Five Civilized Tribes Museum, 1984. Paperback ISBN: 9996688445

Philadelphia Main Line Classics by The Junior Saturday Club of Wayne, PA. 1982. Paperback ISBN: 0965081818

GENERAL

American Cider Book by Vrest Orton. North Point Press, 1995. Paperback ISBN: 0866474842

Food with the Famous by Jane Grigson. Seven Hills Book Distributors, 1991. Hardcover ISBN: 0948817453

The Gentle Art of Cookery by Mrs. C.F. Leyel and Miss Olga Hartley. Originally published in 1925. (out of print)

Great Aunt Jane's Cook and Garden Book by Jane Grigson. Lippincott Company, 1976. (out of print)

Great Dishes of the World by Robert Carrier. (out of print)
See also: *New Great Dishes of the World* by Robert Carrier. Smithmark Publishing, 1998. Hardcover ISBN: 076519127X

James Beard's American Cookery by James A. Beard. Budget Book Service, 1996. Hardcover ISBN: 088365951. Little Brown & Co, 1980. Paperback ISBN: 0316085669

Joy of Cooking by Irma S. Rombauer, Marion Rombauer Becker, Ethan Becker. Scribner, 1997. Hardcover ISBN: 0684818701. Plume, 1997. Paperback ISBN: 0452279151

QUICK MEALS / MICROWAVE

20 Minute Menus by Marian Burros. Fireside, 1995. Paperback ISBN: 0684801353

Fresh 15-Minute Meals by Emalee Chapman. Plume, 1993. Paperback ISBN: 0525482482

The Instant Gourmet by Melissa Clark. Penguin Books, 1995. Paperback ISBN: 014024140X

Let's Eat In: Quick and Delicious Weekday Meals by Brooke Dojny and Melanie Barnard. Prentice-Hall, 1990. (out of print)

Micro Ways: Every Cook's Guide to Successful Microwaving by Jean Anderson and Elaine Hanna. H.P. Books, 1997. Paperback ISBN: 1557882614

Microwave Gourmet: The Only Microwave Cookbook You Will Ever Need by Barbara Kafk. William Morrow & Co., 1998. Paperback ISBN: 0688157920

Microwave Diet Cookery by Marcia Cone and Thelma Snyder. New York, 1988. (out of print)

PRESERVING FOOD/ FOOD GIFTS

Better Than Store Bought by Helen Whitty and Elizabeth Schneider Colchie. Harper & Row and Book-of-the-Month Club, 1979. (out of print)

Country Fresh Gifts: Recipes and Projects From Your Garden and Country Kitchen by Editors of Storey Publishing (out of print)

Gifts of Food by Susan Costner. Crown Publishing, 1984. (out of print)

Keeping the Harvest : Preserving Your Fruits, Vegetables & Herbs by Nancy Chioffi and Gretchen Mead. Storey Books, 1991. Paperback ISBN: 0882666509

Preserving Today by Jeanne Lesem. Knopf 1992. (out of print). **See also:** *Preserving in Today's Kitchen: Easy, Modern Canning Methods-With 168 Recipes* by Jeanne Lesem. Henry Holt, 1997. Paperback ISBN: 0805048812

Putting Food By (4th Edition Newly Revised) by Janet C. Greene, Ruth Hertzberg and Beatrice Vaughan. Penguin USA, 1992. Paperback ISBN: 0452268990

Stocking Up: The Third Edition of the Classic Preserving Guide by Carol Hupping. Fireside, 1990. Paperback ISBN: 0671693956

VEGETARIAN & NON-MEAT

The Edible Mushroom: A Gourmet Cook's Guide by Margaret Leibenstein. The Globe Pequot Press, 1993. (out of print)

Jane Grigson's Vegetable Book by Jane Grigson. Atheneum, 1979. (out of print)

Jane Grigson's Fruit Book by Jane Grigson. Atheneum, 1982. (out of print)

Linda McCartney's Home Cooking by Linda McCartney. Arcade Pub, 1992. Paperback ISBN: 1559701609

The Mushroom Feast, by Jane Grigson. The Lyons Press, 1998. Paperback ISBN: 1558211942

New Recipes from Moosewood Restaurant by Moosewood Collective. Ten Speed Press 1987. Paperback ISBN: 0898152089. Hardcover ISBN: 0898152097

The Vegetarian Epicure by Anna Thomas. Random House, 1972. Paperback ISBN: 0394717848

The Vegetarian Epicure: Book Two by Anna Thomas. Random House, 1978. Paperback ISBN: 0394734157

Victory Garden Cookbook by Marion Morash. Random House, 1982. Paperback ISBN: 039470780X

COOKING FOR KIDS

Betty Crocker's New Boys and Girls Cookbook by Betty Crocker. Golden Press, Western Pub. Co., 1965. (out of print)
See also: *Betty Crocker Kids Cook!* IDG Books Worldwide, 1999. Hardcover ISBN: 0028634063

Jenifer Lang Cooks For Kids: 153 Recipes And Ideas For Good Food That Kids Love To Eat by Jenifer Lang. Harmony Books, 1991. (out of print)

ESSAYS

An Omelette and a Glass of Wine by Elizabeth David. (The Cook's Classic Library) Lyons Press, 1997. Paperback ISBN: 1558215719

The Art of Eating by M.F.K. Fisher. IDG Books Worldwide, 1990. Paperback ISBN: 0020322208

The Curious Cook: More Kitchen Science and Lore by Howard McGee. IDG Books Worldwide, 1992. Papearback ISBN: 0020098014

South Wind Through the Kitchen: The Best of Elizabeth David by Elizabeth David. North Point Press, 1998. Hardcover ISBN 0865475350. Paperback ISBN: 086547575X

With Bold Knife and Fork by M.F.K. Fisher. G.P. Putnams's Sons, 1968. (out of print)

MUSHROOM REFERENCE

A Field Guide to Southern Mushrooms by Nancy Smith. 1st Glance Books, 1985. Paperback ISBN: 0472856154

Growing Gourmet and Medicinal Mushrooms by Paul Stamets. Ten Speed Press, 1994. Paperback ISBN: 0898156084

Mushrooms Demystified: A Comprehensive Guide to the Flesh Fungi by David Arora. Ten Speed Press, 1986. Paperback ISBN: 0898151694

The National Audubon Society's Field Guide to North American Mushrooms. Knopf, 1981. Hardcover ISBN: 0394519922

Index

Index

Acknowledgements

W HEN ROB GRINGLE and Dave Birkhead
promised to gather together some of
Helen's recipes and food writings, little did they
realize what a wealth of material Helen had left
us. As we started this project the editors envisioned
publishing a small piece that would honor Helen,
her family and the exceptional Durham-Chapel
Hill communities she touched.

Helen has graced us with such a bounty of
writings — words that fuel the soul as well as the
soothe the palate — that this book is the result. We
hope we have achieved our goal of producing a
work that does justice to Helen's legacy — a book
edited, designed and produced as a labor of love,
and as a tribute to a friend who left us too soon.

The printing costs are being recouped from
the sale of the book, with the proceeds going to
the Durham-based scholarship foundation that
Helen supported. It took a community of friends
to create *In Helen's Kitchen*, and the editors would
like to thank those who helped make the book
a reality.

For the loving effort, and the skill and knowledge they have brought to this project, we are
especially grateful to:

Tom Campbell and John Valentine,
    Regulator Bookshop
Emily Wexler
Carol Wills

Special thanks go to our reviewers for their gift
of time and their thoughtful comments:

Karen Barker
Greg Cox
Lee Smith

For their generous encouragement, advice
and support, we would like to thank:

Betty and Fred Flemming (Helen's parents)
Liz Whiting, Meg Flemming, and Christian
    Flemming (Helen's sisters and brother)
Lex and Ann Alexander
Carol Anderson
Kim Anderson
Dale Appleman
Azalea Graphics
Bill and B.J. Boyarsky
Duke University Office of Continuing
    Education and Summer Session
Steve Emerson
Mo Ferrell
Dawn Freer
Lynn Hines Harper
Bryant Holsenbeck
The Independent
Martha Maiden and Buddy LeMoyne
Tim and Holly McDonough
Deb Nickell
Regulator Bookshop
Regulator Community Fund
V. Cullum Rogers
Russ Rose
Steve Schewel and Lao Rubert
Ray Simone
Lise Uyanik
Vaguely Reminiscent
Sioux Watson

All proceeds from the sale of this book go
to the Helen Whiting Scholarship Fund, part of
the Regulator Community Fund.